'Providing a lucid account of Lacan and Freud's theorizations of aspects of the visual field from the mirror stage to the gaze as object a, Efrat Biberman's brilliant book shows how painting cannot be thought of separately from the subject of the unconscious and enjoyment. The first book in English to closely engage with Lacan's seminal analysis of Diego Velázquez's *Las Meninas,* it shows the inextricability of painter and observer in the constitution of painting as a site of subjective drama where inside and outside flow into one another'.

Shirley Zisser, *Lacanian Psychoanalyst and Professor of English at Tel Aviv University*

'How do we experience painting's story? In this stimulating and highly original book, Efrat Biberman ensues by astutely surveying the ways in which paintings were historically understood in relation to the verbal arts; from Lessing's *Laocoon,* to the high modernism of Clement Greenberg and beyond, Biberman exposes the flaws they share in subjugating painterly narratives to those of literature, either through comparative (and reductive) opposition, or by way of equally compromised analogies. Instead of this binary model, Biberman brilliantly employs the psycho-analytical toolkit of Freud, Žižek and especially Lacan, to offer a new, fruitful and compelling understanding of visual narrative as standing on its own ground; it is a proposal of visual narrative as multilayered and innately distinct – with incongruity at its very core'.

Roee Rosen, *artist and writer*

Visual Narrative and Lacanian Psychoanalysis

This book analyzes narrativity in painting from a Freudian-Lacanian perspective.

Narrativity in painting is prominently discussed through the disciplinary laws and lens of art history, art theory, poetics and more. Yet such points of view never shed light on its ambiguous status or nature. This book offers a new way of thinking about painting. Its point of departure is the complexity of the term narrative painting, which includes the relationship between painting and literature, as well as the boundaries of each medium. This book develops an alternative way of thinking about narrative painting, in which the viewer constitutes an active part in the visual narrative. Based on Lacanian topology, this book demonstrates how the subject is never distinguished from the painting she is looking at. Moreover, her way of seeing, which constitutes visual narrativity, is not necessarily unequivocal and coherent but partial, scotomized and fragmentary. This form of narrativity is explored through psychoanalytic concepts, such as fantasy, gaze and subject positions, which are discussed in light of their counterparts in the field of art theory.

This book will be key reading for Lacanian psychoanalysts and psychotherapists, as well as art scholars wishing to gain a fresh perspective on narrativity in art.

Efrat Biberman is a Professor of Theory and Philosophy of Art at Beit Berl College. Her research focuses on art and Freudian-Lacanian psychoanalysis. She is the author of *Art, Death and Lacanian Psychoanalysis* (with Shirley Zisser, 2018) and *Weaving a Painting: Israeli Art* and *Lacan's Late Teaching* (2022, in Hebrew).

Visual Narrative and Lacanian Psychoanalysis

Efrat Biberman

Translated by Tamar Gerstenhaber

Routledge
Taylor & Francis Group
LONDON AND NEW YORK

Designed cover image: *An Interior, with a Woman drinking with Two Men, and a Maidservant,* Pieter de Hooch, 1658

First English Edition published 2026
by Routledge
4 Park Square, Milton Park, Abingdon, Oxon OX14 4RN

and by Routledge
605 Third Avenue, New York, NY 10158

Routledge is an imprint of the Taylor & Francis Group, an informa business

First Hebrew edition published by Bar Ilan University Press 2009

British Library Cataloguing-in-Publication Data
A catalogue record for this book is available from the British Library

ISBN: 9781032850795 (hbk)
ISBN: 9781032850771 (pbk)
ISBN: 9781003516446 (ebk)

DOI: 10.4324/9781003516446

Typeset in Optima
by codeMantra

Contents

Figures

Acknowledgments

This book was published with the support of Beit Berl Academic College.

All reasonable effort has been made to identify the copyright holders of the material reproduced in this book. If the authors have inadvertently failed to obtain permission, please contact the publisher so that the necessary arrangements can be made.

2.1 Jan Steen, *The Feast of St. Nicholas,* 1660–1665, Rijksmuseum, Amsterdam.

2.2 Jean-Baptiste Greuze, *A Girl with a Dead Canary,* 1765, National Galleries of Scotland collection.

2.3 Pieter Aertsen, *Market Scene,* 1560–1565, KHM-Museumverband, Kunsthistorisches Museum, Gemäldegalerie, Vienna.

2.4 Rembrandt van Rijn, *The Syndics: The Sampling Officials (wardens) of the Amsterdam Drapers' Guild (The Staalmeesters),* 1662, Rijksmuseum, Amsterdam.

3.1 Thomas Eakins, *The Gross Clinic,* 1875, Jefferson Medical College of Thomas Jefferson University, Philadelphia. Gift of the Alumni Association to Jefferson Medical College in 1878 and purchased by the Pennsylvania Academy of the Fine Arts and the Philadelphia Museum of Art in 2007 with the generous support of more than 3,600 donors, 2007-1-1.

3.2 Hans Holbein the Younger, *The Ambassadors,* 1533, © The National Gallery, London.

4.1 Jean-Baptiste Greuze, *Filial Piety (The Paralytic).* 1763, oil on canvas, The State Hermitage Museum, St. Petersburg. Photograph © The State Hermitage Museum/Photo by Vladimir Terebenin.

4.2 Edouard Manet, *Olympia,* 1863, Musee d'Orsay, Paris. (C) GrandPalaisRmn (musée d'Orsay) - © Hervé Lewandowski.

4.3 Rembrandt van Rijn, *Danaë,* 1636, The State Hermitage Museum, St. Petersburg. Photograph © The State Hermitage Museum/Photo by Vladimir Terebenin.

4.4 Rembrandt van Rijn, *Lucretia,* 1664, National Gallery of Art, Washington D.C. Andrew W. Mellon Collection.

4.5 Rembrandt van Rijn, *Lucretia,* 1666, The Minneapolis Institute of Arts, Minneapolis. The William Hood Dunwoody Fund.

4.6 Rembrandt van Rijn, *Susanna and the Elders*, 1647, Gemäldegalerie, Berlin. Photo credits: Gemäldegalerie, Staatliche Museen zu Berlin / Christoph Schmidt; Public Domain Mark 1.0.

4.7 William Holman Hunt, *The Hireling Shepherd,* 1851–1852, Image courtesy of Manchester Art Gallery, Manchester.

5.1 Samuel van Hoogstraten, *Trompe-l'oeil still life,* 1664, DM/992/691 Dordrechts Museum, purchase with support of Vereniging Rembrandt, Ministry of Welfare, Public Health and Culture, 1992.

5.2 Rembrandt van Rijn, *The Night Watch (The Company of Captain Frans Banning Cocq and Lieutenant Willem van Ruytenburch),* 1642, Rijksmuseum, Amsterdam.

6.1 Rembrandt van Rijn, *Self-Portrait with Bittern*, 1639, Gemäldegalerie, Dresden. bpk / Staatliche Kunstsammlungen Dresden / Elke Estel / Hans-Peter Klut.

6.2 Albrecht Dürer, *Self-Portrait,* 1500, Alte Pinakothek, Munich. © Bayerische Staatsgemäldesammlungen.

6.3 Gustave Courbet, *The Wounded Man,* 1844-1845, Musée d'Orsay, Paris. (C) GrandPalaisRmn - © Hervé Lewandowski.

7.1 Jacques-Louis David, *The Oath of the Horatii*, 1784, Musée du Louvre, Paris. (C) GrandPalaisRmn - © Gérard Blot / Christian Jean.

7.2 Jacques-Louis David, *Bélisaire Begging for Alms*, 1781, Musée Wicar, Lille. (C) GrandPalaisRmn - © Michel Urtado.

8.1 Diego Velázquez, *Las Meninas,* 1656, oil on canvas, 3.2×2.7 m, Museo Nacional del Prado, Madrid. ©Photographic Archive Museo Nacional del Prado.

A previous version of chapter 7 was published in *Image and Narrative*, 2017. "Inside-Out Stories: On Geometrical Perspective and Narrative Representation". *Image and Narrative*. Vol. 18, number 2. Reprinted with kind permission of the editors.

A part of Chapter 6 was published in *Consciousness, Literature and the Arts*, 2005. "The Self as Other". *Consciousness, Literature and the Arts*, Vol. 6, Number 1.

Introduction

In a chapter dedicated to Leonardo da Vinci, Gorgio Vasari, one of the first art historians of the Renaissance, describes one of Leonardo's paintings:

> ...anger, disdain, and vindictiveness are displayed no less by the horsemen than by their horses, two of which with forelegs intertwined are battling with their teeth no less fiercely than their riders are fighting for the standard, which one of the soldiers has seized. While urging his horse to fight, using the power of his shoulders, he has turned around and grasped the staff of the standard, trying to wrench it by brute force from the hands of the four men, while two soldiers defend it with one hand and try with the other to cut off the staff with their swords in the air.[1]

About four centuries later, Jean-Paul Sartre writes the following about a painting by Tintoretto:

> On the left, on the banks of a stinking swamp, we notice a large reptile with branched and dismembered wings. The gaze creates a connection between the vermin and the fugitive; all it takes is a crawl, a flight or leap and it's over: the beast will bite the beauty. This dazzling relationship goes from right to left and front to back; It is not reciprocal. The animal has excellent motives to show a degree of indifference: it is the girl, in her long and ostensible flight, who hints at the dubious intentions of the monster.[2]

A few decades later, art critic Gregory Volk, writes about a painting by contemporary painter, Neo Rauch: "You sense that these two men are destined to battle each other in this idiotic and enervated masculine ritual—or that it's their implacable duty".[3]

It seems as though there is no connection between the three texts, their authors and the reasons they were written, except that all of them relate to

DOI: 10.4324/9781003516446-1

a fictional situation, a moment in a certain plot, and that the origins of these descriptions are paintings. Each of the above excerpts extrapolates a narrative from the painted image. Similarly, the reader of these interpretations, it seems, does not encounter any difficulty in translating the two-dimensionality of the painting into a narrative. These three excerpts are random instances among many. An examination of art books, art critiques or essays in art history and theory reveals that figurative paintings are often seen as narratives or as having narrative aspects. Art critics and art historians often incorporate narrative characteristics in their interpretations of paintings. Some interpretations revolve around a narrative, while others treat it as a matter of lesser importance. In many cases, narrativity is thus an integral part of understanding a painting, even if only as a secondary aspect.

Examining paintings in conjunction with their narrative interpretations evokes a certain ambiguity. On the one hand, looking at a painting as a moment in an unfolding event seems like a natural act that does not require any further explanation. Yet, on the other hand, there is a certain incongruity between the painting and the narrative interpretation that follows it. Although the narrative interpretation of the painting and its connection to the painting itself are clear, there seems to be an inevitable lacuna between them. Narrative interpretation, even when presenting a fantastic fictional state of affairs, generates a stable signification that is accumulated into one solid, coherent, semantic structure. However, the very act of looking at a painting is fragmented. The temporal order of this act is not continuous and linear, and in the process, certain bits of information that are collected do not necessarily constitute a continuation of previous information. Some of the fragments of information sometimes even subvert previous interpretations that arose during the act of looking. It seems as if the juxtaposition of a painting and its narrative interpretation always evokes a visual surplus, which eludes any verbal coverage. That is, there is always an inevitable gap between the two.

This book explores narrativity in painting from the psychoanalytic point of view of Freud and Lacan. One of its main concerns is to shed new light on narrativity in painting and the theoretical discourse around it, while also taking into account the viewer and his relation to the painted scene.[4] In light of various theoretical, historical and interpretative incongruences characterizing the discourse on narrativity in painting, as will be unfolded in what follows, psychoanalysis and its conceptualization of terms such as fantasy,[5] gaze and subject positions offer a fertile ground to analyze this subject. I will, hence, turn to the psychoanalytic discourse for my theoretical framework and focus specifically on the way in which it relates to the concepts that constitute the components for the discussion on the relationship between painting and narrative: narrative, time, vision and the position of the subject in relation to the aesthetic object.

Some theoretical treatises in poetics and aesthetics explore the relations between painting and narrativity, generating diverse references for visual narrative. Yet other treatises explore the boundaries of painting, its narrative insufficiency and even the negative consequences of a narrative apprehension of a painting. These two different approaches seem mutually exclusive. However, they sometimes also appear within the same theoretical framework. For instance, when a painting is discussed as a means of expression that is fundamentally different from literature, while it is also examined through poetic characteristics; or when an intensive theoretical effort is devoted to the negation of the narrative option in painting, yet the very presence of this stubborn negation indicates the possibility of the existence of narrativity in painting.

During the eighteenth century, the conjunction of painting and narrativity was seen as an expression of the conjunction of painting and literature, as implied by the time and space dichotomy. Lessing constitutes the main representative of this approach. He argues that painting is a spatial medium by nature, while literature is temporal.[6] Thus, painting is capable of spatial and simultaneous descriptions, while poetry and prose are destined to unfold within the temporal framework of a plot. According to Lessing, a medium's misuse of the characteristics of a neighboring medium might impair the quality of the aesthetic object. According to this approach, since narrative involves the representation of a sequence in time, painting is limited in its ability to represent a narrative.

The formalist school offers another formulation relating to the boundaries between painting and narrative. This school of thought articulates the differences between the two through the opposition between content and form. In this formulation, literature represents content, which is a marginal or redundant component of painting, while painting, by its very nature, constitutes the material-formal object. In this case, too, the deviation from the boundaries of the medium is understood as an aesthetic deficiency, and here too the conclusion involves a negation or at least a limitation of the narrative capabilities of the painting.[7] Despite the historical differences between them, the various theorizations of the limits of the medium drain the intermedial difference or try to depend on formal characteristics of the object, which vary according to the period and the ideology of the theoretical formulation. The common denominator in all these formulations is that narrative is perceived as external to painting.

The division of the arts according to the boundaries of their different modes of expression has preoccupied aestheticians, while at the same time artists have attempted to exceed these limits or test their flexibility. However, while theoretical debates seem to limit the possibilities of the medium, painting is often perceived as representing a narrative. Hence, the conceptualization of painting as representing narrative is, in many cases, an integral part of its interpretation.

Thus, two opposing theoretical trends can be pointed out. On the one hand, there are aesthetic discussions that explore the boundaries between the two media and view any amalgamation of the two as a negative trend that they must defend against. On the other hand, other aesthetic discussions, and sometimes even the same discussions themselves, raise the possibility of perceiving painting as representing a narrative or examine the painting through literary characteristics. It seems that these two opposing positions, both the understanding of one medium in the tools of the neighboring medium and the criticism of this intermingling, are interlaced with the history and theory of painting. In actuality, these debates testify to the very existence of a kind of "narrative impulse" that accompanies the act of looking at a picture.

Another intricacy concerning narrativity in painting stems from the indeterminate status of this category. While genres such as portraiture or landscape painting group paintings together through a common theme, narrative painting is not a pictorial category in the same sense. The definition of the category of narrative painting is not conclusive. For instance, it may include paintings that refer to a familiar narrative in culture or paintings that represent several situations to be understood as a series of temporal events. Moreover, the value of narrativity in painting is ambivalent. Painterly values such as composition, space organization, materiality or color application have always been perceived as inherent and fundamental to painting. The narrativity of the painting, on the other hand, is optional and subject to ideology and modes of interpretation. These values are often also conceived as marginal or even alien to the painting itself.

As mentioned above, interpreting a painting as a narrative is commonplace, and yet an examination of a painting alongside the narrative interpretation given to it always reveals a certain gap between the two. I would like to argue that the incompatibility between a narrative interpretation of a painting and the painting itself, along with the theoretical ambiguity that has emerged throughout history in relation to narrative painting, points toward the same phenomenon, which is this book's point of departure: the complex nature of narrative in the visual medium is inherent to the image and is not only a product of its interpretation.

Art theories often attribute the problematic nature of narrative painting to a range of factors that are external to the painting itself. I intend to explain this dilemma in a different way and argue that this incongruence is not located in the connection between a painting and something external to it, but rather stems from the structure of the image itself and the mode of looking that it entails. Narrativity, according to this view, is an inherent part of visual logic. However, the characteristics of narrativity, which stem from the relationship between the subject and the image, consist of a fundamental incompatibility. This fundamental incompatibility is hence the source of the failures that emerge from each of the interpretive models that try to deal with narrative painting. In other words, the incompatibility does not stem from the fact that narrativity is external to the image, but, on the contrary, from the very fact that narrativity is inherent to painting, while the incongruence between the two is an integral part of it. Thus, I would like to argue that the boundaries of the medium are not an obstacle that prevents painting from conveying a narrative, but rather they are part of the unique nature of visual narrativity.

The dominant preoccupation with the disciplinary affiliation of the term "narrative painting" has shifted the focus away from fundamental questions relating to painting such as: Why are paintings read as narratives? What is the nature of the narrativity that arises from them? And in what way is narrativity present in them?

This book traces a transition from a predetermined conception of narrative, which is attributed to painting through interpretation, to a narrative that is established through the exchange of gazes between the looking subject and the fictional world. This narrative is built into the image and is a product of a subjective mode of looking.

I intend to answer questions and explain phenomena that, in my opinion, have been left without an adequate response on the part of the fields of art history and theory and aesthetics. This book is, therefore, essentially interdisciplinary. Its point of departure is based on discussions from the fields of art theory, literary theory and aesthetics, which will be analyzed in what follows from a psychoanalytic perspective. As I will show, the psychoanalytic framework makes it possible to explain this fundamental discrepancy as an inherent part of the image and of the ways of looking at it.

The concept of narrativity is not foreign to psychoanalysis, even if it is not one of its main concepts. Since the early days of the psychoanalytic clinic, Freud formulated his case studies using narrative constructions, and he even noted that the case study of Dora, for instance, could be read as a novella.[8] Indeed, all his case studies may be read in a similar fashion. Moreover, Freud's paper on family romances explicitly presents the affinity between the psychic reality of the subject and the fictional narrative he attributes to his family.[9] The same applies to the Freudian term fantasy, which is a fictional script in which the subject is the protagonist.[10] The fundamental concept of construction in psychoanalysis is also based entirely on narratives that the subject reconstructs during analysis.[11]

Furthermore, Freud often turned to literature in order to theorize psychoanalytic topics, for instance, in "The Uncanny",[12] or in his essay on Jensen's Gradiva.[13] Lacan also frequently turned to writers and poets, including Shakespeare, Racine, Gide and Poe. At the same time, both Freud and Lacan often discussed painting and sculpture.

Moreover, the tension that underlies the various interpretations of narrative painting, between word and image and their meeting points, preoccupies psychoanalytic discourse, from Freud's early distinction between object-representation (*dingvorstellung*) and word-representation (*vortvorstellung*),[14] to the encounters between word and image that take place with in the "means of representation" as part of the dream work in *The Interpretation of Dreams*.[15] Lacan also discusses the relationship between word and image, for instance, in his reading of Caravaggio's two paintings *The Sacrifice of Isaac* in his seminar *The Names of the Father*,[16] in the seminal essay about the instance of the letter,[17] or in his analysis of the written formula in Freud's dream of Irma's injection.[18] Hence, psychoanalytic thinking offers fertile conceptual grounds for the discussion of visual narrativity. Moreover, psychoanalytic discourse enables us to explore the concept of "narrative painting" while not adhering to a traditional genre or disciplinary lens.

I will make use of the psychoanalytic framework to focus on the concepts that constitute the components of visual narrativity: narrative, temporality, the looking subject and his position in relation to the painting. This approach is intended to answer concrete questions and explain phenomena that have been left without an adequate answer on the part of the fields of art history, art theory and aesthetics.

Thus, this book aims to take the debate on narrative painting beyond its genre or disciplinary position and explore the relationship between painting and narrative from the psychoanalytic perspective by reexamining the meeting point between painting, the looking subject and narrative, in their relation to concepts such as the gaze, desire, phantasm and subject positions.

The theoretical discussion that distinguishes between literature and painting can be channeled into three paradigmatic cases throughout history: Lessing's treatise *Laocoon* of the mid-eighteenth century,[19] Greenberg's essay "Towards a Newer Laocoon" of the mid-twentieth century[20] and W. J. T. Mitchell's discussion of *Laocoon* from a postmodern point of view.[21] The first chapter examines the problematic nature of the discussion of narrative painting in all its aspects, as they emerge from the three *Laocoons*. These three *Laocoons*, I argue, share an isomorphic structure, as all three simultaneously refute the possibility of narrative painting and point to it. The problem of narrative painting, therefore, continues to appear in various formations despite its alternating formulations throughout history.

The second chapter examines three models of narrative painting. While the first two models locate the source of the narrative value of a narrative painting in an anterior verbal text, the third model points toward a different narrativity, which is a result of the encounter between the looking subject and the object of his observation. This narrativity is characterized by a way of looking in which the visual field contains both the looking subject and the object he is looking at, and it serves as a point of departure for examining how narrative can be thought of in the visual field. This narrative does not stem from a verbal narrative, but rather from a meaning-generating mechanism that emerges from the encounter between the viewer and the painting.

An examination of this narrative possibility raises a question: how can this situation, in which the subject and the aesthetic object are not sharply distinguished, be theorized in a way that goes beyond perceiving it metaphorically? In order to conceptualize a pictorial arena in which the looking subject and the object are not sharply distinguished, I turn to the Lacanian psychoanalytic concept of the gaze.

The third chapter examines the Freudian-Lacanian concept of fantasy and draws possible connections between fantasy and painting. The concept of narrative painting as constituted by the relations between the painting and its spectator, so it seems, is similar to the way psychoanalysis defines fantasy: an imaginary script in which the subject is the protagonist. A close reading of Slavoj Žižek's essay on the seven veils of fantasy can help me examine the concept of fantasy and show its relevance to narrative painting.[22] The chapter traces this intricate concept, reconfiguring concepts such as vision and seeing, temporal ordering and subject's position in relation to painting, and the term "narrative" itself.

The fourth chapter explores narrativity that is relevant to the visual image through the concept of the split image, which I coined. I turn to Žižek's discussion of the phantasmatic aspect of narrative as a cover for paradoxical situations to argue that the visual medium makes it possible to preserve this paradoxicality, which verbal narrative structures seek to disguise. I illustrate this paradoxicality through interpretations of paintings that expose a contradiction or inadequacy that cannot be unequivocally determined. I delineate this phenomenon through a temporality unique to psychoanalysis, using Žižek's discussion of Alfred Hitchcock's cinema.[23]

The fifth chapter examines Lacan's conceptualization of the gaze.[24] I isolate three aspects of the gaze: temporality, reflexivity and blindness as sight. I examine Lacan's discussion, alongside those of Norman Bryson and Maurice Merleau-Ponty (to whom Lacan himself refers) to shed light on Lacan's theorization and to show its relevance to painting.[25] This analysis makes it possible to formulate a unique perception of time relevant to visuality, which is not derived from the space–time opposition set by Lessing, in which the visual medium emerges as insufficient. The same applies to the psychoanalytic conception of the structure of the gaze, which defines a complex and anti-dualistic process of looking. The idea of blindness as an essential component of a dynamic visual process offers yet another aspect of vision, differing from the traditional visual perceptions laid down by art theories.

The sixth chapter examines the way the object of vision is an integral part of the looking subject. The chapter begins with a theoretical discussion of the Lacanian subject, the role that vision plays in his constitution, and the relationship between the subject and the object according to Freud and Lacan. Then, I turn to the painterly genre in which the subject, with all his complexities, is embodied in the most explicit way: self-portraiture. First, I examine interpretations from the field of theory of art given to self-portraits, and then I show how different psychoanalytic discussions shed new light on these interpretations and their relevance to painting in general.

The position of the subject toward the painted object, to which I refer in the sixth chapter through the genre of self-portraiture, is addressed in art history and theory in the discussion on geometrical perspective. The seventh chapter explores perspective as an artistic manifestation of subjectivity in the visual field, while highlighting the connection between perspective and narrativity. On this matter, opinions are diverse. Some theorists claim that perspective paintings focus on the story the picture represents, hence supporting narrativity. Others argue that, as a formal device, perspective is inherently at odds with narrativity. Still others claim that perspective plays a dual role in objectifying and subjectifying the pictorial space. I show how perspective painting operates as an inverting apparatus that allows narrative meaning to emerge from lapses in representation, points in which the painting fails to obey the strict rules of perspective.

The final chapter explores Lacan's analysis of Velázquez' painting *Las Meninas*. Lacan's analysis makes it possible for me to articulate the place of narrativity in the visual field. Narrativity is not a literary supplement to a painting to which it is heterogeneous by nature. Rather, narrativity is inherent to the very structure of the visual field, of which the looking subject is as much a constitute as the object he sees, and it emerges as an effect of the act of seeing.

Basing its insights on the psychoanalytic discourse, this book presents a reformulation of concepts such as temporality, narrative, gaze, subject positions, representation and perspective, enabling us to think differently about narrative painting. Thus, narrativity is returned to painting not as an external addition to it, but as an immanent component of the painting, as a product of the unique way of looking at it. Narrativity is, thus, a painterly value, a component in the understanding of painting as a complex, dynamic and changing structure of sense. It is the result of the process of looking at a visual object by a particular subject.

Rather than considering interpretive models regarding painting merely as a tool for attaining meaning, the research method employed here differs in principle: I examine both the painting and the ways in which it was interpreted previously. Thus, to a large extent, I analyze the ways we look at paintings. This method allows me to examine paintings based on the way they are understood and interpreted and to critically illuminate existing interpretive models.

Notes

1 Vasari, Gorgio. 1991. *The Lives of the Artists*. Trans. Julia Conaway Bondanella and Peter Bondanella. Oxford: Oxford University Press, p. 295.
2 Sartre, Jean-Paul. 1972. "Saint George et le dragon". *Situations*, IX. Paris: Gallimard, pp. 203–204.
3 Volk, Gregory. 2010, "Neo Rauch", edited by Marcia Vetrocq. In: *Art in America*, Brant publications.
4 Throughout the book, I relate to the subject as both male and female, so that the masculine grammatical form "he" and "his" is used as gender neutral.
5 The term "fantasy" is written interchangeably as both fantasy or phantasy. I chose to spell it according to the relevant author. That is, in Freud's English translations, it spelled as phantasy, while Žižek writes it fantasy and so forth.
6 Lessing, Gotthold Ephraim. 1887 [1766]. *Laocoön: An Essay upon the Limits of Painting and Poetry*. Trans. Ellen Frothingham. Cambridge: Cambridge University Press, John Wilson and Son.
7 Greenberg, Clement. 1986 [1940]. "Towards a Newer Laocoon". *The Collected Essays and Criticism: Vol. 1 Perceptions and Judgments, 1939–1944*. Chicago and London: The University of Chicago Press, pp. 23–38.

8 Freud as quoted by François Regnault. Regnault, François. 1991. "Lacan and Experience". In *Lacan and the Human Sciences*. Edited by Alexandre Leupin. Lincoln: University of Nebraska Press.
9 Freud, Sigmund. [1908]. "Family Romances". *SE* 9: 237–241.
10 Freud, Sigmund. [1919]. "A Child is being Beaten". *SE* 17: 179–204.
11 Freud, Sigmund. [1937]. "Constructions in Analysis". *SE* 23: 257–269.
12 Freud, Sigmund. [1919]. "The Uncanny". *SE* 17: 219–256.
13 Freud, Sigmund. [1906]. "Delusions and Dreams in Jensen's *Gradiva*". *SE* 9: 7–93.
14 Freud, Sigmund. [1915]. "The Unconscious. Appendix C: Words and Things". *SE* 14: 209–215.
15 Freud, Sigmund. [1900]. "The Means of Representation in Dreams". *SE* 4: 310–338.
16 Lacan, Jacques. 2005. *Des Nomes-du-Père*. Paris: Seuil.
17 Lacan, Jacques. 2006 [1957]. "The Instance of the Letter in the Unconscious or Reason since Freud". Écrits. Trans. Bruce Fink. New York and London: Norton and Company, pp. 412–441.
18 Lacan, Jacques. 1988. *The Ego in Freud's Theory and in the Technique of Psychoanalysis 1954–1955: The Seminar of Jacques Lacan, Book II*. Trans. Sylvana Tomaselli. New York and London: W.W. Norton and Company.
19 Lessing, 1766.
20 Greenberg, 1940.
21 Mitchell, William John Thomas. 1986. *Iconology: Image, Text, Ideology*. Chicago and London: University of Chicago Press.
22 Žižek, Slavoj. 1998. "The Seven Veils of Fantasy". In *Key Concepts of Lacanian Psychoanalysis*. Edited by Danny Nobus. London: Rebus Press.
23 Žižek, Slavoj. 1992. "In his Bold Gaze My Ruin Is Writ Large". In *Everything You Always Wanted to Know about Lacan but Were Afraid to Ask Hitchcock*. Edited by Slavoj Žižek. London and New York: Verso.
24 Lacan, Jacques. 1981 [1964–1965]. *The Four Fundamental Concepts of Psychoanalysis: The Seminar of Jacques Lacan, Book XI*. Trans. Alan Sheridan. New York and London: W.W. Norton and Company.
25 Bryson, Norman. 1983. *Vision and Painting: The Logic of the Gaze*. New Haven: Yale University Press.
Merleau-Ponty, Maurice. 1997 [1968]. *The Visible and the Invisible*. Trans. Alphonso Lingis. Evanston: Northwestern University Press.

1 Beyond Laocoon

Lessing published his essay *Laocoon* in 1766, and it has since become one of the cornerstones of the theoretical debate on the limits of the medium.[1] Lessing separates poetry and painting as two distinct artistic expressions and argues that each medium has abilities that stem from its distinct character. Thus, to create a beautiful object of art, an artist must adhere to the limits of each medium. Lessing equates the distinction between poetry and painting to the distinction between time and space. He locates the "root of all evil" in narrative painting in the attempt to represent, through painting, not only space but also time. However, Lessing also articulates the possible ways art can go beyond the boundaries of every medium without hurting the aesthetic qualities of the object.

A little under 200 years after Lessing, Clement Greenberg published an essay entitled "Towards a Newer Laocoon".[2] Like Lessing, Greenberg warns against confusing the different media of the arts. He praises painting as devoid of any external attributes, including literary attributes. This claim leads him to favor form over content in painting. Thus, Greenberg substitutes Lessing's opposition of time and space with a different one – content versus form. Now, the root of the problem in narrative painting is in the idea of painting as a bearer of content, since the interest in content stems from a confusion between poetry and painting. Greenberg argues that in painting, form needs to take precedence over content. He believes that this new order would eliminate, once and for all, the unwanted amalgamation of literature and painting, allowing each art to remain within the material boundaries of its own medium.

Forty years later, another chapter was added to the Laocoon series. W.J.T. Mitchell, a cultural critic, rereads *Laocoon* and returns to the opposition between the verbal medium and the visual medium.[3] However, unlike his predecessors, Mitchell does not sketch the opposition to discuss the possibility or impossibility of painting to represent narrative. Rather, he explores the connection between image and word, while undoing the two previous oppositions. The connection Mitchell draws relates to a broader trend that took shape during the twentieth century, which strived to undo the differences between the media and found narrativity in almost everything.[4]

DOI: 10.4324/9781003516446-2

Despite its liberal nature, though, this trend also limits thinking on narrative painting, not because it confines it within the borders of the visual medium, as the first two *Laocoons* do, but because it empties the very concept of narrative of its meaning by creating an "inflation of narrativity" that exists everywhere.

The three Laocoons constitute paradigmatic cases that reflect the way Western culture treats the possible connection between narrative and painting. The first two *Laocoons* situate this relation in two pairs of oppositions, time-space and content-form. The third *Laocoon*, as stated, unravels the opposition yet without solving it, since when everything is narrative, thinking about narrative painting is virtually emptied of all meaning.

In what follows, I will show how each *Laocoon* negates narrative painting or makes its existence possible only under certain conditions. I will point toward the way narrative painting is examined as an opposition between two components such as poetry-painting, time-space or content-form, and I will show that even when these oppositions are undone in the third *Laocoon*, the problem of narrative painting remains.

The first *Laocoon*: the oppositions painting-poetry, space-time

One of the claims regarding the differences between poetry and painting is that, up until the eighteenth century, the two were seen as sister arts, different only in their manner of expression but not in their goals or contents.[5] Both arts are a mimesis of a noble human action; hence, the objects of their mimesis are culturally familiar mythological, biblical or historical events. These arguments stem from earlier theoreticians who read Aristotle and Horatius's comments on painting at face value and concluded that both *The Poetics* and *Ars Poetica* equivalate the two media.

Lessing's essay, *Laocoon*, constitutes an attempt to articulate, through formal means, the differences between poetry and painting, fix the boundaries of each, and set the conditions for the possibility of each medium to exceed what has been marked as its limit. In many respects, the aim of the essay is to regulate the distinctions of each medium that should bind each artistic expression. Thus, Lessing claims that we find poetry filled with descriptions and paintings that are flooded with allegories, thereby tarnishing the beauty of the object.[6] Lessing's fundamental presupposition is that there must exist a certain relation between representation and the thing it represents. He distinguishes between spatial objects, which exist side by side and can be represented through a spatial object, that is, painting, and temporal objects, which exist sequentially and can be represented through a temporal object, that is, poetry.[7] Thus, Lessing claims that poetry is limited in its ability to describe space, and the poet must take necessary precautions so that a description of space will not harm the beauty of the poem. Just as he places limitations on poetry in its ability to describe space, Lessing also limits painting in its ability to represent time.[8]

We could claim that the negation of the possibility of representing time through painting does not necessarily prevent its narrative capabilities, since they could exist through alternative visual means. However, Lessing does not reach this conclusion. He does not completely negate the possibility of narrative painting and claims that the painter has at his disposal certain means that make it possible for him to represent a partial and limited narrative. Yet this very point leads to a conflict that characterizes Lessing and other art theorists who follow him. Despite his proclamation at the beginning of his essay to regulate the confusion between poetry and painting, Lessing mostly uses literary characteristics to examine painting. He mostly compares the abilities and limitations of painting in relation to poetry and only discusses actual painterly characteristics, such as perspective, in sparse instances. That is, Lessing's point of departure is positing a dichotomy between poetry and painting. We could have expected that, from this point onward, his discussion would diverge into two parallel lines: an analysis of the verbal medium, its characteristics, abilities and limitations, alongside a similar analysis of the visual medium. However, alongside the basic dichotomy he proposes, Lessing mainly examines painting through characteristics that he borrows from poetry. This issue, in which theories posit a dichotomy between painting and poetry, yet at the same time discuss one field through the tools and characteristics of the other, appears in various theoretical debates that followed Lessing and examined the visual medium through literary characteristics.

As stated, Lessing argues that painting cannot describe a sequence in time, which is the distinct field of poetry and literature. However, despite this limitation, he finds a way for painting to depict some narrative attributes: the possibility of representing a "fruitful moment". A fruitful moment is one from which we may deduce a certain sequence of actions, even though the painting only depicts a part of it. Therefore, the artist should not choose a moment of culmination beyond which there is nothing, but rather "the more we see, the more we must be able to imagine; and the more we imagine, the more we must think we see".[9] That is, if the artist can represent in the painting a piece of the plot that implies the previous event and the later one, the viewer can infer a sequence of temporal and causative events and thus employ a narratological reading of the painting.

Thus, the "fruitful moment" constitutes a compensation for a temporality that is neutralized through painting. It is a distillation of a sequence of events into a single moment, which compensates for the painting's inability to represent a sequence of developing events. The hidden supposition, then, is that the goal of painting is to achieve, even if only partly and in a limited way, what literature does. However, due to the limitations of the medium, it must make do with the fruitful moment as a substitutive means for this task.

The supposition regarding a sequence of temporal events as the fundamental characteristic of literature is, of course, taken from Aristotle. In the opening chapter of the *Poetics*, Aristotle distinguishes between the various means by which the different art forms create their imitation. Later, he isolates the "structure of the incidents" as the most important and significant component of tragedy: "It follows that the incidents and the plot are the end at which tragedy aims, and in everything the end aimed at is of prime importance. Moreover, you could not have a tragedy without action".[10] That is, incidents that make up the plot of tragedy are the starting point from which all the components of the tragedy emanate and to which they are subjected. Thus, the plot is the most fundamental element of tragedy, and even the characters and thoughts are of lesser importance. Aristotle compares this to the components of painting: the structure of the plot is similar to the outline of the painting, and the characters to the brushstrokes against the chalk outline.[11] Like the drawing, the structure of the plot may also exist without its "filling materials".

If we go back to the dichotomy Lessing proposes, we could expect that when he turns to the characterization of painting, he will offer a certain spatial, painterly characterization that would be visually parallel to Aristotle's incidents. However, the fruitful moment that he articulates can only be a "visual parallel" to a limited extent. The fruitful moment is more like a shortened and partial version of incidents from which we can extrapolate the entire plot. That is, the power of the fruitful moment is not measured by its visual values, such as perspective or composition, but rather by representing a sequence. Thus, the fruitful moment reflects the way in which Lessing examines painting through literary values.

In addition to limiting painting to a single moment, Lessing points toward another difficulty in representing complex situations, which stems from the limitations of the medium: in his efforts to represent a certain character the viewer would recognize, the painter must concentrate his efforts on characterizing the figure. This characterization does not leave him room to elaborate on and describe the character in complex situations.[12] Thus, the supposition behind the fruitful moment regarding the limitations of the visual medium in comparison to the verbal medium also applies to the construction of characters. Here, too, Lessing believes that the poet has more possibilities than the painter, and so the painter makes do with his limited means. For instance, the painter must always represent Venus as a beautiful woman; otherwise she would not be recognized as Venus, whereas the poet can represent her from less flattering angles as well.[13] That is, again, Lessing does not offer an alternative expressional channel for the visual medium, which makes use of spatial means; rather, he examines its possibilities strictly within the framework of verbal ones.

Lessing's other remarks on the characterization of figures relate to proportions. He claims that through painting it is difficult to represent scale. He gives the manner in which Homer describes Minerva lifting an enormous stone with her hand as an example. When trying to depict this situation, the painter will encounter a problem: if he paints both the stone and Minerva in fantastic size, "all marvel ceases". This is the marvel that characterizes the lines from *The Iliad*, since it is reasonable to suppose that a giant can lift such an enormous stone. So, if the artist paints only the stone as enormous, he will create an insufferable incoherence, since "on canvas we lose everything which in poetry exalts the gods above mere godlike men".[14] In other words, verbal representation generates in the reader a marvelous, divine sensation, while the visual representation of the same wonder exposes it in a way that divests it of the wondrous element or creates confusion. Lessing attempts to demonstrate here the limitations of the visual medium and its dependence on an anterior verbal text, to which the painting is supposed to refer. However, beyond this, there is also an appeal to a distinct Aristotelian element, that is, the representation of characters.

The imitation of characters, according to Aristotle, is the second most important element in tragedy, after the structure of incidents.[15] He enumerates four rules for the representation of characters: they must be fitting for tragedy, they must fit the type they portray, they must resemble the specific detail they represent, and they must be consistent. Moreover, the imitation of a character must always follow what is necessary or probable.[16]

If we return to Lessing, who is disturbed by the inability to represent Venus in a less favorable light, it seems that there is a direct connection to Aristotle's rules for the representation of characters. Because of its temporal abilities, poetry can describe how, in her anger, in the blink of an eye, Venus does not look her best. The reader would understand this as a momentary lapse in her otherwise perfect appearance. Yet, if Venus is represented in a painting with her face distorted in horrible rage, it would irreparably damage the representation of Venus's character and would, hence, not adhere to the Aristotelian rules. And this is the verdict in the case of Minerva and the stone. By examining painting through its ability to meet Aristotelian criteria, Lessing again reveals that he examines painting through literary devices and is disturbed by the inability of painting to conform to the verbal text. The lack of proportion that he refers to in the example of Minerva and the stone also does not stem, as he himself states, from an aesthetic flaw but from the fact that the painting would represent a nonsensical state of affairs.

Lessing also relates to painting through a non-Aristotelian literary device, which in the twentieth century will be defined as "point of view", "perspective" or "focalization". According to Lessing, literature or painting may depict a situation in which one of the fictional characters is invisible to the other characters, yet present to the reader or the viewer. Homer demonstrates this situation when he refers to the mist surrounding the characters. Lessing argues that this is a metaphoric speech that aims at demonstrating the invisibility of the character. In painting, he argues, it is impossible to distinguish between figurative and literal speech, and that is why the painter represents the invisible character as immersed in an actual cloud.[17] That is, Lessing points toward two advantages of the literary medium over the visual medium: the literary medium has the ability to speak in a metaphoric language, and it can also describe a situation in which only some of the characters in the fictional world are aware of what is happening. The visual medium cannot use metaphoric language; it can only describe the situation in a direct manner. Moreover, when trying to describe a state of affairs in which only some of the characters are aware of the things around them, the visual medium has awkward means. As Lessing states, "It is no better than the rolls of paper with sentences upon them, which issue from the mouth of personages in the old Gothic pictures".[18]

The concept of "focalization" denotes a narrative principle that makes it possible to determine which elements in a fictional world are organized from a certain point of view or position.[19] Narratological theories distinguish internal focalization, as the point of view of one of the characters in the fictional world, from external focalization, as the point of view of a character who is external to the fictional world. Another distinction is between a fixed internal focalization, in which the text is consistently narrated from the point of view of one character, and changing internal focalization, in which the focalization passes through several characters, or many focalizers, such as in cases where the story presents different versions of the same events.[20]

When Lessing describes a scene in which a certain fictional character is invisible to the others, he is, in fact, referring to this narrative principle. And in the example depicted above, the focalization is internal, since the painted situation is shown from the partial point of view of one of the characters, who cannot see the character immersed in the cloud. Here, too, Lessing relates to the limitation of painting while also claiming that the attempt to depict a partial point of view ends up awkward and simplistic. It seems that Lessing is disturbed more by the painting's incongruency with the verbal text, or its inability to represent fiction as it was written than by any visual-aesthetic flaw that might stem from this.

The echoes of literary principles in Lessing's descriptions of paintings show that, despite his professed aim to separate the artistic mediums, his interpretation does the opposite: painting is examined through literary characteristics and through distinct painterly values, such as composition or colorfulness. Mitchell's criticism of Lessing, which I will later discuss, touches on this very point. According to Mitchell, the root of the problem in the distinction between painting and literature is not located in the inability of one medium to use the characteristics of the neighboring medium, but the opposite, in this very ability.

We could claim that the echoes of literary characteristics in Lessing's discussion of painting stem from the fact that he was a man of literature and theatre, and not an art critic. However, interpreting painting with terms taken from literary theory is not unique to Lessing. We can see this manner of interpretation in the works of theoreticians and critics such as Denis Diderot, Alois Riegl, Heinrich Wölfflin and Erwin Panofsky.

Almost 200 years after Lessing, Panofsky writes about iconography and iconology. However, despite his historical and theoretical distance from Lessing, and even though his theoretical credence is dedicated to painting, Panofsky's discussion still resonates with Aristotelian principles.[21]

According to Panofsky, the interpretation of painting passes through a system composed of three layers of understanding. The first layer relates to the initial way in which certain forms appear before the eyes of the viewer. The second layer, which he calls iconography, relates to the manner in which these forms receive meaning. The third layer, which he names iconology, relates to the manner in which the meaning is distributed through cultural and social contexts. In the process of understanding a painting, the interpreter moves between the different layers while drawing from his own subjective experience. However, according to Panofsky, the interpreter must not stop at his subjective experience; rather, he needs to base his interpretation on the historical and social contexts of the work of art.[22] Panofsky, then, distinguishes between iconographic analysis and iconological analysis. Both are supposed to function as tools that help the interpreter identify elements of the work. He exemplifies the two forms of analysis through an interpretation of Leonardo da Vinci's painting, *The Last Supper*, from 1495 to 1498. The iconographic analysis relates to the painting as a representation of *The Last Supper* and analyzes the compositional and iconographic characteristics of the painting. An iconological analysis takes place when we relate to a painting as a symptom of something else. That is, in iconological analysis, the interpreter views details in the painting as symbols of meanings that were often unknown even to the artist himself.[23]

When the iconographic and iconological analysis encounters difficulties of identification, the interpreter must turn to previous works of the artist, a literary text that has an affinity with the painting and works of other artists from the period. Panofsky hence shows how the meaning of a painting does not rely only on a prior verbal text but may also be extrapolated from previous paintings and conventions of representation that appear in them. However, his most basic premise is that the interpretation must account for the meaning of the represented character and its qualities, which are supposed to be coherent in accordance with the Aristotelian demands. In other words, Panofsky may claim that painting can somewhat exceed the boundaries of the verbal text that is part of its background, but it also must be consistent with other paintings. That is, Panofsky adheres to the basic principle of unity of characters, only he also relies on a pictorial corpus and not solely on a literary corpus. The fact that we can find the echoes of a literary theory, even if only tacitly, in the work of a canonical theoretician of art such as Panofsky is important in this context, since it demonstrates my general claim that the visual medium and its narrative aspect are often examined through literary concepts and characteristics.

Two other Aristotelian principles that can be found in theories of art are unity and causality. In his discussion on painting during the age of Diderot, Michael Fried claims that various theoreticians in the eighteenth century posed the demands of unity and causality for painting.[24]

The demand for unity became a cornerstone in the painterly theories of the end of the seventeenth century and the beginning of the eighteenth century. As Rensselaer Lee claims, the assertion that a certain painting obeys the principles of unity was seen at that time as a compliment to the artist.[25] In accordance with this idea, painter Charles Le Brun praises Nicolas Poussin's painting *Israelites Gathering Manna* from 1639,[26] for the unity of its action. Poussin, as Le Brun states, carefully arranged all of the characters in the painting, with their actions and expressions, so that every detail was tied to another detail in a causal relationship, thereby serving the general idea of the painting.[27] Diderot takes this demand even further, and sees it as a call to expel from the painting anything that does not directly contribute to the represented dramatic action. He concludes this idea with the words: "nothing is beautiful without unity, and there is no unity without subordination. This appears contradictory, but it is not".[28] That is, each painterly detail must work toward a single unified idea, and any blemish to the representation of unity of action in the painting would hurt the entire painting.

The demand for unity, like the other characteristics I have presented so far, also relates to the demands Aristotle places for tragedy:

> As then in the other arts of representation a single representation means a representation of a single object, so too the plot being a representation of a piece of action must represent a single piece of action and the whole of it; and the component incidents must be so arranged that if one of them be transposed or removed, the unity of the whole is dislocated and destroyed. For if the presence or absence of a thing makes no visible difference, then it is not an integral part of the whole.[29]

The principle of unity also plays a part in Alois Riegl's discussion of Dutch painting, albeit in an indirect fashion.[30] Riegl examines group portraits spanning over 150 years in Amsterdam and Haarlem, and through them, he marks several developments that took place in group portraiture paintings. Riegl outlines the direction toward which this painterly genre developed in stages: achieving internal coherence, which relates to the manner in which the characters in the painting are organized around one central character or more, while one of the ways of achieving this internal coherence is external coherence, which means opening the pictorial space toward the subject that is looking at it.[31] It seems that the use that Riegl makes of the concept of "coherence" is somewhat analogous to the Aristotelian principle of unity since it is designed to organize all the elements in the painting into a single meaning and purpose.

In his book *Principles of Art History: The Problem of the Development of Style in Later Art,* Heinrich Wölflin also applies the principle of unity as a property of painting.[32] Wölflin makes unity one of the fundamental concepts with which he analyzes Renaissance and Baroque art. He claims that sixteenth-century art is characterized by what he calls "multiple unities", while seventeenth-century art is characterized by "unified unity". That is, Wölflin proposes two painterly states: one in which every detail in the painting is subordinate to the painting as a whole, and the other in which the details of the painting are part of a whole while also retaining their own independent presence. It should be noted that Wölflin presents the principle of unity as a fundamental concept to understand painting as a whole and not just its narrative aspect. However, within this prism, the principle of unity also brings about the unity of the fictional story, as can be seen from the way in which he interprets Leonardo da Vinci's *The Last Supper*. According to Wölflin, the painting represents the moments after Jesus spoke of the act of betrayal. So as to attain the spiritual unity in which the disciples of Jesus are gripped, Leonardo expels from the painting anything that does not directly relate to the general story.[33] In this interpretation, Wölflin, much like the other art historians I mentioned, applies the Aristotelian principle of unity, which is supposed to work both for tragedy and for painting.

As Fried shows, various thinkers in the eighteenth century also applied to painting the demand for causality. He argues that we may use the principle of causality to distinguish between Diderot's conception of painting and the conception of other painters and theorists such as Le Brun and Roger de Piles. Thus, for instance, de Piles claims that painting must function as a machine in which every part is designed for the other, and all the parts work together to produce a single effect. However, while various thinkers conceived of painting as a machine that coordinates the parts of the painting, Diderot thinks of this idea in the sense of an internal and inherent causality, which is necessary for painting. According to Diderot, "A composition must be organized so as to persuade me that it could not be organized otherwise; a figure must act or rest so as to persuade me that it could not do otherwise".[34] Painting is hence conceptualized as a kind of microcosmos of an overall causal system. The demand for causality leads Diderot to prefer historical and genre paintings over landscape paintings for the simple reason that paintings representing human action and desire can also represent causal relations more distinctly than landscape or still-life paintings.

Diderot here, again, turns to Aristotle, who argued that events in tragedy should exceed expectations but stem from each other.[35] The principle of causality that may be extrapolated from this argument constitutes one of the cornerstones with which a narrative structure is examined within literary theories, narratological theories and cognitive sciences. We can also find this principle, according to which painting is supposed to obey a certain causal order, explicitly expressed in Diderot's analyses of the French Salon paintings from the eighteenth century. However, the causality Diderot demands of painting is different from Aristotelian causality. Causality, according to Diderot, does not relate to the causal order within a sequence of events, but to an overall causality that subjugates all the details of the painting to a single purpose.

Lessing himself does not explicitly mention causality, but his "fruitful moment" includes causality. If the viewer is supposed to infer a certain cause or effect of the represented event, we may assume that there is a causal order between the represented event and the event that the viewer is supposed to be able to imagine the more he sees, as he argues.[36] The principle of causality is also intertwined into Riegl's discussion in his analysis of Rembrandt's painting *The Night Watch* from 1642. Riegl shows how every character in the painting is subjugated to the central scene, while another character, the captain of the night watch, constitutes the cause of the events. This is how Riegl suggests we understand Rembrandt's pictorial conception, in which the very cause of the painting, the call to march, is expressed by the hand of the captain, showing how the group is heading toward the viewer.[37]

Different theoreticians, then, make use of certain terms with sources rooted in various literary theories. The theories I have outlined above preserve, to a certain extent, the conflict that I pointed out in Lessing's argument. Yet, in his attempt to confine each medium within its own borders, and despite his explicit intention, Lessing continues to examine painting with literary tools. Thus, he places painting in an inferior position to literature. The various theories that examine the theoretical aspects of painting continue, to a certain extent, to uphold this hierarchy when analyzing painting through literary terms.

As I have claimed, a narrative reading of painting is fundamentally an almost spontaneous activity, which characterizes a wide variety of looking at figurative paintings. The fact that different theoreticians choose to examine painting through literary terms, whether directly or implicitly, shows that they believe there is a fundamental affinity between painting and narrative. Thus, they strengthen the claim that narrativity is a characteristic that emanates from the painting, as many interpretations of paintings spontaneously conceive of it as a narrative. That is, these theoreticians sense the narrative option that emanates from painting and identify it with literature. Their use of literary characteristics, then, is not because the painting is "literary", but because narrativity is exclusively identified by them with literature.

Does making use of literary terms to analyze paintings indeed shed light on the narrativity in painting? As I have shown, from Lessing's articulation of the "fruitful moment", it seems that applying literary characteristics to painting eventually demonstrates its inferiority in relation to literature. Moreover, in what sense does applying literary characteristics to painting coincide with its inherent properties? Is not this form of analysis fundamentally foreign to painting? In other words, relating to painting through literary characteristics, on the one hand, strengthens its narrative potential, yet on the other hand, it diminishes it and demonstrates its limitations since comparing it to the narrative possibilities that the verbal medium possesses.

The question at stake here is to what we may attribute this complexity. Is this a use of a form of analysis that does not comply with the object it analyzes? After all, the search for a representation of a continuous sequence of events or an extrapolation of causal relations from the painted situation cannot explain the immediate narrativity that emanates from the painting; its presence is also clear to a random viewer who is not familiar with its different narrative aspects. Or perhaps the reason for the difficulty in defining narrative painting lies elsewhere? As we will see, both answers are equally true: literary characteristics are indeed not an adequate criterion for the examination of narrative painting, yet beyond this, one of the characteristics of narrativity in painting is its ability to offer a complex structure of meaning, whose incongruity is its most fundamental element.

The first Laocoon showed how the boundaries of the visual and verbal medium are articulated through the opposition of poetry versus painting and through the distinction between time and space. However, just as Lessing himself sketches boundaries on the one hand, while on the other breaks them, so do theories of art continue to make ample use of literary characteristics when discussing painting.

The manner in which the narrative abilities of painting are examined through literary narrative is multifaceted: on the one hand, it underscores the fact that there is a basic intuition to understand painting as a story. Yet, on the other hand, examining painting through literary characteristics turns it into a pale version of literature. The combination of the two dimensions, applying literary principles to painting with the inability of painting to fully comply with these principles, fashions a complex relationship between painting and narrative, which is characterized by a fundamental failure. Thus, it appears that there is a need for a new and fundamentally different way to think of narrativity in painting, one that would comply with the characteristics of narrativity that are relevant to painting.

The second *Laocoon*: the formalist discussion and the form-content opposition

Despite the various problems of the first *Laocoon*, it did not negate narrativity in painting. The second Laocoon demonstrates a univocal and amplified trend in relation to the first Laocoon, in which theories of art attempt to rid themselves completely of poetic characteristics and offer characteristics that they see as "pure", in the sense that they are strictly painterly. These are the formalist theories from the early twentieth century and Clement Greenberg's later critical writing. That is, while the discussion so far has shown how theories of painting have entered a dialogue with literary theories and view narrativity as one of the components of painting, even if they attribute it to characteristics that are foreign to it, the formalist discussion lands a winning blow over narrativity by viewing it as a redundant component of painting.

Even though these formalist positions were mostly articulated in the first half of the twentieth century, it seems that they continue to percolate, often unconsciously, within theoretical debates to this day. The discussion of the second Laocoon demonstrates another aspect of the particularity of the relations between painting and narrative, which cannot be resolved by the negation of the option of narrative painting. In this case as well, the claim would be that this complexity points toward an essential characteristic of narrativity in the visual field and constitutes a part of it.

In what follows, I will examine formalist theories and their implications for narrative painting from two different vantage points. The first point will focus on how these theories use Immanuel Kant's aesthetics. However, I would like to show that Kant does not provide them with the theoretical reference they believe he does. The second point will examine the basic distinction between content and form, a distinction on which Clement Greenberg bases his negation of narrative. Yet, as I will show, traces of narrative still manage to infiltrate Greenberg's formalist discussion despite his explicit reservations.

In 1940, Greenberg published an essay entitled "Towards a Newer Laocoon". Greenberg opens the essay by presenting the arguments for the superiority of abstract art, as well as the calls for the expulsion of literature and subject matter from plastic art.[38] He argues that for centuries, painting has disavowed its own medium while trying to work against its basic properties, that is, the flatness of the canvas, and has aspired to create the illusion of a three-dimensional space. He views the positions that demand purity in painting as expressions of a positive trend that works against the literary conception of painting. This purity is expressed in two ways: in the sense of exploring painting for painting's sake and not in the service of something external to it, and in the sense of a purity that refers to the medium, according to which painting must focus on the characteristics of its medium and not make use of characteristics taken from a neighboring medium, such as literature or sculpture. Like Lessing, Greenberg also protests against the intermingling of poetry and painting. However, he criticizes Lessing for his inequitable stance toward painting and poetry and claims that Lessing turns more to the verbal medium while neglecting the visual medium.[39]

According to Greenberg, literature was viewed as the dominant artistic medium during the seventeenth and eighteenth centuries. As a result, forms of artistic expression, mainly painting, were forced to imitate the characteristics of the dominant form of expression, often at the expense of their own internal characteristics.[40] Hence, "painting and sculpture in the hands of the lesser talents... become nothing more than ghosts and 'stooges' of literature".[41] Romanticism, which identifies the essence of art with the power to express emotion, also suppressed the characteristics of the medium, specifically because it viewed the feeling of the artist as the focal point of artistic interest. And thus, claims Greenberg:

> By the second third of the 19th century painting had degenerated from the pictorial to the picturesque. Everything depends on the anecdote or the message. The painted picture occurs in blank, indeterminate space; it just happens to be on a square of canvas and inside a frame. It might just as well have been breathed on air or formed out of plasma. It tries to be something you imagine rather than see – or else a bas-relief or a statue. Everything contributes to the denial of the medium, as if the artist were ashamed to admit that he had actually painted his picture instead of dreaming it forth.[42]

Greenberg's words show that, for him, narrativity in painting is intertwined with other ailments of the medium, such as imitation or illusion. And the connecting thread of all these ailments is their conception of painting as a means of transporting something else with an aspiration to deny and cancel its materiality.[43] Greenberg finds the solution to this problem in the avant-garde:

> As the first and most important item upon its agenda, the avant-garde saw the necessity of an escape from ideas, which were infecting the arts with the ideological struggles of society. Ideas came to mean subject matter in general.[44]

He mentions Courbet as someone who tries to free himself from this "infection" through a form of painting that is reduced to the data of the senses without the mediation of the mind. Greenberg explains this as the reason Courbet chooses to depict everyday routine, since the topic is not the main focus of his paintings.

Greenberg then claims:

> The arts, then, have been hunted back to their mediums, and there they have been isolated, concentrated and defined. It is by virtue of its medium that each art is unique and strictly itself. To restore the identity of an art the opacity of its medium must be emphasized. For the visual arts the medium is discovered to be physical.[45]

Painting and sculpture reach their purity by looking like what they are; they exhaust themselves in the visual sensation they produce, without anything beyond this. Thus, painting is rid of imitation, of poetry, and of its fusion with sculpture. Color becomes pure color rather than shades, light and shade are replaced with brushstrokes that are defined for themselves, and the outline is present in the painting as it is. The only possible plane for painting is the picture-plane that takes the place of the illusion of depth.[46] In other words, pictorial elements such as contour, colors and brushstrokes are no longer enlisted to create an imitation and an illusion of reality but now stand in and for themselves.

While Lessing sketched the difference between painting and poetry through the opposition time-space, Greenberg locates the intermedial difference in the opposition of content versus form. He identifies narrativity with the painting's dimension of content, which is of lesser importance to him. It seems that Greenberg's position, that the immanent components and values of painting can be found in its materialistic qualities, is related to the writings of Formalists such as Clive Bell. Bell identifies the essential value of a painting with pure form without a theoretical, narrative or informative context. Bell and Greenberg then identify narrativity with the dimension of content, a dimension that they value less than the formal-material dimension, which they regard as the heart of painting.

Bell and Greenberg base their arguments on Kantian aesthetics and derive from it the negation of narrativity in painting alongside other of its characteristics, such as the representation of subject matters or imitation. As I will show, this negation is founded on a partial reading of the Kantian debate on the judgment of taste. I will introduce Bell's position and then explore the relation between Greenberg, Bell and the Kantian debate so as to show that their negation of narrativity, which is based on Kant, is problematic, and does not stem, as they believe, directly from Kant's conceptualization of the beautiful.

Bell argues that, in order to appreciate a work of art, we must approach it with minimal knowledge, which includes only "a sense of form and color and a knowledge of three-dimensional space".[47] He argues that in our evaluation of a work of art, we need to leave behind any idea or knowledge of life, since "art transports us from the world of man's activity to a world of aesthetic exaltation".[48] Thus, if the viewer wishes to experience "aesthetic emotion", he must relinquish all previous knowledge in his encounter with the art object. The term "aesthetic emotion" was coined by Bell to describe a reaction that a work of visual art awakens in the viewer. In Bell's words, it "is a personal experience of a peculiar emotion. The objects that provoke this emotion we call works of art".[49] Bell does not elaborate on the definition of aesthetic emotion and its qualities, but only asserts that anyone who is sensitive to the work of art will sense it.[50]

Bell distinguishes between descriptive painting, which provides information or tells a story, and art whose forms are "objects of emotions". Descriptive painting could interest the viewer but does not move him aesthetically.[51] Bell, then, supposes a clear distinction between the formal aspects of a painting and other aspects of it, which include content, descriptions or story-telling. These aspects, he claims, are not counted among the qualities that would make the painting into a work of art and are not related to its "significant form". The "significant form" is a combination of lines and shapes that are responsible for provoking "aesthetic emotion" in the viewer, a quality that is common to all works of art.

Descriptive painting, which constitutes, according to Bell, a meta-category that also includes, among others, narrative painting, is not a work of art. The informative content that accompanies a painting has only a secondary significance and should be stripped away from the painting so as to experience its "significant form", which is its essence. While he does state that descriptive painting may, in principle, contain a "significant form", he also argues that many descriptive paintings do not.[52]

Bell, then, distinguishes between the components of content and the components of form in painting. He counts the narrative value of painting as part of the dimension of content while ascribing the gravitational center of the painting to its formal dimension. The encounter with the formal dimension of the painting is spontaneous and does not require the viewer to use any prior knowledge. The encounter with the dimension of content, on the other hand, requires a different kind of activity, one that is not the spontaneity of the aesthetic emotion. Bell does not explicitly state the nature of the encounter with the dimension of content within the painting, yet his intention may be deduced from the way he describes the aesthetic emotion, which characterizes the encounter with its formal dimension. As stated above, Bell does not elaborate on the qualities of this emotion but states that it is a "personal experience of a peculiar emotion".[53] That is, this is a particular and subjective emotion that can be provoked within people with strong visual sensitivity. The encounter with the painting's dimension of content, then, should be very different. If we attempt to articulate it through the negation of the aesthetic emotion, then it seems that this dimension is not related to subjective experience but objective; it is not emotional but intellectual, and it is not particular but general.

Bell goes on to present what he calls the "metaphysical hypothesis", in which he refers to another characteristic of an object of art. He argues that an artist is someone with the ability to see pure forms beyond their everyday use, as ends in themselves.[54]

After establishing the foundation for his "aesthetic hypothesis" as an unspecified emotion that is provoked in the subject by the object of art, and having stripped the object of all its informative, descriptive, narratological and associative qualities, which he views as marginal and "not artistic", and after pointing to the most significant component left in painting, Bell presents another quality that characterizes the object of art, its end for itself. This quality is internal to the object and is related to the fact that we see in it an end for itself, disconnected from the object as a means for anything. Since Bell explained the nature of the aesthetic object and its significant form in his aesthetic hypothesis, when he claimed that it is a relation of lines and shapes disconnected from having to represent or describe anything, it seems that this end for itself again relates to the fact that it is grasped outside any structure of meaning. If we return to Bell's definition of "significant form", we can infer from his words that what he calls "descriptive painting", which also includes narrative painting, serves a goal external to it and lacks an end in itself.

Although Bell, on the one hand, not directly refer to Kant, the formalism he articulates seems to be based on Kantian aesthetics. Greenberg, on the other hand, directly references Kant. In the following pages, I will outline the Kantian traces in Bell and Greenberg's arguments. Moreover, I will show that the negation of narrativity is not a necessary derivative of Kant, since an examination of his argument shows that the values of narrative painting do not necessarily contradict his judgment of taste.

Bell's argument is founded, as stated, on the supposition of an aesthetic emotion that cannot be described in positive terms. At this point, it is difficult not to think of the Kantian sense of pleasure that characterizes the judgment of taste toward the beautiful. Like Kant, whose aesthetic credence focuses on the process of consciousness that characterizes the judgment of taste yet does not concretely define the sense of pleasure that testifies to the existence of the judgment of taste, Bell also does not relate to the concrete expression of aesthetic emotion. Greenberg also speaks of the experience of looking at art, in a way similar to the Kantian emotion of enjoyment. As he claims, "art is a matter strictly of experience, not of principles".[55]

Moreover, Bell's concept of "significant form" relates to Kant's proposition that what characterizes the judgment of taste is the lack of concepts. According to Bell, the "significant form" that characterizes a work of art and provokes aesthetic emotion in the viewer is a form that is "arranged and combined according to certain unknown and mysterious laws".[56] And indeed, according to Kant, "the judgment of taste determines the Object, independently of concept, in respect of delight and of the predicate of beauty".[57] That is, just as Kant believes that the pleasure we derive from the object of art stems from the beauty of the object irrespective of any concept, so Bell relates the aesthetic emotion to an object that is free from concepts of content. The lack of concepts is seen by Bell as a preference for form, which can be conceived only through the internal elements of the painting, without external context. Bell, and later Greenberg, identify Kant's formal preferences with the formal attributes of the aesthetic object. Thus, in his essay on avant-garde and Kitsch, Greenberg claims that "the avant-garde poet or artist tries in effect to imitate God by creating something valid solely on its own terms, in the way nature itself is valid.... something *given*, increate, independent of meanings, similar or originals".[58] That is, like Bell, Greenberg also identifies the aesthetic with formality independent of an external meaning that is given to the form.

One of the conclusions of the judgment of taste, according to Kant, is that "the beautiful is that which, apart from a concept, pleases universally".[59] However, this does not necessarily mean that the beautiful object must be completely severed from all conceptual context, but that the act of judgment itself does not rely on the object's conceptual links. It seems that Bell and Greenberg give a literal interpretation to Kant and thus reduce the beautiful object to forms stripped of any concept. The beautiful object, according to Kant, is beautiful without a reason we may point to.[60]

However, Kant's refusal to characterize the beautiful object and its various concrete actualizations in a positive manner shows that these formalist interpretations reduce the spirit of his aesthetics. According to Kant, the beautiful object's independence from concepts is a condition that liberates the object rather than limit it. Thus, the judgment of taste is not dependent on concepts as such.

Another affinity between Bell and Kant can be found in the way Bell describes the inner finality of the aesthetic object. As stated, Bell claims that there is an inner finality that characterizes pure forms, and which is not related to the form as a means but is an end in itself. Again, it is difficult not to think, at this point, of Kant's finality without an end. As Kant states: "*Beauty* is the form of finality in an object, so far as perceived in it *apart from the representation of an end*".[61] This is a subjective finality in which the viewer "either has no concept of this end, or else makes abstraction from it in his judgment".[62] Kant calls this kind of finality formal finality.[63] However, it seems that the form he speaks of does not relate to the formal aspects of the beautiful object but to the form that characterizes the cognitive process involved in the judgment of taste.

In his writing, Greenberg also relates to the finality without an end of the aesthetic object. He claims that an aesthetic observation never constitutes a means toward something else but is an end in itself.[64] Greenberg gives the example of looking at the sky: "the intuition that gives you the color of the sky turns into an aesthetic intuition when it stops telling you what the weather is like and becomes purely an experience of color".[65] That is, he understands finality without end as a reduction of the aesthetic object to its formal elements, as the sky is turned into a pure "experience of color". Looking at the sky to tell the weather does not constitute a judgment of taste according to Kant; however, this does not mean that, for this act of looking to be aesthetic, it must be confined to the color of the sky or any other of its formal elements. Rather, for the act of looking to be aesthetic, according to Kant, it must be pleasurable for the viewer. That is, Kant's judgment of taste is not limited to the formal values of the object or any other *a priori* limitation of the aesthetic object.

Bell and Greenberg's arguments, then, relate to Kant in three main aspects: the way they describe aesthetic emotion, which corresponds with Kant's emotion of pleasure; the way they both reduce the aesthetic object to its formal characteristics; and the way they both locate in the aesthetic object a certain kind of finality, which is detached from any reliance on concepts. Bell and Greenberg rely on the latter two points to argue that the essence of the aesthetic object can be found in its formalist values and not in its content. This assertion shaped the discourse of art throughout the twentieth century, which rarely relates to the content of modern paintings, and even less so to their narrational values. However, as I have stated, this is an incomplete reading of Kant. The lack of conceptuality for Kant relates to the judgment of taste and does not constitute an attribute of the object itself. Their reading of the finality of the object is also a partial reading of Kant. As stated, form, according to Kant, relates to the cognitive process and is not a formal attribute of the object.

Is there a connection between narrativity and finality? Once we conceive of narrative painting as an adherence to a priori literary principles imposed on it, this form of painting contains an "objective finality", which is alien to the judgment of taste. However, if we think of narrativity as an attribute that is an integral part of the image, then narrative painting can be seen as having a finality without an end. That is, narrativity in painting can be an expression of a finality without an end, if it emanates from the painting and from the process of looking at it. Although Bell and Greenberg use finality without an end in its Kantian articulation as another way to negate the dimension of content in the painting, this conclusion does not necessarily stem from Kant's discussion.

Another issue that emerges from the comparison of Bell and Greenberg's arguments with Kant relates to the very opposition they pose between content and form in painting. As shown, it seems that both Bell and Greenberg rely on Kant's discussion of the beautiful when they pose this opposition. However, in the few places in which Kant relates to the object of beauty, he distinguishes between the outline and the filling of colors, two attributes that Greenberg and Bell associate with the formal aspects of painting. Kant does not distinguish between form and content in the sense that Greenberg does. That is, Kant's distinction between the essential and marginal aspects of the object is fundamentally different from the distinction that Greenberg and Bell draw between the formal aspects of the object and its content.

A conception of narrativity in painting as an application of anterior literary principles is indeed antagonistic to the Kantian perception of beauty. However, the a priori assumption that the narrative values of paintings are less valuable or "not artistic" also does not adhere to the Kantian perception of the beautiful. The Kantian judgment of taste should be liberated from any previous fixations, free and open to any singular observation in which the subject experiences pleasure. It seems that Bell does the exact opposite by imposing limitations on the object of beauty and by placing predetermined demands on its essential components. Greenberg goes even further, imposing even stricter limitations on painting than Bell.

As shown, Greenberg views the essence of painting in its material and formal values. This position is founded on the supposition that a painting can be divided into form versus content, while narrativity is seen as one of the pictorial components of content. It seems that the very distinction between "content" and "form" is considered obvious, just as Bell viewed it before him and just as Lessing treated the distinction between time and space as a "real" stable and a priori distinction.[66] However, what is the nature of this distinction, and is it possible? Where do we locate the line between form and content? And to what extent may we apply this distinction to our interpretations of painting?

The language of Greenberg's discourse discloses the difficulties that can arise from this distinction. Does not the use Greenberg make of metaphors testify to the very lack of a fundamental ability to determine a clear border between "form", as something that exists in the painting itself, and "content", as something external that is attributed to it? Although the significance of narrativity is indirect, the main argument here is in putting into question the very distinction between form and content that leads him to negate narrativity or, at the very least, see it as something redundant.

In his analysis of Jackson Pollock's paintings, Greenberg claims that:

> An "all-over" Pollock makes the impression of being chaotic because it promises the order of mechanical repetition only to betray it. An "all over" Pollock is only vaguely, ambiguously symmetrical. When it is

> pictorially effective and moves and excites the viewer, it does so in the same general way in which all pictorial art does, by disrupting and restoring, by unbalancing and balancing.[67]

Later in the same article, he writes:

> Ostensibly, the impersonality of handling that reigns in avant-garde art of the sixties is like Mondrian's. But it does not *feel* like Mondrian's, and this has to be explained in good part by the different interpretation of impersonality found in Pollock's "drip" paintings....Ruled or compass-plotted edges don't feel as rigidly geometrical today as they did in geometrical art done in the past. The practice, descended from Pollock, of soaking pigment into raw canvas ***deprives these edges of their "cutting" power by making them bleed ever so slightly***.[68] (My emphasis – E.B.).

What are these bleeding edges? And what is their place in Greenberg's conception of modernist painting as pure? And if this is a treatment solely of form and material, as that which is present in the painting, what is the place of this metaphoric language?

In other words, the effect of a line drawn with a hand, shaking or fluctuating, is different from the effect of a straight line. If we adhere to Greenberg's distinction between content and form, then his very definition belongs to the painting's dimension of form. The problem appears when we use concepts such as "bleeding edges" to treat this difference of forms since the place of this metaphor can no longer be so clearly placed on the side of the "purer form". A pure form can indeed have different sizes, colors and surfaces, and it can indeed also bleed, but that, then, begs the question of whether it is still a pure form.

Does Greenberg meet the demands of the purity of the medium, or does the metaphoric speech indicate the hidden presence of a conception of painting as representing something else? I do not claim that Greenberg's metaphoric language somehow turns his interpretation into a narrative one. I wish to show that the line between the purity of the medium, which Greenberg aspires to articulate, is problematic in its definition. Moreover, the very opposition of content versus form, which is at the heart of his debate, is also complicated.

Greenberg's analysis of Winslow Homer's figurative painting discloses another problem. Greenberg writes:

> It was in the 1880s that Homer adopted something of the sentimental, middle-keyed genre style that had then become popular among post-Barbizon French academic painters, and which took for its principal subjects melancholy landscapes and peasants....Afterward, or even concurrently, he may have come under the influence of the Whistlerian

> tone poem. At any rate, he lowered his color key further, confining himself to cool and neutral tones and emphasizing relatively subtle shifts of light and dark- in reaction perhaps against the violence with which he had previously treated value contrasts. There were certain rewards: scenes of beaches at dusk rendered in deep blues, violets, mauves and tinted grays, with one or more figures of women silhouetted in the foreground. The poetry of these pictures was all the more genuine for its being unforced concomitant of a manner that betrayed, and through all of its changes was always to betray, a certain nostalgia for the literal or even pedestrian.[69]

Greenberg speaks about the way these paintings overcome a verbal, nostalgic tendency and thus achieve a more reliable and original poetic. In other words, Greenberg does not ignore the poetic aspect of these paintings; however, he does not ascribe this poetics to the painterly subject; rather, he shows how it stems from formalist decisions, such as lowering the color key or the use of delicate transitions between shades. Greenberg's words imply that this poetics is more successful than the poetics of "content", which is contrived, verbal and cliché. And it is at this point that the problem with the distinction between content and form is more clearly visible: can we indeed distinguish, as Greenberg proposes, between "verbal poetry" and "poetry of colors and shapes"? Can we determine that the effect of the painting indeed stems from his form despite its contents? And in what sense are these contents indeed verbal?

Greenberg continues:

> Homer had his share, nevertheless, of the popular and romantic taste of his time for melodrama. It was at Tynemouth that he seems to have acquired that fascination with the menacing aspects of the sea which was not to leave him for the rest of his life. Perhaps there was some unconscious connection for him (as for Poe) between the sea and sex. One of his frequent subjects in the eighties was women being saved from drowning or shipwreck, with wet clothing clinging to their bodies in a surreptitious approximation of the nude – which he hardly ever attempted to do directly. Later on, the raging surf would hold the center of his attention, with women's figures appearing less often in the foreground. Homer's presumably matter-of-fact vision, like that of Stephen Crane, another "literal" realist, would, when directed out of doors, usually alight on something that moved dramatically, were it but waves or a leaping fish.[70]

Greenberg later shows how Homer's most significant artistic breakthrough occurs later, in his watercolors, and he analyses this breakthrough in strictly formalist terms, such as the treatment of the medium, the transparency of color or the use of the texture of the white paper.

That is, according to Greenberg, Homer's narrative paintings constitute part of his "melodramatic inclination" and the popular aspect of his art. It seems that Greenberg does not value this aspect of the paintings, and he quickly moves on to describe Homer's later, more important achievements that take place because of their formal advantages. Nevertheless, Greenberg does not ignore the presence of narrativity in these paintings, even when he tries to reduce it to the places where it is most ostensibly present and explains it apologetically. In other words, even a modernist like Greenberg fails to completely eradicate narrativity from painting, and a remainder of it remains in his discussions.

Like the first Laocoon, the second *Laocoon* also attempts to redefine the boundaries of the medium. However, while the first *Laocoon* is based on the opposition of time and space, and its problem lies in the way it examines the narrative painting through literary characteristics, the problem in the second Laocoon, which is based on the opposition of content and form, may be in this very distinction, which is neither univocal nor a necessary derivative of Kant's aesthetics.

The third *Laocoon*: the collapse of the boundaries of the medium

In the mid-1980s, W.J.T. Mitchell published his book *Iconology*, which explores the relationships between image, text and ideology.[71] Mitchell shows how the conception of the image throughout history is used as a way to link the different theories of art, language and consciousness with social, cultural and political conceptions.[72]

One of the texts that Mitchell examines is Lessing's *Laocoon*. Mitchell shows how even Lessing's most severe critics do not undermine his fundamental distinction between time and space, which they grasp, just like Lessing, as "natural" or "real". Mitchell attempts to expose the nature of this distinction. He shows that this is not an innocent distinction but one that contains social, political and gendered positions.[73]

Mitchell argues that if, as Lessing claims, there were two distinct modes of representation, temporal and spatial, and two types of artistic objects, each complying with only one representational mode, then there would be no problem. The question of the limits of the medium arises exactly because, despite Lessing's argument, each medium can trespass into the neighboring medium, even if it is a more complicated or less economic mode of representation.[74] This does not mean that the two arts are fundamentally the same but that the distinction between time and space cannot provide the basis for the distinction between them.[75] In a certain sense, claims Mitchell, the limits of each medium only challenge each field to cross its borders.

The significant point, according to Mitchell, is that the distinction between painting and poetry is not as objective and absolute as Lessing attempts to show; rather, it is constructed from a political, religious-Protestant position, which leads Lessing to go against anything he views as Catholic idolatry.[76]

Lessing's opposition can eventually boil down to an opposition to a narrative representation in painting, as part of a Protestant struggle against the Catholic representation of religious stories in paintings. Thus, this opposition constitutes a rationalization of the fear of the icon. While the icon was perceived, in certain historical periods, as a characteristic of primitivity and femininity, thought was perceived as pure, abstract and logocentric.

In this matter, Norman Bryson's debate of still-life paintings seems particularly relevant.[77] Bryson relates to a painterly trend in Dutch paintings during the sixteenth century. In still-life painting, in the background, behind the mundane objects placed at the forefront, the artists would place tiny characters representing a familiar scene from the New Testament. The narrative part of the painting is pushed to the background and can only be seen after a careful examination of the painting. According to Bryson, this trend reflects the Protestant aversion to figurative visuality, which was seen as carnal and associated with Catholicism. Bryson argues that the fundamental ideology of these paintings is that the God of Reformation is a hidden God and can only be seen in a fleeting glance beyond the physical life. Spirituality cannot be manifested visually since visibility does not have direct access to the spiritual world.[78] That is, Bryson points toward a transition from religious paintings in which the narrative scene is placed at the center, to still-life paintings, which are not considered narrative paintings, in which the narrative scene is pushed to the background and diminished in size, making it difficult to perceive at a first glance. What is relevant to this discussion is that the resistance to pictoriality, which Mitchell and Bryson relate to the Reformation, is expressed through an extreme diminishment of the narratological elements in the painting. Thus, the aversion to the image is not an aversion from the picture as an object but from its narrative aspect, from its ability to represent fiction, just as the prohibition against idolatry does not go against the sculpture as an object but against ascribing divine character to it.

This relates to Greenberg's claim against perceiving the painting solely as a means to transfer an external meaning, as if "it just happens to be on a square of canvas and inside a frame".[79] That is, in this sense, Greenberg points to a problem similar to the one that drives the Protestant rejection of painting as a representation of fiction. Greenberg and Bell advocated a return to the perception of painting through "what it is" and not as a representing means. According to Bryson, questions related to the tension between painting as a material object in a world of objects and its ability to transfer something beyond its own materiality appeared already in the mid-sixteenth century. The interesting fact is that in both cases, and despite the vast differences between them, their solution is the rejection, or at the very least, reduction of narrativity in painting.

Yet is the source of the rejection of narrativity in painting indeed social-historical as Mitchell supposes? And if so, then why does Greenberg also, to a certain extent, adhere to it? If the space-time opposition is rooted in a cultural-political context, how does it remain stable throughout centuries in which cultural, political and artistic perceptions have changed so deeply?

I believe that the two cases point to a complex, yet indelible, knot in the relationship between painting and narrativity. In this sense, we can think of Greenberg as a representative of a more complex version of the Reformation. The two positions which, for different reasons, reject the ability of painting to transfer something beyond its material presence, reflect an aversion to these very capabilities of painting while also pointing to their very existence. This aversion points toward the complex relationship between painting and narrativity and is directly linked to the nature of narrativity in painting.

By doing away with Lessing's distinction between time and space, Mitchell seems to open a path to think anew of narrative painting, since its limitations have been removed, or at least exposed as incompatible. However, despite his criticism of Lessing, the reasons Mitchell suggests for the limitations of the visual medium are strikingly similar to Lessing and Greenberg. Mitchell suggests that the limitation of the visual medium is an iconophobia rooted within broad social contexts. In that sense, he constitutes another link in a chain, placing the problematics of the relationship between painting and narrativity in reasons that are external to painting.

However, Mitchell eventually gives space for a more "liberal" state of affairs than the two previous Laocoons. Painting is no longer under any prohibition to represent narrative. How, then, can we think of narrative painting now that the strict limitations placed by the two *Laocoons* have been lifted? It is here that we find another problem related to narrative painting: the broader trend of the twentieth century, in which the applicability of the very concept of narrativity in general is extremely expanded. Mitchell, as stated above, undoes the distinction between the arts of time and the arts of space as a "truth". One of the results of this undoing is that the verbal medium is no longer in a state of "natural" compatibility with narrativity, as Lessing believed. Mitchell is not the only one to arrive at this conclusion; rather, he adds his position to a variety of theoretical stances that expanded the application of the concept of narrativity during the twentieth century. This expansion stemmed from parallel developments in different fields. The thinkers in these fields, each in his own fashion and for his own motives, reached a similar conclusion, according to which narrativity is not the sole property of literature, but can be ascribed to a variety of fields of human activity.

One of these fields of research is semiotics, which argues that all forms of signification can create meaning, including narrative meaning. Unlike traditional theories that thought of narrative as a literary form of textual organization, semiotic theories conceive any system of signs as a text and grasp narrative as a fundamental and universal semantic structure underlying the text. As Roland Barthes states: "Caring nothing for the division between good and bad literature, narrative is international, transhistorical, transcultural: it is simply there, like life itself".[80] This fundamental semantic structure is not only independent of the qualities of the object but is also not limited to a certain form of expression; it can be expressed in pantomime, in a series of pictures, in a single picture, in dance or in any other way.

Another field of research that has contributed to the expanding applicability of the concept of narrative is cognitive science. The point of departure for this field is the assumption of universal capabilities that are common to all human beings. Thus, much like linguistic theories that assume an inborn universal grammar, which is at the basis of every human language, and with which each of us is equipped, these theories assume that narratological capability, just like linguistic capability, is a universal human attribute. Narratological capability is not limited to the arts or to verbal means, and it appears in various ways in pedestrian life. These studies claim that language speakers can create a story, identify a story as such and improve an unsuccessful story.[81] Thus, narrativity expands beyond the scope of literature by becoming a basic human cognitive ability. Moreover, narrativity is no longer restricted to the verbal dimension and can also exist in a series of paintings or in pantomime.

Cultural studies have also examined narrativity in a plethora of contexts as a non-medium-specific concept. According to these studies, narrative is not only one code among many but a meta-code. Narrativity is the way experienced events are rewritten, highlighting the importance of the concept of narrative in the representation of reality and in historical research.[82] This theorization of narrative constitutes another addition to the inflation of narrativity that characterizes the end of the twentieth century, and in which narrativity becomes an almost essential component of a variety of human activities. In this case, narrativity also finds a place in fields traditionally seen as anti-narrative, such as exact sciences.

Another sense of the concept of narrative that emerged after the mid-twentieth century ties it with political power and ruling ideology. This critical position views narrative as a structure of meaning that is meant to retroactively justify control and the erection of certain ideologies. These theories do not set strict preconditions for narrativity; rather, they ascribe narrativity to every coherent structure of meaning.

What these various theories have in common is the extreme expansion of the concept of narrativity. The significance of the debate on narrative painting is twofold: it seems as though it is now possible to locate narrativity in a variety of fields, including, of course, painting. There has been a considerable easing of the conditions that define narrativity since literary markers are no longer treated as the paradigmatic characteristics of narrativity. This facilitation of the conditions according to which narrativity is examined, on the one hand, and the supposition that narrativity can essentially be found in every field, on the other, seem to constitute an unequivocal answer to the first two *Laocoons*, which restricted and even rejected the possibility of thinking about narrative painting.

However, the expansion of the definition of narrativity, along with its conceptualization as an elementary structure of human activity, is a double-edged sword. This expansion eventually empties narrativity of any meaning since everything can be narrative, and narrativity is identified with everything. How, then, can we specify a discussion on narrative painting and its characteristics when narrativity is immersed in everything? This problem is, in a certain sense, the inverse of the problems of the previous two *Laocoons*: the third *Laocoon* seems to open the door to narrative painting, but it also lets in almost every form of human expression and leaves almost no possibility to think of narrative painting as a productive concept.

Beyond *Laocoon*

Each *Laocoon* I have examined here cancels, in its own fashion, the possibility of narrative painting while also pointing toward this very possibility. According to the first *Laocoon*, narrativity is attributed to a literary aspect that is added to the painting. This *Laocoon* overlooks the unique attributes of narrative painting and also points to the incompetence of painting in the face of literature. Moreover, it creates a gap between the theoretical attempt to extract from the painting complex literary characteristics and the spontaneous way paintings are read as a narrative.

The second *Laocoon* seemed to present a simpler relationship between painting and narrativity by negating narrativity in painting. The problem in the second Laocoon relates to the manner in which, like the first Laocoon, narrativity is ascribed to an external aspect of painting, in this case, to content. The second Laocoon, which is supposed to constitute a better and more relevant version of Lessing's Laocoon, eventually suffers from similar problems: just as Lessing treated the distinction of time-space as natural and neutral, so Greenberg regards the distinction between content and form as two separate and distinct aspects of the paintings, although they are, to a great extent, products of interpretation.

The problems of each Laocoon reveal a question which relates to the character of the relation between painting and narrativity. As shown, the option of narrative painting eventually appears in each of the *Laocoons*, but it is not a simple relationship in which narrativity is expressed in various ways. Rather, it appears through the attempts to negate or devalue it. How may we, then, interpret this dual relationship, which has been preserved throughout the vicissitudes of the theories of art and literature?

I wish to show that the source of the problem that characterizes the relationship between painting and narrative does not stem from the limits of the medium or from the fact that narrativity is fundamentally alien to painting, but, on the contrary, that the problem arises from the fact that narrativity constitutes an inherent part of the image. As this book will show, the narrativity inherent to the image is a multi-layered narrative that is unstable, a structure whose incongruency is its constituting characteristic. That is, this narrativity emanates from processes of looking that, by their very nature, are not stable and continuous, rather they belong to a dynamic and fragmented vision that is constructed and veiled in pulsations by the particularity of the looking subject.

Notes

1 Lessing, Gotthold Ephraim. 1887 [1766]. *Laocoön: An Essay upon the Limits of Painting and Poetry*. Trans. Ellen Frothingham. Cambridge: Cambridge University Press, John Wilson and Son.
2 Greenberg, Clement. 1986 [1940]. "Towards a Newer Laocoon". In *The Collected Essays and Criticism*. Vol. 1. Edited by John O'Brian. Chicago and London: The University of Chicago Press, pp. 23–38.
3 Mitchell, William John Thomas. 1986. *Iconology: Image, Text, Ideology*. Chicago and London: University of Chicago Press.
4 It should be noted that Mitchell himself does not claim that there is no difference between the visual and the verbal medium, rather that the distinction between time and space cannot be used as a basis for the inter-medium distinction. Mitchell, 1986, pp. 102–103.
5 Lee, Rensselaer W. 1967 [1940]. *Ut Pictura Poesis: The Humanistic Theory of Painting*. New York: Norton Library, p. 3.
6 Lessing, 1887, p. IX.
7 Lessing, 1887, p. 91.
8 Lessing, 1887, p. 90.
9 Lessing, 1887, p. 17.
10 Aristotle. 1932. *Poetics*. Aristotle in 23 Volumes, Vol. 23. Trans. William Hamilton Fyfe. Cambridge: Harvard University Press; London: William Heinemann Ltd. https://www.perseus.tufts.edu/hopper/text?doc=Perseus%3Atext%3A1999.01.0056%3Asection%3D1450a [section 1450a].
11 Aristotle, 1932, 1450a.
12 Lessing, 1887, p. 58.
13 Lessing, 1887, p. 59.
14 Lessing, 1887, p. 79.
15 Aristotle, 1932, 1450 a1.
16 Aristotle, 1932, 1454 a1.
17 Aristotle, 1932, p. 80.
18 Aristotle, 1932, p. 81.
19 Ronen, Ruth. 1994. *Possible Worlds in Literary Theory*. Cambridge: Cambridge University Press, p. 179.
20 Genette, Gerard. 1980. *Narrative Discourse*. Trans. Jane E. Lewin. Ithaca, New York: Cornell University Press, p. 189.
21 Panofsky, Erwin. 1955. "Iconography and Iconology: An Introduction to the Study of Renaissance Art". In *Meaning in the Visual Arts*. New York: Doubleday Anchor Books, pp. 26–54.
22 Panofsky, 1955, p. 39.
23 Panofsky, 1955, p. 31.
24 Fried, Michael. 1988. *Absorption and Theatricality: Painting and Beholder in the Age of Diderot*. Chicago: University of Chicago Press, p. 83.
25 Lee, 1967, p. 62.
26 Musée du Louvre, Paris.
27 Lee, 1967, p. 62. See also Fried, 1988, p. 83.
28 Fried, 1988, p. 84.
29 Aristotle, 1932, 1451 a1.
30 Riegl, Alois. 1999 [1902]. *The Group Portraiture of Holland*. Trans. Evelyn M. Klein and David Britt. Los Angeles: The Getty Research Institute for the History of Art and the Humanities.
31 Riegl, 1999, p. 20.
32 Wölflin, Heinrich. 1929 [1915]. *Principles of Art History: The Problem of the Development of Style in Later Art*. Trans. Marie Donald Hottinger. New York: Dover Publications, p. 155.

33 Wölflin, 1929, p. 174.
34 Fried, 1988, pp. 85–86.
35 Aristotle, 1932, 1452 a1.
36 Lessing, 1887, p. 17.
37 Riegl, 1999, p. 275.
38 Greenberg, Clement. 1986 [1940]. "Towards a Newer Laocoon". In *The Collected Essays and Criticism*. Vol. 1. Edited by John O'Brian. Chicago and London: The University of Chicago Press, pp. 23–38.
39 Greenberg, 1986, p. 25.
40 Greenberg, 1986, p. 24.
41 Greenberg, 1986, p. 25.
42 Greenberg, 1986, pp. 28–29.
43 However, Greenberg concludes this discussion by noting that his enjoyment from Rembrandt is still rooted more in his expressional abilities than in his abstract values, p. 37.
44 Greenberg, 1986, p. 28.
45 Greenberg, 1986, pp. 32–33.
46 Greenberg, 1986, p. 35.
47 Bell, Clive. 1961 [1914]. *Art*. London: Arrow Books Ltd, p. 37.
48 Bell, 1961, p. 36.
49 Bell, 1961, p. 21.
50 Bell, 1961, p. 22.
51 Bell, 1961, p. 29.
52 Bell, 1961, p. 30.
53 Bell, 1961, p. 21.
54 Bell, 1961, pp. 58–59.
55 Greenberg, 1965, p. 133.
56 Bell, 1928, p. 25.
57 Kant, Immanuel. 1952 [1790]. *The Critique of Judgment*. Trans. James creed Meredith. Oxford: Clarendon Press, pp. 59–60.
58 Greenberg, Clement. 1986 [1939]. "Avant-Garde and Kitch". In *The Collected Essays and Criticism*. Vol. 1. Edited by John O'Brian. Chicago and London: The University of Chicago Press, p. 8.
59 Kant, 1952, p. 60.
60 Kant, 1952, p. 31.
61 Kant, 1952, p. 80.
62 Kant, 1952, p. 74.
63 Kant, 1952, p. 64.
64 Greenberg, Clement. 1973. "Seminar One". *Arts Magazine* 48: 44–46, p. 44.
65 Greenberg, 1973, p. 44.
66 I will elaborate on this topic later when I outline Mitchell's reading of Lessing.
67 Greenberg, Clement. 1995 [1967]. *The Collected Essays and Criticism: Volume 4 Modernism with Vengeance, 1957–1969*. Chicago and London: The University of Chicago Press, p. 246.
68 Greenberg, Clement. 1965 [1944]. *Art and Culture: Critical Essays*. Boston: Beacon Press, p. 186.
69 Greenberg, 1965, p. 186.
70 Greenberg, 1965, p. 186.
71 Mitchell, 1986.
72 Mitchell, 1986, p. 2.
73 Mitchell, 1986, p. 110.
74 Mitchell, 1986, p. 104.
75 Mitchell, 1986, p. 103.

76 Mitchell, 1986, p. 106.
77 Bryson, Norman. 1990. *Looking at the Overlooked: Four Essays on Still Life Painting*. Cambridge: Harvard University Press.
78 Bryson, 1990, p. 150.
79 Greenberg, 1986 [1940], p. 29.
80 Barthes, Roland. 1977. *Image, Music, Text*. Trans. Stephen Heath. New York: Hill and Wang, p. 79.
81 van Dijk, Teun. 1980. "Story Comprehension: An Introduction". *Poetics* 9: 1–21, p. 3.
82 White, Hayden. 1987. *The Content of the Form: Narrative Discourse and Historical Representation*. Baltimore and London: Johns Hopkins University Press, pp. 1–2.

2 Three models of narrative painting

Despite its problematic status, historians and art theoreticians have occasionally related to the possibility of narrative painting. This chapter explores the different ways in which art theory and art history conceive of narrative painting. These disciplines usually define narrative painting either as a form of painting with a strong affinity to a verbal text or as a painting that relates to a more general framework of knowledge that provides it with its narratological possibility. In both cases, narrative painting is analyzed according to a prior verbal text. However, there is another option in which narrative painting is not conceptualized in its relation to a verbal text. Aesthetics, feminist criticism and other theories of painting conceive of visual narrativity as the product of the encounter between the viewer and the painting, in which the viewer becomes an active component in the represented scene. According to them, narrativity is constructed within the image and constitutes a necessary part of it, which is the product of the act of looking at the image.

From various theories of art, I have extrapolated three models of narrative painting. The first two models conceive of narrative painting in relation to an anterior verbal text, at varying levels of proximity to it. These two models encompass most of the ways in which the theory of art treats narrative painting. The first model examines painting in relation to the verbal text to which the painting alludes, and even though there may be slight visual deviations or supplements to the verbal story, the painting clearly relates to a text that predates it. In the absence of an anterior text, the second model examines painting in relation to a general framework of knowledge or a meta-story. Within the framework of these two models, narrativity is seen as dependent on an external context, such as canonical verbal text, a familiar system of symbols or schemes of representation, which are situated outside the visual representation.

The third model offers a different relationship between the viewer, narrative and painting. Narrativity, here, stems from the relation between the viewer and the painting, and the viewer is perceived as an inseparable part of the represented fiction. This type of narrativity is not a coherent structure that should be appropriated to certain painterly details, but rather a presence of a story that is not necessarily coherent to the viewer. Moreover, sometimes, the

DOI: 10.4324/9781003516446-3

painting even points toward another narrative, which undermines the official narrative that it also references, so the painting fashions a contradictory and antagonistic structure of meaning. Narrativity, within this model, is produced through means that are internal to the painting; it cannot necessarily be verbally articulated and is fashioned by purely pictorial means. This is a form of narrativity unique to pictorial representation.

I have termed these three models: conditional narrative painting, independent narrative painting and narrative painting through the expanded arena. In this chapter, I will outline these models and distinguish between the first two and the third, which I will later connect to the psychoanalytic thinking of Freud and Lacan.

I will show how thinking of narrative painting in relation to a verbal text is antagonistic to the nature of the visual medium and to the viewer's dynamic process of looking at a painting. However, an interpretation of a narrative that is constructed through the process of looking, and does not rely on a text external to the painting, shows that the very relations between the viewer and the painting are responsible for both the narrative effect and its complex structure. In such paintings, the viewer simultaneously sees and is seen at once, looks and participates in the visual scene.

Narrativity in painting, as fashioned through the relations between the viewer and the image, originated in aesthetic traditions that conceive of an unmediated relation between the subject and the object of art, for instance, Friedrich Nietzsche's *The Birth of Tragedy*.[1] In his book, Nietzsche describes the artist as a figure who is "like the weird picture of the fairy tale which can at will turn its eyes and behold itself; he is now at once subject and object, at once poet, actor, and spectator".[2]

Nietzsche articulates a state of affairs in which the subject forms an inseparable part of the object of art. Although Nietzsche does not discuss painting in this work, his conceptualization of art can be seen as analogous to the way in which pictorial space is perceived as containing the viewer within it. Adapting this form of thought to painting means that the viewer actively participates in the represented scene by exchanging glances with the painted characters. Thus, narrativity is the product of the viewer's perception of himself as an active participant in the painted scene.

Two problems may be gleaned from this supposition: how can you think of a structure in which the viewer and the object of his observation are not clearly distinguished from each other, in terms that will not be imaginary or metaphorical? Another problem is that this position, in its various articulations based on the subject's identification with the object, rests on the supposition of a complete correspondence between the viewer and the object of his observation. Thus, it does not explain the inherent incongruity that I argue narrativity makes appear and that characterizes the visual medium.

As I will show, psychoanalytic discourse offers a theoretical framework that can address both of these problems. It can help explain the way in which the viewer cannot be distinguished from the object of his observation and show how this relation is not based on harmony but on a fundamental incongruence.

Conditional narrative painting

"Ajax was not represented at the moment when, raging among the herds, he captures and slays goats and oxen, mistaking them for men. The master showed him sitting weary after these crazy deeds of heroism, and meditating self-destruction".[3] This interpretation, which Lessing quotes, is attributed to Flavius Philostratus, and it demonstrates a conception of a conditional narrative painting that relates to a canonical narrative. The viewer of the painting identifies the image of Ajax and understands the painting as a representation of a specific scene from the canonical text. The painterly narrative, according to this conception, is a preexisting unit that the viewer is required to identify. Lessing provides examples of paintings that depict various mythological scenes. Yet, while Lessing only recommends that the painting refer to a familiar text, he does not obligate the artist to do so. According to him, it is preferable for both the poet and the artist to treat familiar topics in original ways; since, in this way, the poet

> can omit a hundred tiresome details otherwise indispensable to an understanding of the piece. .... The same advantage is possessed by the painter when his subject is so familiar to us that we take in at a glance the meaning and design of his whole composition, and can not only see that his characters are speaking, but can even hear what they say.[4]

Although this is a recommendation, Lessing does not relate to the other option, in which the painting constitutes a narrative with no connection to an antedating text.

This conception of painting is prevalent among art historians and theoreticians. Thus, for instance, Leon Battista Alberti describes Timantes's painting *The Immolation of Iphigenia* as a developing narrative that describes a familiar story.[5] In his discussion of the theory of humanist painting, Rensselaer Lee explains that, in the sixteenth century, people believed that the topics of paintings should be taken from history and be familiar to every European, just as the mythological stories or the Bible are familiar to all. This is because the painter has a didactic role and, in a certain sense, is supposed to serve as an example. The French academy inherited this view and divided painting into various hierarchical categories in accordance with it. Thus, the most esteemed genre of painting, according to the French academy, is historical painting.[6] That is, the ubiquitous tendency is to view narrative painting as a text-dependent painting.

Conditional narrative painting constitutes Richard Brilliant's subject of inquiry. Brilliant analyzes Pompeii's frescoes as a developing narrative that represents various episodes from the *Iliad*.[7] Brilliant's aim is to develop a methodology to analyze painting, which would unveil the ways in which the artist creates a sense of continuity for the viewer of the series of paintings. He wishes to show how classical artists could transpose the viewer from the limitations of description to the representation of continuous actions in visual works of art. Brilliant believes that, despite the fundamental difference between painting and poetry, there is still a strong relation between them in cases in which the artist wishes to create a narrative through a visual image.[8] The process of depicting the narrative requires a translation from words to visual images, which would be comprehensible for both viewer and artist and is made possible because they both share the same cultural perception of the world. However, Brilliant examines various cases in which the word and the image do not necessarily only complete each other, but in which the visual artist has rhetorical intentions, which he achieves through the image. In these cases, according to Brilliant, the combination of various episodes can convey an allegorical or ironic message, as a certain episode from the *Iliad* is juxtaposed with another episode.

To a certain extent, Panofsky also conceptualized narrative painting as conditional, specifically of his definition of iconography and iconology, and the extensive use he makes of symbols when describing the visual medium. Panofsky articulates a process of understanding a painting that is based on visual codes, through which the viewer may connect the different pictorial details to a culturally familiar text to which these details refer. As I mentioned earlier, according to Panofsky, narrative painting can be understood through constant or varying characteristics. Panofsky analyzes paintings through their painterly details and based on the painterly phenomenon he wishes to identify, while drawing on the extensive knowledge at his disposal. The painterly details in themselves do not constitute an independent narrative. They may point toward an earlier narrative structure that exists in culture. Panofsky, then, does not negate a painting's ability to produce a narrative. However, according to him, the production of such a narrative must be carried out by mapping and attributing the painting to a familiar text or by comparing the painting to other paintings that represent a similar scene. In this manner, understanding a painting as a narrative relies on external sources that predate the painting. A painting, in this formulation, then, does not produce a narrative independently through its own particular details. The painterly arena, according to Panofsky, is internal to the painting, and the viewer does not take an independent part in the production of the painterly narrative, but only in its reconstruction. That is, the painterly meaning is a fixed and preexisting structure and can be reached through an iconographic and iconological analysis.

All these various critics, then, think of painting in relation to an anterior text, which provides the key to the interpretation of the painting. This is, to a great extent, another aspect of the same trend sketched in the subchapter on the first *Laocoon*, in which paintings are examined through literary characteristics.

It seems that the very need to rely on texts external to the painting points to the inability to see painting as able to constitute an independent narrative through the visual means that are internal to it. However, not one of the theoreticians claims that the need to turn to an antedating text stems from the painting's inability to represent a narrative.

Independent narrative painting

"St. Nicholas has just paid his pre-Christmas visit to the household, leaving toys, candy, and cake for the children. Everybody is jolly except the bad boy on the left, who has received only a birch rod".[9] Art historian H.W. Janson

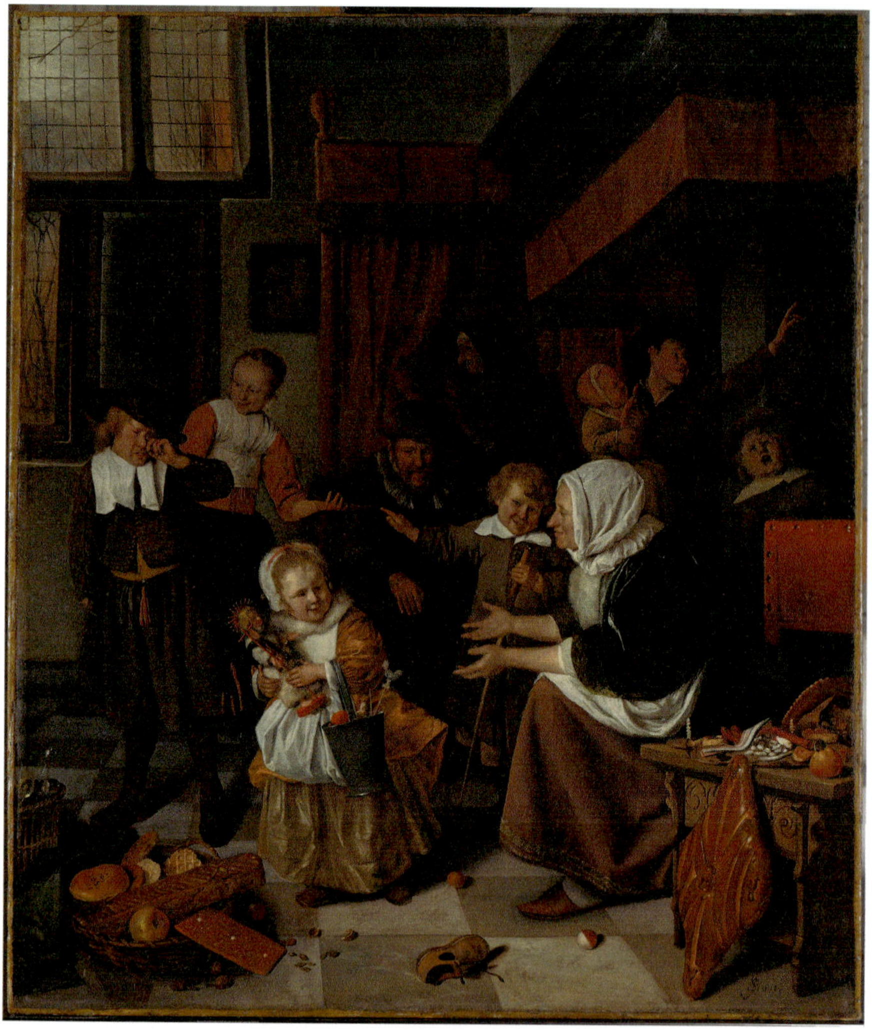

Figure 2.1 Jan Steen, *The Feast of St. Nicholas*, circa 1660–1665.

analyzes here Jan Steen's painting *The Feast of St. Nicholas* circa 1660–1665. In this case, the painting does not relate to a specific antedating text. The narrative is produced through the representation of a few of the stages of the story through the gestures of the painted characters.

This painting declares its narrativity through an abundance of painterly details that make it possible to reconstruct a kind of sequence of events. Narrativity, in this approach, appears as an implicit template and is not associated with a specific narrative.

Another example of a narrative interpretation that does not directly relate to a prior text is Diderot's reading of Jean-Baptiste Greuze's painting *The Girl weeping for her Dead Bird*, circa 1765. The painting is a portrait of a sad girl whose hand covers part of her face; before her is a bird cage with a dead bird on it. Diderot develops from this painting a complex narrative, with a sequence of events related to each other through temporal and causal order.

Thus, Diderot constructs an intricate love story whose protagonists are the crying girl, her lover and her mother, even though the latter two are not present in the painting.[10] Diderot, then, supposes a narrative painting that is not dependent on a prior verbal text, although the relation of this narrative to the situation represented in the painting seems accidental and completely dependent on the interpretive maneuvers of the creative viewer.

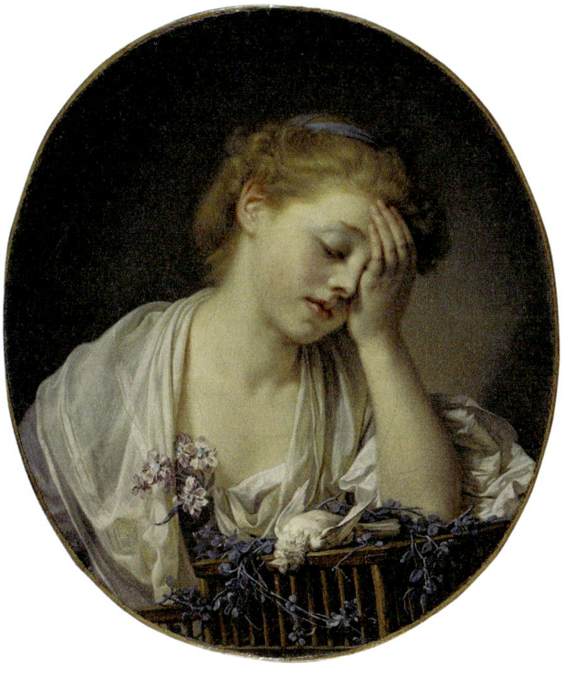

Figure 2.2 Jean-Baptiste Greuze, *A Girl with a Dead Canary*, 1765.

In his analysis of English painting from the end of the nineteenth century, Ernst Gombrich also raises the theoretical possibility of an independent narrative painting. For instance, in his interpretation of Sir William Quiller Orchardson's painting *The First Cloud*[11] of 1887.[12] Gombrich states that there is an essential difference between a painting that relates to a familiar text and a painting that tells its own story. This painterly category has not received much attention in the history of art, also due to the overwhelming reservations twentieth-century critics have shown toward these paintings.[13]

Yet, are these two models genuinely different? Both cases attempt to offer a coherent and complete narrative structure. Both models also attempt to extrapolate from the painting a narrativity that would obey literary characteristics. Both models essentially rely on a verbal text or its clues at the expense of picturality. These kinds of readings assume that the narrativity produced by the paintings is essentially similar to the narrativity produced through textual means, while ignoring the very process of looking, which is, after all, essentially different from reading a text, and the difference between the material presence of the painting as an object and the presence of the verbal text.

As I have shown in my discussion of the third *Laocoon*, different studies throughout the twentieth century have reached the same conclusion from different directions – that narrativity is not a strictly literary asset. This line of thought indicates that painting possesses narratological abilities that are not dependent on the literary text but are produced by the painting through its own means. This option cannot be found in any of the discussions I have outlined so far, and, to a certain extent, these studies also follow the assumption shown in the first two *Laocoons*: that narrativity is an external addition to painting.

Narrative interpretations of painting, which rely on an anterior text, present a coherent structure, with a clear internal logic, clear causal order and an adherence to a certain global structure, such as a transition from complication to solution. At the beginning of this book, I pointed toward the phenomenon of alienation that exists between a painting and the narrative interpretation given to it. I intend to point toward a possible relation between the coherency of the narrative interpretation and the effect of alienation that emanates from the relation between the painting and its interpretation. I wish to show that the gap between a narrative interpretation given to the painting and the painting itself stems from a forced connection between the painting and an a priori verbal text.

The expanded pictorial arena

In his discussion on the connection between painting and theatre, Michael Fried analyzes the way in which Diderot outlines the relations between the viewer and the painted figure through the concept of absorption.[14] This concept relates to the painted characters who are completely absorbed in a human action, focusing on something spiritual and mental, religious or moral, and while the viewer is also carried away into the represented scene. As an example of paintings that represent this absorption, Fried cites Jean-Baptiste-Siméon Chardin's painting *Un Philosophe occupé de sa lecture*, from 1753, in which a male figure is absorbed in reading.

Another type of absorption can be found in historical paintings depicting characters in the midst of an intense activity. Yet another kind of absorption may be found in landscape paintings. Thus, for instance, in the salon of 1763, Diderot describes landscape paintings that present a human activity and describes himself as entering the fictional scene and taking part in it.[15] The process of looking at a painting is not described as an experience of looking at a painterly object located before the viewer and is separated and distinct from him; rather, the viewer experiences the painterly landscape as a physical place that surrounds him.

What is common to all the paintings that absorb the viewer is that they also ignore him. Thus, they make their viewer feel like a voyeur who is looking at a scene that does not present itself to his gaze, but rather the opposite: a scene that closes itself before his eyes. There are different versions of this painterly style, such as genre painting or allegorical scenes, historical painting or landscape painting. Absorption, according to Fried, constitutes a common denominator for a plethora of French paintings that were showcased in the salons of Paris in the eighteenth century. One of the effects that are attributed to these paintings is the way in which the viewer enters the painting. Fried presents many examples from Diderot's texts, among them his interpretation of Greuze's painting of *The Girl Weeping for Her Dead Bird*, to which I related earlier. In his interpretation, Greuze describes a process of looking in which the viewer is present in the painterly scene, fashions relationships with the characters, speaks with them and participates in the fictional world. In this way, the viewer who has been absorbed into the paintings takes on the role of one of the protagonists in the scene.

Fried underscores the seemingly paradoxical nature of the relationship Diderot proposes between the viewer and the painting. On the one hand, Diderot emphasizes that it is important for the painted characters to ignore the viewer, and on the other hand, he claims that the viewer is absorbed into the painterly scene precisely because the characters ignore him. According to Fried, this is true for both the theatrical medium and painting and in both cases, the characters should act as if the curtain has never been lifted. By ignoring the viewer, the painted character answers the condition that Diderot and his contemporaries articulate for painting: to draw in, fascinate and charm the viewer.[16]

According to Diderot, the act of looking is founded on absorption, denial, negation and fascination. Only a painting that denies its viewer can fascinate him. Thus, when Susanna exposes her naked body to the viewer, she remains modest since she hides herself from the elders.[17] The painter and Susanna do not acknowledge the existence of the viewer. This act of ignoring, Diderot argues, guarantees the quality of the painting and its strong effect on the viewer. The aim of the painting, according to this stance, is the existence of a viewer who is not indifferent or alienated. Rather, precisely because the painting does not suppose his existence or acknowledge him, the viewer can function as a hidden yet inherent part of the painterly scene. In other words, the viewer, whom Diderot sketches, is a voyeur, an observer who believes that no one sees him looking.

Absorption, according to Fried, has two characteristics: it relies on the assumption of an unmediated relation between the viewer and the painting, while the viewer in this equation is not external and indifferent but is, in a certain sense, internal to the painting. Moreover, this absorption is an activity that produces a narrative, while the interpretation that follows turns the viewer into an active participant in the painterly scene.

Margaret Iversen's commentary on Riegl's writing offers another reading of the relation between absorption and narrativity.[18] Iversen, who analyzes the differences between Riegl and Fried, underscores the voyeuristic aspect that Fried attributed to absorption and connects absorption to narrativity. According to Iversen, absorption promises a narrative when the characters do not present themselves to the eyes of the viewer, since they are not aware of his presence. This lack of awareness makes it possible for the viewer to fall under their spell.[19] What is significant for this debate is that, even though Fried's argument relies on a salient link between painting and theatre in Diderot's work, in his conceptualization of absorption he nevertheless articulates an aspect of narrativity that uniquely belongs to the visual field.

I find in Riegl's analysis of Dutch group portrait paintings the buds of an alternative narrativity that emerges from the visual medium, and is related to the viewer's position as an integral part of the painting.[20] In his analysis, Riegl points toward an alternative narrative perception that emanates from the visual medium and that conceives of the viewer as an integral part of the painting. Riegl demonstrates how Dutch group portrait paintings, which do not portray an action but focus on describing a group of working people, generate a narrativity that is not dependent on a prior known text. This narrativity is achieved through two sets of relations – the relations between the characters themselves and the relations between the characters and their viewer. Moreover, and most importantly for our purposes, Riegl substitutes the explicit characteristics of narrativity with other characteristics, which are not ostensibly narrative, yet create a narrative effect.

Riegl coins the term "external coherence", which is different from "internal coherence". External coherence relates to the way the painting turns to the viewer. Riegl enumerates a few possibilities for expanding the painterly space: when the characters in the painting exchange glances with the viewer, as is the case in many portraits; when they look "beyond the viewer" to a third party who is not in the painting, as in the case of Rembrandt's *The Syndics* circa 1662; or when the painterly characters are about to perform an action that will take place "outside the painting", for instance, when the characters march in *The Night Watch*. Riegl demonstrates the distinction between internal and external coherence through two painters, Pieter Bruegel and Pieter Aertsen. Bruegel demonstrates an internal coherence in which the characters are busy with their own world. Aertsen, however, demonstrates an external coherence in which the characters are disconnected from each other and directly turn toward the viewer.

We may see this in Aertsen's painting *Market Scene*, circa 1560. Aertsen isolates the characters in the painting, and each of them fashions their own independent relation with the viewer. In the center of the painting is a bird seller who is in search of customers. Rather than turning to the characters in the painting, claims Riegl, he turns to the viewer as a potential customer. Next to him stands a servant who seems to have just bought a pair of birds from him. She is separated from the seller and also turns to the viewer to show him her purchase. Thus, Aertsen separates characters that are otherwise linked through a narrative from each other and connects them with the viewer.[21] This is similar to group portraits in which external coherence stands instead of internal coherence until painters reach the stage in which both coherences can coexist in their paintings. That is, according to Riegl, Dutch group portraiture reaches this optimal state when the paintings contain both internal coherence between the painted characters and external coherence between the image and the viewer, and the two operations complement each other.

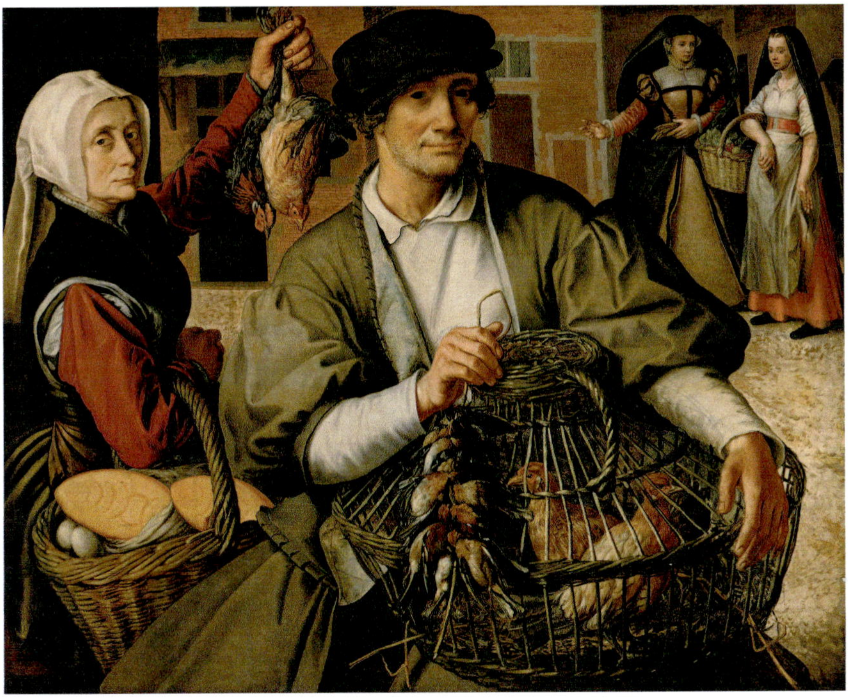

Figure 2.3 Pieter Aertsen, *Market Scene*, 1560–1565.

Riegl outlines the development of group portrait paintings. In this process, external coherence becomes more and more specific in terms of space and time. The span of the activity that binds the painted characters to the viewer is contracted to a single moment, and the characters in the paintings who turn toward the viewer assume a specific viewer. Riegl argues that the choice of a single moment also affects the internal coherence of the painting, since it also supports the external coherence.[22]

According to Riegl, the paintings that best represent the later stage in the development of group portrait paintings are Rembrandt's *The Night Watch* and *The Syndics*. Riegl argues that what is unique to *The Night Watch* is the way in which Rembrandt resolves external coherence. Not one eye is turned to the viewer, not one ear is attuned to him, but the entire guard is about to march toward the viewer and break into his space. As Riegl argues, Rembrandt breaks here a thousand-year-old tradition, in which movement in painting exists solely within the surface of the painting. What is important for this discussion is not the way Rembrandt represents movement, but the psychological aspect of the intention of the characters to act and the expression that indicates this intention.[23]

The second example of a painterly space extending toward the viewer is the painting *The Syndics*. According to Riegl, this painting represents the apex of the late period in group portrait paintings. Rembrandt, in this painting, finds a solution to the two types of coherence. Internal coherence is achieved by subjugating the characters to the character of the spokesman,

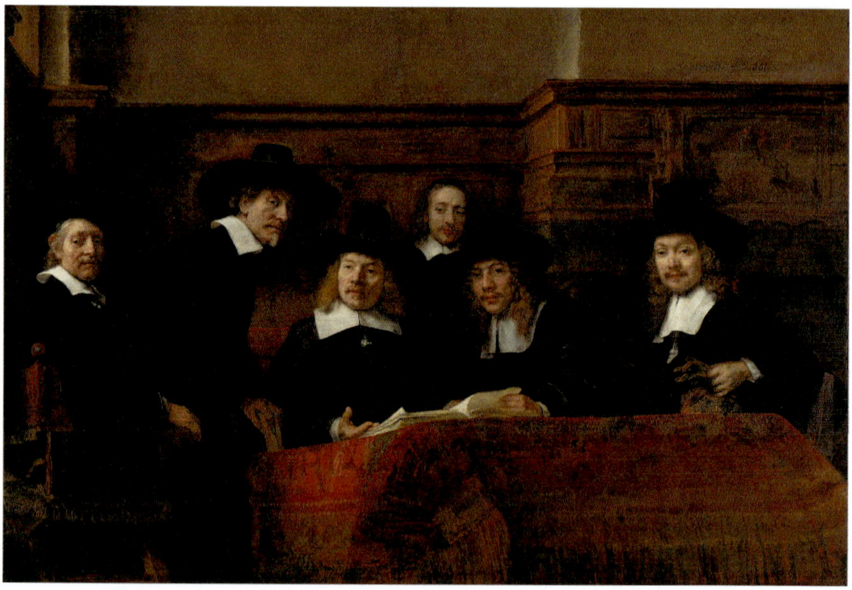

Figure 2.4 Rembrandt van Rijn, *The Syndics: The Sampling Officials (wardens) of the Amsterdam Drapers' Guild (The Staalmeesters)*, 1662.

and external coherence is achieved through their appeal to the viewer. The characters are in a state of dividing their attention between the inner character and the viewer. Thus, the two types of coherences, both internal and external, are achieved in a single moment of time and space.[24]

Both Fried (who draws, as stated, from Diderot) and Riegl discuss the expansion of painterly space and the viewer. In both cases, the limits of the painted canvas are traversed, whether the viewer enters the painting or vice versa, since the painted space aspires to encompass the world around it.

Both theoreticians attribute the expansion of the painterly space to the way in which the characters turn their gaze either toward the viewer or away from him. They both connect the conflation of the painterly space and the world beyond it with the exchange of glances between the painted characters and the viewer. However, they reach the same conclusion through opposite routes. For Diderot, the viewer is "drawn" into the painterly space when the painted characters ignore him by turning their gaze to the intense work that absorbs them. For Riegl, the boundaries between the viewer and the painting are conflated when the painted characters turn their gaze either directly to the viewer or to someone standing behind him, and the limits of the picture expand to encompass the space of the viewer as well.

To what extent, then, does the expansion of painterly space and the conflation of its limits function as a way of constituting a narrative? And is it possible to conceptualize narrative painting not through the text that it represents, or at least points toward, but rather through the active the relations of looking that are fashioned between the viewer and the painting? It is important to note that despite their initial differences, both Diderot and Riegl articulate an aspect of painting that involves the conception of the viewer as an inseparable part of the painting. To clarify the relation between the act of looking described here and visual narrativity, I will outline Mulvey's feminist argument on Hollywood narrative cinema.[25] Although Mulvey's research revolves around cinema and not painting, she still draws a link between the gaze she describes and narrativity.

Mulvey claims that the viewer in Hollywood cinema identifies with the fictional male character. The male character functions as the viewer's surrogate by turning the feminine character into his object of enjoyment. Hence, the visual field contains both the viewer and the object of his gaze, while this visual construction relates to narrativity.[26]

Another, more specific connection between the act of looking and narrativity emerges from Laura Mulvey's claim that realistic cinematic modes of representation make it possible to relate vision to self-identity. The process of identification, which is carried out through the gaze of the viewer, is directed at the fictional character and leads to the dissolution of the cinematic arena as separate from the viewer. According to Mulvey, various photographic technologies are ultimately used to blur the spatial boundaries projected on the screen.[27] Mulvey isolates yet another link in the relation of looking that is intertwined in the identification with an existing narrative. She argues that narrativity appears so as to treat the anxiety that is produced from the act of looking itself. The gaze directed toward the female character also circumscribes another aspect of this character beyond her being an object of enjoyment for the male gaze, and that is her lack of a penis. This lack awakens castration anxiety, and one of the ways to cope with this anxiety is through a sadistic fantasy that is fashioned into a narrative.[28]

Like Diderot and Riegl, Mulvey also points to a structure in which unmediated relations of looking function as part of the constitution of the image as narrative. Mulvey takes this one step further, though, by showing how the act of looking itself generates narrativity. However, is this indeed, as Mulvey argues, a social product of power and control? Can we not explain this construct in a way that does not reduce its relevance to the field that Mulvey examines, and thus also understand narrativity not only in its relation to a sadistic form of enjoyment? Mulvey bases her arguments on an act of looking that generates a form of narrativity in which the viewer constitutes one of the protagonists. This phenomenon can also be found in other debates, such as Diderot and Riegl. Thus, we may conclude that the phenomenon Mulvey points at is not unique to the cinematic genre nor to feminist critique.

The similarity between the relations of looking in Diderot's work and the male gaze which Mulvey discusses points to a more crucial point: these discussions open the possibility of theorizing narrativity as a product of an act of looking in which the viewer and the object of his gaze are seemingly located in the same visual field. Diderot and Riegl already showed how the act of looking can expand the painterly arena. Mulvey's description of the cinematic gaze makes it possible to take a step further and to grasp the act of looking itself as a narrative action. That is, the act of looking is seen as a narrative act, an act in which the looking subject becomes one of the protagonists. Looking, in this context, is no longer merely an act of reception, in which the viewer processes the painterly details before him; rather, the act of looking is, in fact, one of the activities that are involved in the narrative. In other words, Mulvey considers the act of looking as an event that generates anxiety, and the way to treat this anxiety is through a phantasmatic script with a narrative structure. She distinguishes between the act of looking, which constitutes the cause of the anxiety, which she attributes to a social construct, and the narrative that is formed to silence the effect of the act of looking. If we take Mulvey's logic a step further, we can understand the act of looking itself as an inseparable part of the formation of a narrative, as taking an active part in some story.

A conception of narrativity constituted through an exchange of gazes is essentially different from the previous conceptions I presented, which conceive of narrativity as a supplement that is external and foreign to painting. Narrativity that is part of the act of looking is unique to the visual medium. It is a narrativity that constitutes an inseparable part of the act of looking that generates it. This form of narrativity connects the two seemingly disparate aspects of narrative painting: painting as a representation of fiction and painting as a material object. Moreover, this narrativity is an inherent component of painting and stems from the act of looking.

Traversing the pictorial arena as an aesthetic device

What is the significance of stretching the painterly arena toward the viewer and including him within it, of undermining the boundaries between the viewer and the object of his gaze? Is this a mental activity, an emotional position, a metaphorical articulation or maybe a hallucination? This model offers an essentially different act of looking than those I extracted from the previous two models, and beyond the question of narrativity, it raises a question regarding the very ontological status of the artistic object and the way we conceptualize it.[29]

Scholars such as Riegl and Fried, who conceive of painting as an expanded arena, try to explain this expansion through a theorization of painting and its significance. However, questions concerning the ontological status of the relations they outline remain outside the scope of their research due to their disciplinary definition. Moreover, an examination of Riegl's and Fried's arguments shows that even though they point toward a certain amalgamation between the viewer and the painter, eventually, they rely on a conventional Albertian conception of space, which they challenge, each in his own fashion. In other words, though different theories of art speak of the possibility of the conflation of the boundaries between the viewer and the painting, they focus only on the conflation as a way to interpret the painting. They do not interpret the ontological and epistemological status of the act of looking that arises from this conflation.

Investigating narrative painting as a form of painting that is constituted through an act of looking that traverses the boundaries between viewer and object can make it possible to see in narrativity something that is imminent to painting and not an external addition to it. How, then, can the concept of the expanded arena offer a solution to the problem of narrative painting while also explaining this traversal? Moreover, how can we characterize this expanded arena through a narrativity that is unique to the visual medium in a way that articulates the problematics in the relationship between painting and narrativity?

At this point I would like to turn to the psychoanalytic thought of Freud and Lacan, which offers a non-dualistic approach to subject-object relations. As I will later show, psychoanalysis can help answer the problem I delineated above: the psychoanalytic framework can make it possible to articulate the logic of the "traversal", in which the viewing subject is not separated from his object of observation. Unlike the theoreticians outlined above, the psychoanalytic discourse of Jacques Lacan does not consider the act of looking to be a harmonious process of complete assimilation. Instead, the relation between the looking subject and the object is characterized by its asymmetry.

Moreover, psychoanalytic theory will make it possible to explain the act of looking as a complex and layered act, which is part of the very construction of narrativity. The juxtaposition of these two aspects, namely the complexity of the act of looking and the incongruency that it entails, can show how the problems in the discussion of narrative painting and the fundamental gap that exists between a painting and its narrative reading are two sides of the same coin: narrativity is constructed into the image, and the looking subject is an inseparable part of it. The complex and unstable character of the image stems from the inevitable connection between the viewing subject and its object of observation. That is, narrativity in the visual field is derived from a complex act of looking, which is not necessarily progressive or coherent. As I will show later in this book, the importance of this conception of narrativity lies in the manner in which it aligns with the failures and incongruencies that have characterized the theoretical debate on narrative painting.

In the first chapter of this book, I noted that one of the traditional ways of thinking about narrative painting is to apply literary theories to painting, and I highlighted the problems in thinking about the visual medium using tools that are foreign to it. This begs the question, then: in what way is the psychoanalytical approach essentially different from applying literary theories to painting? The second, and more significant, problem relates to the very justification for using psychoanalytic theories, which are originally centered on the clinic, to conceptualize painting.

As for the first problem, the attempt to explain narrativity in painting through literary principles contains the assumption of a similarity between one medium and the other, and this similarity should justify the application of the principles of one medium to another. I believe that this assumption is false and does not properly answer the complexities of both the visual and the verbal medium. However, the use of psychoanalytic theory does not attempt to apply its observations to painting but makes possible a new way of thinking about basic themes that are situated at the heart of the investigation of both the visual and the verbal medium, such as sight, representation and narrative structure.

As for the second problem, the turn to psychoanalysis makes it possible to rethink the structure of the expanded painterly arena delineated above. Several disciplines have already pointed toward this structure. However, they cannot explain it beyond a metaphorical or emotional level. The act of looking that Lacan describes, which is founded on a certain conceptualization of the subject, offers a similar structure with essentially different logic. At this point, we may say that although the various theories I outlined above, from Alberti to Mulvey, supposed that the expanded arena is based on the gaze of the looking subject, the Lacanian conception of the subject rests on a completely opposite state of affairs, in which what looks at the subject from the painting is not the gaze of the subject but the gaze as object. The gaze as an object is exactly that which escapes representation, as the subject is necessarily captured in the act of looking. Since, as Lacan claims: "No doubt, in the depth of my eye, the picture is painted. The picture, certainly, is in my eye. But I am in the picture".[30] That is, along with the complete image that the picture provides, it also offers the opposite, the possibility that there is a visibility that escapes me, which I do not possess but is attributed to me by an Other who is looking at me. The significance of this to the expanded painterly arena is crucial: there are no longer two distinct fields that should be traversed since the subject is bounded in one of them, but, in a certain sense, the subject inhabits both.

Notes

1 Nietzsche, Friedrich. 1910 [1872]. *The Birth of Tragedy.* Trans. William A. Haussmann. Edinburgh and London: T.N. Foulis.
2 Nietzsche, 1910, p. 50.
3 Lessing, Gotthold Ephraim. 1887 [1766]. *Laocoön: An Essay upon the Limits of Painting and Poetry*. Trans. Ellen Frothingham. Cambridge: Cambridge University Press, John Wilson and Son, p. 19.
4 Lessing, p. 74.
5 Alberti, Leon Battista. 1966 [1435–1436]. *On Painting.* Trans. John R. Spencer. New Haven: Yale University Press, p. 85.
6 Lee, Rensselaer W. 1967 [1940]. *Ut Pictura Poesis: The Humanistic Theory of Painting*. New York: Norton Library, p. 18.
7 Brilliant, Richard. 1986. *Visual Narratives: Storytelling in Etruscan and Roman Art.* Ithaca and London: Cornell University Press.
8 Brilliant, 1986, p. 53.
9 Janson, Horst Woldemar. 1995. *History of Art.* London: Thames and Hudson, p. 585.
10 Diderot, Denis. 1994. *Selected Writings on Art and Literature*. Trans. Geofrey Bremner. London: Penguin Books, pp. 236–239.
11 The Tate Gallery, London.
12 Gombrich, Ernst. 1994 [1982]. *The Image & the Eye: Further Studies in the Psychology of Pictorial Representation*. London: Phaidon Press Limited, p. 102.
13 Gombrich, 1994, p. 101.
14 Fried, Michael. 1988. *Absorption and Theatricality: Painting and Beholder in the Age of Diderot.* Chicago: University of Chicago Press.
15 Fried, 1988, pp. 119–120.
16 Fried, 1988, p. 92.
17 Fried, 1988, p. 96.
18 Iversen, Margaret. 1993. *Alois Riegl: Art History and Theory*. Cambridge: MIT Press.
19 Iversen, 1993, p. 133.
20 Riegl, Alois. 1999 [1902]. *The Group Portraiture of Holland*. Trans. Evelyn M. Klein and David Britt. Los Angeles: The Getty Research Institute for the History of Art and the Humanities.
21 Riegl, 1999, p. 169.
22 Riegl, 1999, pp. 221–223.
23 Riegl, 1999, p. 271.
24 Riegl, 1999, p. 285.
25 Mulvey, Laura. 1989. *Visual and Other Pleasures*. Bloomington and Indianapolis: Indiana University Press.
26 It should be noted that Mulvey makes use of Lacanian psychoanalytical conceptualizations to present her claims. At this point, I am focusing on the process of

looking she sketches and its relation to narrativity and not yet entering into the psychoanalytic context, which will later receive a central role.

27 Mulvey, 1989, p. 20.

28 Mulvey, 1989, p. 22.

29 On the expansion of the painterly arena, see also: Bryson, Norman. 1988. "The Gaze in the Expanded Field". In *Vision and Visuality*. Edited by Hal Foster. Dia Art Foundation. Seattle: Bay Press, pp. 87–108.

30 Lacan, Jacques. 1981 [1964–1965]. *The Four Fundamental Concepts of Psychoanalysis: The Seminar of Jacques Lacan, Book XI.* Trans. Alan Sheridan. New York and London: W.W. Norton and Company, p. 96. There is often a certain discrepancy between the English translations of Lacan and the French source. This quotation, like the other quotations of Lacan, is based on the French source.

3 Looking at a painting as a phantasmatic structure

Theon of Samos first revealed to a crowd his painting of a soldier running to save his homeland to the sound of a trumpet. Thus, he created a vivid impression. As Brilliant, who relates this story, notes, the Greek word for "impression" or "appearance" is "phantasia", a term with a complex history in Greek and Roman criticism, whose meaning oscillates from the sense of "appearance" to "imagination" or "creative imagination" and later imaginary visualizations.[1] The word fantasy, in its early articulations, relates, then, to vision and its effect.

Following in Sigmund Freud's footsteps, psychoanalysts Jean Laplanche and Jean-Bertrand Pontalis define fantasy as an "imaginary scene in which the subject is a protagonist".[2] Indeed, according to Freud, fantasy is a script of organized scenes that are usually manifested visually and in which the subject of the fantasy is, in a certain way, included.[3]

Interpretations of paintings that base their argument on the supposition that the viewer grasps himself as the hero of the painted scene are structurally similar to the way fantasy works. Fantasy operates mainly in the visual field, while the subject perceives himself as part of a script. Unlike the artistic and aesthetic positions outlined in the previous chapter, which argued that the spectator is fully and harmonically immersed in his object of observation, the psychoanalytic discussion of fantasy exposes an essentially different relation between the subject and the phantasmatic script, since it is not based on symmetry and harmony.

Fantasy is a central concept in psychoanalysis, from its early conceptualization in Freud's writing to its Lacanian articulations and the way in which Žižek interprets them. The psychoanalytic discussion in this chapter will enable me to articulate the relation between the gaze, narrativity and the subject looking at the scene in which he himself is included.

In his article "The Seven Veils of Fantasy", Žižek, who explores the relation between Lacanian psychoanalysis, popular culture and art, outlines seven aspects of fantasy as they appear in Lacan's teaching.[4] Although the object of his research is fantasy, his discussion makes it possible to conceptualize painting in a similar fashion. Žižek's discussion of the characteristics

DOI: 10.4324/9781003516446-4

of fantasy is fruitful for understanding narrativity in painting for two reasons. The first relates to the similarities between the characteristics of fantasy and the processes of looking at a painting from a Lacanian position. The second relates to the imaginary structure of narrativity as one of the veils of fantasy. As we may glean from Žižek's discussion, narrativity, as a veil of fantasy, is an imaginary order that is imposed on reality so as to make it coherent.

Žižek's conceptualization of the characteristics of fantasy makes it possible to both articulate an alternative model of looking at a painting and reaffirm the criticism of traditional narrative theories and various theories of art, which offer interpretive practices that are incompatible with pictorial representation. I have chosen to present the veils of fantasy not in the order that Žižek presents them, but in accordance with the relevant order of the argument before us: I will open with the veil of fantasy that relates to the concept of narrative, continue with the veil of fantasy that relates to the concept of the gaze and the manner of looking at a painting, and conclude with the veil of fantasy that is relevant to the concept of the positions of the subject.

As stated, fantasy is a central concept in psychoanalysis, which is rooted in Freud's work. At a certain point in his practice, Freud reached the conclusion that the testimonies his patients reported of experiences of sexual seduction from their childhood were often phantasmatic and did not necessarily take place. Yet, from a psychoanalytic vantage point, the distinction between an imaginary-phantasmatic world and reality is impossible, since for psychoanalysis there is no such thing as an objective "reality". Rather, reality, like fantasy, is structured through discourse. Freud's conclusion, then, is not hinged on the distinction between truth and imagination, but on the fact that the memories of the past are structured through language and are established anew in accordance with unconscious desires. The concept of fantasy, for Freud, relates to a scene presenting an unconscious desire. The concept of fantasy in its Lacanian articulation is based on Freud's theorizations while underscoring the fact that fantasy constitutes a defense in the sense that it veils castration.[5] Fantasy, then, makes it possible for the subject to not encounter trauma and other repressed elements.

As seen in the previous chapters, the term narrative has been interpreted in various ways. Žižek, drawing on Lacan, defines narrative as a construction of sense with unified, coherent and hermetic characteristics. These characteristics have been identified with narrativity since Aristotle, through various theoreticians throughout history, to our own time. For Žižek, narrative is a necessary condition for the construction of meaning, despite its internal failures. The starkest characteristic of narrativity, according to him, is not storytelling, but rather the imaginary appearance of a hermetic structure of meaning. I will make use of these different aspects of narrativity to offer a model of the relation between the subject and the painting, in which narrativity is structured during the process of looking at a painting.

Fantasy is a narrative

The term narrative, which Žižek makes use of, refers, as stated, to a construction of meaning that is a product of a textual object. Narrative is a product of a textual object with a temporal sequence that is unified, coherent and hermetic. This kind of narrative makes possible the emergence of a phantasmatic sense, while the very attempt to construct meaning brings to the fore something of the unconscious. That is, the narrative structure itself points toward repressed content which narrativity strives to cover.

As Žižek argues, Lacan is a radical *anti-narrativist*. Lacan does not simply claim that the narratives that emerge during psychoanalytic treatment are "false" and based on the expulsion of traumatic events from the patient's past and the suturing of the gaps that remain from this operation. As he states:

> ...the answer to the question 'Why do we tell stories?' is that narrative as such emerges in order to resolve some fundamental antagonism by rearranging its terms into a temporal succession. It is thus the very form of narrative which bears witness to some repressed antagonism.[6]

Narrative is a kind of a "package deal", and whoever participates in it pays the price of temporal organization, coherency and unity so as to gain sense. The very existence of this "package deal" indicates that it veils something repressed. In other words, despite its pretense to unfold a "realistic" description of a chain of events, narrative is, in fact, a phantasmatic and imaginary construct.

Narrativity, in psychoanalytic terms, is a representation with a limited capacity for description, yet it is necessary, since it fashions its object through its very appearance, the very object that escapes its narrative representation. Narrativity cannot describe a paradoxical state of affairs like that of the Lacanian *object petit a* – the object cause of desire, which is made present only when it is lost.[7] According to Lacan, the *object petit a*, by its very definition, eludes representation and is never attainable. The *object petit a* is only possible as a representation of lack a cover for what cannot be represented. Unlike the traditional relations of representation, in which the signifier signifies something else, the *object petit a* does not represent something that is lost but points toward the lack, and hence only appears in the wake of its loss. Narrational representation does not make this type of paradoxicality possible, and the only way for it to treat it is to place it within a temporal sequence in which the object first appears and is lost only later.

Žižek shows that narrative follows a certain logic, which does not necessarily comply with history. History contains contradictory situations, like a loss that has a gain, and these situations do not obey narrational logic.[8]

Žižek's criticism of narrativity is founded on its conception as an imaginary pattern masquerading as compatibility with a changing reality. The problem that arises does not end with the limit of the narrational conception, but rather with the pretense it poses to give an answer to contradictory situations, to place impossible situations in one single unified frame. Narrative is necessary for there to be understanding; however, it will forever continue to fail in its task to describe what it invents. The very existence of a narrative testifies, as stated, to the repression it is meant to veil, and through the attempt to construct meaning, narrative makes it possible for something from the unconscious to emerge to the surface.

Žižek provides an example of the paradoxicality of narrative through a reading of a criticism of Descartes, which accuses him of "anthropocentrism". Žižek shows how, even though this criticism tries to claim that Descartes places man at the center, it also raises the opposite claim – that Descartes actually devalues man. As he states: "Does the Cartesian subjectivity… not involve the 'Copernican turn? does it not decenter man and reduce him to insignificant creature on a small planet?".[9] In other words, following Lacan, Žižek claims that the Cartesian reduction of man to a signifier, to a self-relating negativity, corresponds, in fact, to the position that is opposite of anthropocentrism, in which man is reduced to "a grain of dust in the infinity of the universe".[10] These are two sides of the same coin. In the same sense of placing man at the center, Descartes also functions as a "radical anti-humanist, i.e. he dissolves the Renaissance humanist unity of man as the highest Creature, the top of creation, into pure *cogito* and its bodily remainder".[11] In other words, not only can we not fix the Cartesian *cogito* within unequivocal meaning, but the articulation of this kind of interpretation eventually brings about the emergence of the opposite sense.

Žižek finds yet another example of the paradoxicality of narrative representation in relation to Descartes in the criticism that accuses Descartes of identifying the *cogito* with male attributes. These critics assume an initial state of affairs in which man and woman complete each other in harmony, but Descartes's *cogito* disrupts this harmonious relation and instead places male conceptions at the center. However, at the same time, the conception of man as pure and genderless thought marks the first crack in an otherwise ostensibly male perception of the world. That is, like the previous example that relates to the status of man in the world, here too we have two opposite versions that come to describe the same object.

These cases represent situations in which narrative representation includes its inverse, and narrativization makes it possible for each of them to represent a different "truth" without settling between them, as the different narratives relate to the same reality that they aspire to define. Moreover, the attempt to represent a story of progress from one state of affairs to another, for instance, a transition from a primitive and sexist worldview to modern neutral thought, is itself distorted. However, this distortion also takes place in the opposite narrative when describing a regression from thinking of man and woman as completing each other to a patriarchal point of view that identifies the woman with the "natural". The two versions blur the simultaneity of the incongruity at hand. The paradox is that a certain historical moment is conceived as a loss of a certain quality; we may see that the lost quality only appears at the moment in which it is allegedly lost. Thus, for instance, in the case of Descartes's conception of sexuality, the crack in the centralization of male thought appears at the very moment in which male consciousness is defined and identified as central. The conclusion of this synchronicity is not that there is no history or that the various and contradictory states are a priori, but that historical processes do not adhere to the logic of narrativity. As Žižek argues:

> The actual historical breaks are, if anything, *more* radical than mere narrative deployments, since what changes in them is the entire constellation of emergence and loss.... a true historical break does not simply designate the 'regressive' loss (or 'progressive' gain) of something, but the shift in the very grid which enables us to measure losses and gains.[12]

Žižek's description of the phantasmatic aspect of narrative structure is essential to the manner in which we may think of narrative painting. Examining the very concept of "narrative painting" through this veil of fantasy makes it possible to think in a similar fashion about the way different theories of art apply narrativity to painting while attempting to make it adhere to literary principles. As I stated in the introduction, the relation between painting and narrativity is not simple since it entails problems on different levels. Žižek's discussion raises the possibility that this difficulty, that is, the gap between narrative interpretation and the painting to which it refers, stems from the very same incongruity as the one between a coherent and semantic interpretive structure and a painting that does not necessarily follow this structure. Thus, can we not understand the narrative interpretations of the painting as a veil to what cannot be articulated, since the very presence of the narrative interpretation testifies to its own impossibility?

This raises another question: can a painting, through a single image, make possible the very same simultaneous, paradoxical situation that narrativity aspires to veil? Can it not bring these situations to the surface and thus make possible a complex form of narrativity that would be unique to the visual field? As Žižek's examples show, the temporal sequence that characterizes narrative structure, in all its formulations, constitutes, to a great extent, the very same unified standard to which we adjust complex and paradoxical situations, while the attempt to make them fit the standard distorts them. Reality cannot always be captured through a simple development from state A to state B that follows the demands of narrative structure.

How does Žižek's argument, then, shed light on narrative painting? In the discussion of the first Laocoon, I showed how different theories of art examine narrative painting by imposing literary principles on it while extrapolating from it a temporal sequence. However, in this matter in particular, it seems that the single image of a painting reveals a paradoxical state of affairs, which narrativity seeks to veil.

Fantasy stages castration

The relation between fantasy and castration stems from the fact that unlike the common belief according to which fantasy is used to fulfill forbidden satisfactions, the phantasmatic narrative does not present the transgressions of law and order, but rather the reverse, an adherence to the law and its formation. This fashions an ironic state in which the pervert, who is usually considered as the one who breaks the law, actually yearns for it.[13] The phantasmatic narrative displays castration in the sense that it presents us with a yearning for a state of prohibitions and limitations. Žižek provides historical examples of attempts to find phantasmatic points in time that describe an imagined turning point and thus offer an imposed order. Thus, for instance, the attempt to pinpoint the exact historical moment in which Germany "turned in the wrong direction" and the different options proposed to answer this question, or the attempt to answer the question "When exactly did patriarchal oppression coincide with the repression and exploitation of nature?".[14] Eco-feminist positions provide various answers to this question, such as the dominance of capitalism in the nineteenth century, modern Cartesian science which objectifies nature, and so forth. As Žižek argues, these answers express the desire for order, while these points in time, which ostensibly mark a turning point, are, in fact, the phantasmatic products of this desire.

This argument presents another criticism of narrative structure. Beyond the fact that narrativity is presented as a phantasmatic product of an illusory answer and imagined wholeness, it also shows that organizing information in a narrative structure expresses a desire for an imposed order, one that is not the product of a particular observation but rather stems from the presupposition of a general order. If we accept this supposition, then narrative interpretation of a picture, both in the sense of a story and in the sense of a coherent structure of meaning that Žižek describes, is an attempt to organize fragmented information into a unified structure whose purpose is to create a coherent meaning and not necessarily to describe the object. I am referring to cases in which certain practices of interpretation in which the aspiration for a coherent and cohesive meaning causes the interpretation to miss the object partially or fully, in this case, the interpreted picture.

A visual example of the manner in which fantasy functions as castration can be found in Fried's analysis of Thomas Eakins's painting *The Gross Clinic*, from 1875.[15] Fried offers a Freudian reading of Eakins's painting. According to him, the painting revolves around the relationships between a son and his father, a mother and her son, homosexuality and castration. I claim that Fried's attempt to adjust the painting to the Freudian interpretation can be read as a staging of a phantasmatic castration to which Žižek refers.

For his analysis, Fried connects various biographical details of the artist and his other paintings. Thus, for instance, he connects Eakins's almost compulsive attraction to written letters, which he argues can be seen in Eakins's other paintings to Eakins's close relationship with his father, who

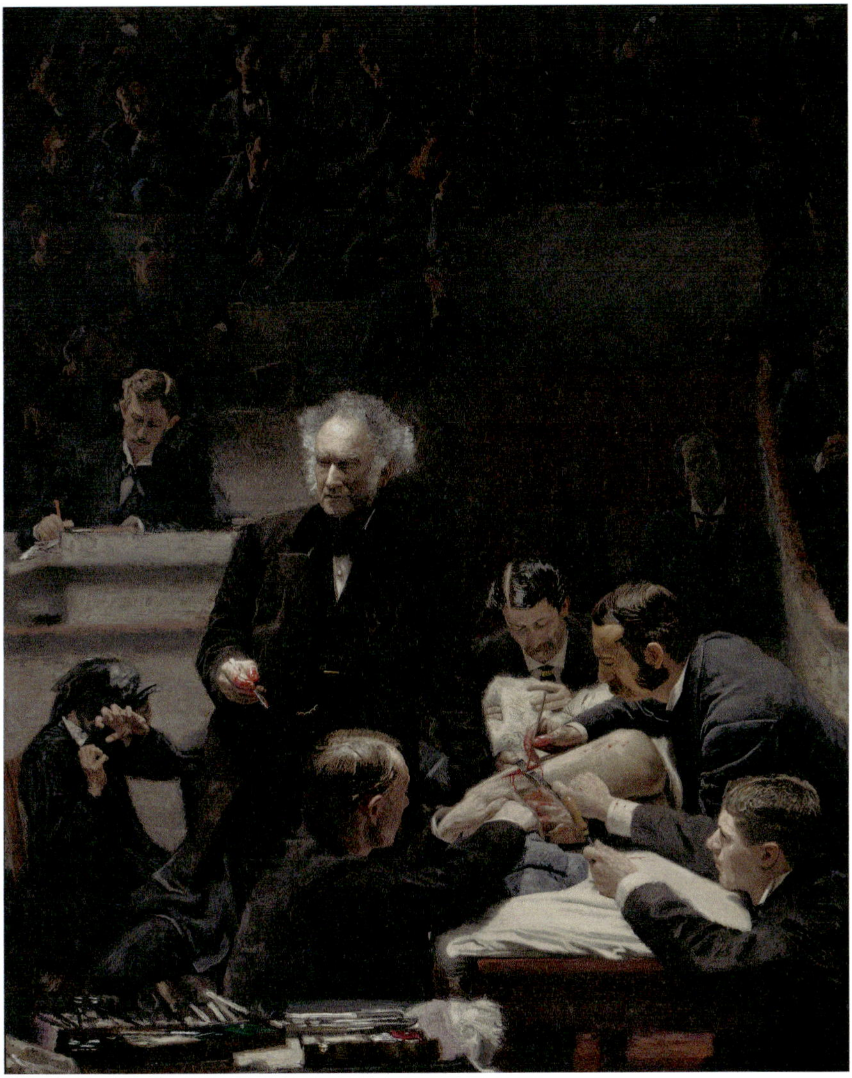

Figure 3.1 Thomas Eakins, *The Gross Clinic*, 1875.

was a writing master and taught fine penmanship.[16] Fried outlines the similarities in the way the character of the surgeon is painted and a painting depicting Eakins's father and interprets the character of the surgeon in *The Gross Clinic* as a version of the character of the father.[17] Thus, he reads *The Gross Clinic* as dealing with the artist's family, in which Eakins himself appears as one of the characters in the audience. Fried reads this as the opposition between the surgeon, who is the father, and the patient, who is

Eakins himself, while the knife in the hand of the surgeon symbolizes castration. Fried bases his argument on Eakins's other paintings, such as *The Artist and His Father Hunting Reed Birds* from 1874, in which Eakins's father appears as a hunter standing on the boat and shooting. Fried locates another isomorphism between the character of the surgeon in *The Clinic* painting and the character of Eakins's shooting father, as the act of shooting is again interpreted as an act of castration.[18] He argues that the position of the patient being operated upon can be interpreted, within a psychoanalytical context, as a homosexual fantasy akin to what Freud found in the case of Schreber. Schreber's fantasy was to become a feminine figure and be ravaged by a male figure. The position of the patient in the painting of *The Clinic*, argues Fried, refers directly to Schreber's description of his own fantasy.[19] Another indication of the subject of castration in this painting can be seen, according to Fried, in the depiction of the mother without a face and with a claw-like hand. The nonhuman mother represents another aspect of castration and aligns with the Freudian concept of anxiety or hatred toward the mother, from a homosexual position.[20]

This interpretation demonstrates the specific manner in which Fried looks at a painting. However, if we return to the painting itself, we will find a gap between the painting and its interpretation. It should be noted that Fried's analysis includes other aspects of the painting, such as questions concerning realism, absorption, perspective and more. However, Fried, in fact, conducts a series of arbitrary decisions to justify his interpretation. To prove his argument, Fried chooses painterly details from Eakins's other paintings with the guiding principle of his initial argument. Fried further supports his claims by presenting the painter's various biographical details, but, again, these details only support the initial interpretation of the painting.

The purpose here is not to refute Fried's interpretation but to shed light on the manner in which it is founded as an attempt to make the painterly object fit into a given model. The interpretation is used as a realization of the phantasm of a unity of meaning, of a theme that is woven into every detail of the painting. Eakins's painting of *The Clinic* is complex and disturbing. Fried's analysis of this painting reflects a desire to organize the disturbing painterly information into a preexisting meaning, which is the fruit of his choice, yet does not necessarily fully describe the object.

Fantasy is a transcendental schematism

This screen refers to the supposition that fantasy is not a simple fulfillment of a desire that generates hallucinations; rather, it functions in a fashion similar to Kant's transcendental schematism and constitutes desire.[21] The concept of desire in its Lacanian articulation refers to an unconscious desire, which is, according to Lacan, who quotes Spinoza, "the very essence of man".[22] Lacan distinguishes between three concepts: need (*besoin*), demand (*demande*) and desire (*désir*). Need is a biological instinct that reaches its satisfaction the moment it is fulfilled. Demand is the articulation of the need; for instance, a hungry infant's cry articulates his need for milk. Since the fulfillment of the need can only be realized through the Other, that is, the breastfeeding mother, the fulfillment of the need becomes an expression of the Other's love. While the Other may fulfill the need, she cannot perfectly fulfill the unconditional love for which the subject longs. Desire, then, is the gap that exists between need and demand, which can never be fulfilled, and which emanates from the Other.[23] This distinction clarifies the object that generates desire, which is none other than the *objet petit a*, which appears only in the wake of its loss. That is, desire itself has no object that can fulfill it, but rather an object cause of desire that continues to propel it.

Thus, the relation Žižek finds between fantasy and Kantian schematism is based on the fact that both are devices that mediate between two inherently different elements. Just as schematism mediates between the pure and a priori concepts of understanding and intuitions,[24] fantasy mediates between the subject and the object cause of his desire. Just as, according to Kant, experience is only possible in light of the conditions that constitute it, so desire is constituted through fantasy.

Fantasy constitutes desire in the sense that it "teaches us how to desire".[25] Žižek bases this aspect of fantasy on Lacan's claim that there is no sexual relation between subject and subject, but only between a subject and the object of his desire. Since a universal formula that would ensure a harmonic relation between the sexes does not exist, each individual invents his own fantasy, and the function of this fantasy is to justify the fixation on a specific object. This aspect of fantasy encompasses two sides: fantasy is what constitutes desire and what teaches us how to desire, and fantasy is a justification of the fixation on the object; not the cause of this fixation. To implement this logic in the visual field, we need to examine how Lacan conceptualizes the act of looking at a picture.

Looking at a picture, claims Lacan, is not exhausted by the physiognomic activity of the eye that supposes a single, constant and universal sight. Rather, the subject who looks at a picture is manifested in it. Unlike traditional theories of art, which suppose universal practices of observation and interpretation, Lacan's concept makes every sight a particular sight, while there is a structure that characterizes the various acts of looking. Thus, just as fantasy teaches us how to desire, so looking at a painting teaches us how to look. That is, since the picture manifests something of the particularity of the subject, looking at a picture is never universal and predetermined. Rather, the painting itself constitutes the act of looking at it. Each painting constitutes the act of looking at it, and as a result, every instance of a viewer standing before a painting creates a particular observation. This means that we cannot speak of interpretive models that would be valid for an entire corpus of paintings, or of general practices of analyzing a picture.[26] Moreover, this position is antagonistic to the manner in which theories of art usually perceive narrative painting as corresponding to a prior verbal text.

Lacan's position is antagonistic not only to iconography, which interprets a picture based on a given set of symbolic values that can be interpreted in advance, but also to various structural theories in poetics. According to these theories, while there may be different possible readings of a given text, there is a more successful reading; for instance, a reading that would more thoroughly exhaust the text. The Lacanian conceptualization of the subject's relation with a picture also opposes these theories since it negates the possibility of determining a hierarchical order among the various operations of looking. Such relations make it impossible to determine a more successful act of looking than another. However, this does not mean that any interpretation is possible. The picture is not open to all readings; rather, each viewer makes use of his own particular way of looking, which stems from the way he fixates on a particular painterly detail. Thus, it follows that the painterly logic has something that determines the subject's relation to the picture. In light of this stance, the possibility of a narrative painting is not negated, but can be theorized in a different way. This does not mean a set of signs with a meaning that would be known and shared among various viewers, but a particular way of looking that fashions its own narrative while the structure of the process of looking remains similar.

This characteristic of fantasy makes it possible to extrapolate an isomorphism between fantasy and the visual field, since fantasy is rooted in a fixation on an object, while the phantasmatic narrative is generated in the wake of this fixation, as a way to justify the choice of that object. In other words, the narrative is what constructs the object as prior to the narrative. A similar process takes place in the field of vision, where the narrative meaning given to a painting constitutes the product of looking, rather than the condition for that object. This position is fundamentally different from the literary conceptualization of narrativity as a characteristic of the object rather than its result.

This position is based on Lacan's conception of the "anterior future" (*futur antérieur*). Lacan theorizes a kind of reversed time in which the present constitutes the past and not the other way around, so as to explain the return of the repressed. As Lacan claims, Freud explains repression as a fixation. However, if, at the moment the fixation takes place, nothing of the repressed appears, how can we explain the return of the repressed? The answer Lacan proposes is that, in a paradoxical fashion, the repressed does not emerge from the past but rather from the future.[27] This is because the return of the repressed makes appear an erased mark that receives its meaning only through the future, through its incorporation into the subject's history.[28]

The source of the "anterior future" can be found in Freud's concept of the "retroactive" (*nachträglich*). Freud claims that the subject reconstructs, in retrospect, events from his past, and that their rewriting is what gives them meaning. He refers to the manner in which a traumatic event of a sexual nature, which the child experiences at an early stage, is repressed and registered in the unconscious as a senseless trace due to the impossibility of coping with it in the real time of its occurrence. Years later, when the child has grown, an event that has an associative relation to the primary and repressed event, which is not inherently sexual, receives its sense in light of the first event. Following Freud, Lacan claims that there is no direct access to repressed events, which can be represented only through a "representative of representation" (*Vorstellungsrepräsentanz*), and that this representation cannot lead to what has been repressed but can only present itself. Hence, the repressed is not what is represented; rather, what is represented is a representative of representation.[29] Thus, the symptom appears in the beginning as senseless. Only at a certain stage does it suddenly point toward something. In his remarks on Lacan's paradoxical perception of time, Žižek explains that, in this manner, "analysis is conceived as a symbolization, a symbolic integration of meaningless imaginary traces".[30] The unconscious is made of imaginary fixations that have not found their place in the symbolic development of the subject's history, and, as analysis progresses, they find their place. The repressed, according to Žižek who follows Lacan, returns from the future. The interpretation of these repressed traces is not revealed but retroactively constructed. Analysis produces truth by assigning symptoms their symbolic place and meaning. The meaning of these traces is not discovered; it is reconstructed retroactively.[31]

As Žižek explains, the construction of the meaning of what has been repressed transposes us, in a certain sense, to the future and not to the past. This is because, according to Lacan, the symptom exists as a result that predates its cause.[32] This logic takes the shape of the number eight, in which we return to the place we have already been. The transition to truth must move through illusion, "the truth arises from misrecognition".[33] This takes place in stories of destiny, such as the tragedy of Oedipus. Oedipus's father knows, through the prophecy, what is to come in the future. His attempts to prevent what is to come are precisely what brings about the fulfillment of the prophecy.[34]

This position relates directly to traditional distinctions between verbal and visual media. These distinctions assume that the encounter between the viewer and the visual medium takes place "all at once", while reading processes unfold over a sequence of time. Theories based on this assumption draw far-reaching conclusions regarding the differences between the media. A conception that views narrativity as the product of the object takes away the very foundation of these distinctions.

Fantasy has two dimensions

Fantasy has a stable dimension, which is governed by a dream state without interruption.[35] At the same time, it also has a dimension of instability, whose elementary form is envy. The unstable dimension includes everything that annoys me about the Other, everything that the Other does beyond my range of vision. Totalitarian regimes hinge on the codependence of these two aspects. On the one hand, they underscore the ideal essence, which is the stable aspect of fantasy, and on the other hand, they persecute minorities so as to explain the failure of this ideal essence, which is the unstable aspect of fantasy. This, for instance, was the case in Nazism and Stalinism. While the Nazis presented a harmonic "folk community (*Volksgemeinschaft*)", the other side of this folk community was their paranoid obsession with the Jewish plot. In a similar fashion, the compulsive need of the Stalinists to locate new enemies for socialism is, in essence, an attempt to define the ideal of the "New Social Man". That is, the articulation of the ultimate model is completely isomorphic to the definition of its threat. In both examples, there are two aspects of the same thing, one with a positive value and the other with a negative value, which function like two sides of the same coin. Žižek calls the two dimensions of fantasy "fantasy 1" and "fantasy 2". "Fantasy 2" is what makes possible the existence of "Fantasy 1".[36]

The two dimensions of fantasy are, to a certain extent, similar to the two aspects that exist in painting. According to Lacan, the two aspects of looking at a picture stem from the split between the eye and the gaze. Through this split, Lacan explains the complexity of the relations of seeing and being seen.[37] He describes two aspects of the field of vision: in the first, the subject governs the field, which is the object of his sight, while in the second, the subject becomes the object; he is seen from a place he cannot control. These two aspects operate simultaneously. Lacan demonstrates these relations of vision through three diagrams: the first diagram describes the relation between object, image and the geometric point.[38] This is the vision model articulated by Albertian perspective. The geometric point is the place from which the painter looks and in which the eye and the gaze work together. Lacan undermines this state of affairs and claims that the geometric point is only a partial dimension in the scopic field, since Albertian perspective maps space rather than vision and does not exhaust subjective vision.[39] He shows how, in perspective, the subject, whose vision is articulated through the vanishing point, himself vanishes.

To articulate the aspect of subjective vision, which escapes the geometric articulation of Albertian perspective, Lacan presents a second diagram, which is the reverse of the first. Lacan articulates the diagram as follows:

> The correlative of the picture, to be situated in the same place as it, that is to say, outside, is the point of the gaze, while that which forms the mediation from the one to the other, that which is between the two, is something of another nature than geometral, optical space, something that plays an exactly reverse role, which operates, not because it can be traversed, but on the contrary, because it is opaque – I mean the screen.[40]

In other words, in the second diagram, the subject no longer controls the visual field. The subject has now become the object that is seen. This reversal undermines the meaning that stems from the observation articulated in the Albertian model. The image, which is first identified with the object of vision, is substituted by an opaque screen. The gaze is now seen as external to the subject, who is no longer in control of the visual field. If, in the first diagram, the subject was unified with the gaze, in the second, he becomes the object of vision.[41]

The third diagram is comprised of the overlapping of the two previous ones. It shows how the place of the act of looking is in constant oscillation between the object of looking, that is, the picture, and what makes it an object, that is, the gaze. The subject cannot be fixed in any position, and he constantly oscillates between the two.

This model of vision, then, points to a state in which vision encapsulates two aspects: the illusionary sight, which gives a sense of control of the visual field and according to which the one who looks from a certain vantage point can see the world as an external space that sprawls out before his eyes, and alongside it a vision in which the subject's gaze is returned to him from the picture on which he looks. The object of the gaze is not neutral, and once the subject looks at it, something from within it returns his gaze, since he finds there something of himself.[42]

The two aspects of vision are manifested in Lacan's distinction between the good eye and the bad eye. The good eye sees the painting as a calming thing. This refers to the figurative aspect of the painting, which provides the viewer with material that can be interpreted and hence gives the illusion of controlling the visual field. The calming effect of the painting stems, then, from the idea that the painter provides the viewer with material for observation, or, as Lacan describes it, the painter "invites the person to whom this picture is presented to lay down his gaze there as one lays down one's weapons".[43] It seems Lacan refers to the appeal of the painter toward the viewer to succumb to the illusion of control over the visual field, to be captured by the option of representation. We can see the good eye, described in the relation of sight of the first diagram, as the parallel of the stable side of fantasy.

The process of looking also encapsulates the evil eye, which can generate evil through the gaze. Lacan turns to Augustine's *Confessions* to explain the essence of the evil eye, specifically in the scene in which the young child looks at his mother breastfeeding his younger brother and grows pale with envy.[44] The meaning of the example is rooted in a certain aspect of vision in which the object is closed off to the viewer and represents something that he once owned but lost to him. The evil eye sees the painting as a whole image that is closed before it. Here, like the models of vision described in the second diagram, it is not about the relations of sight and vision, in which the visual image is identical to the represented object. The evil eye's sight can only be possible if we follow the logic of the Lacanian sight, in which the image is projected onto a screen, while the field of vision is not accessible to the observer but flickers before him from within the opaque screen. The evil eye is analogous to the envious side in fantasy, which includes everything that annoys me about the Other. This sight is demonstrated in the second diagram, and we can see in it an expression of Lacan's idiom: "what I look at is never what I wish to see".[45] In this form of vision, I do not see everything; there is always something that falls from my gaze. As in the two dimensions of fantasy, so in the field of vision, we can see these two aspects as two sides of the same coin, while each aspect makes possible the existence of the other. The process of looking is Janus-faced and makes possible the simultaneous existence of the two aspects of vision.

Hans Holbein's painting *The Ambassadors* from 1533 exemplifies the simultaneous existence of the two aspects of vision through anamorphosis. The painting depicts two men standing against the backdrop of objects: books, musical and scientific instruments. Seemingly, this is a group portrait that obeys the painterly conventions of its time. The assorted objects belong to the tradition of *vanitas* paintings,[46] while the relation between the still-life objects and the characters symbolizes the high social class of the ambassadors. At the bottom of the painting appears an oval disk, which is supposedly painted from another perspective, from a vantage point that does not correspond with the entire painting. A frontal look at the painting reveals the characters of the ambassadors at their best, and the disk looks meaningless. However, when looking at the painting from the side, in accordance with the alleged perspective of the disk, one can clearly see a skull, but then the

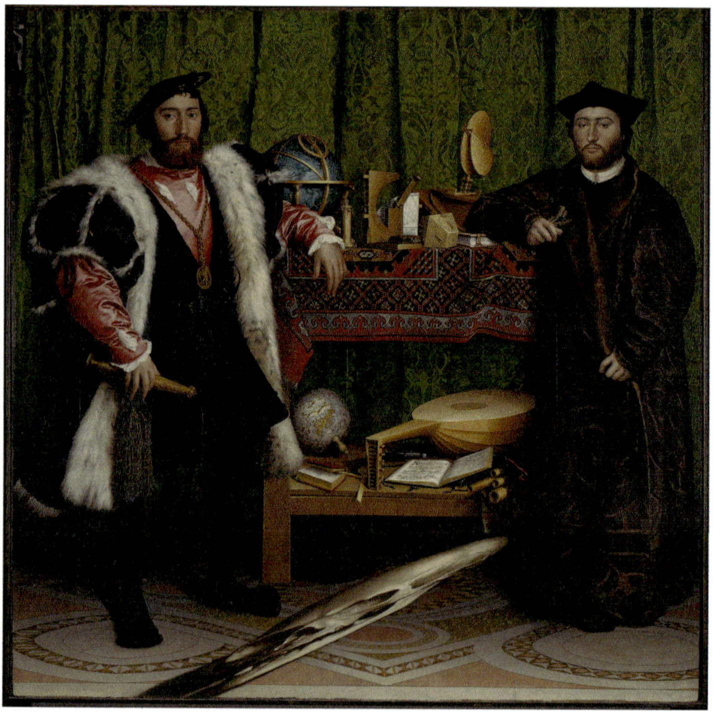

Figure 3.2 Hans Holbein the Younger, *The Ambassadors*, 1533.

characters of the ambassadors become blurry. As Lacan states in his interpretation of the painting:

> at the very heart of the period in which the subject emerged and geometral optics was an object of research, Holbein makes visible for us here something that is simply the subject as annihilated – annihilated in the form that is, strictly speaking, the imaged embodiment of… castration.[47]

In other words, while the characters of *The Ambassadors* constitute an affirmation for the subject who is in control of his field of vision, the anamorphic skull marks the opposite, the subversion of the viewer's control.[48] We can understand this seeming paradox through the comparison made by Miran Božovič makes between the anamorphic skull and a photograph of a race car accident, which appears at the beginning of Alfred Hitchcock's *Rear Window* from 1954.[49] The film revolves around Jeff, a photojournalist who broke his leg in an accident, spends his time confined to a wheelchair watching his backyard, and witnesses a murder. At the beginning of the film, the camera focuses on Jeff's broken leg that is placed in a cast. The camera moves to a close-up of his shattered camera and then focuses on a photograph hanging on the wall, and in the background of this photograph is a racetrack. The photograph captures the moment in which a race car flips over. The photograph shows a car wheel that was detached from the car, at the moment of the crash, as it is seen from the side as an oval disk. Later in the film, we witness a phone call between Jeff and his editor, and in it, we discover that the race car crash was the last photograph Jeff took. The wheel of the car hurled in the air toward Jeff, who insisted on photographing the accident that injured him. As Božovič claims, while Holbein's skull can only be seen as a skull from the side, the wheel can manifest the sight of death, the last sight that someone who insists on looking straight at it will see.[50]

In *The Ambassadors*, and in a similar fashion also in the photograph of the race car crash, there exist two modes of looking, described through the diagrams by two visual areas. The subject looking at the characters of the ambassadors in the foreground of the painting, who looks directly at him, demonstrates what happens in the field of vision when the viewer governs it. The anamorphic skull at the bottom of the painting demonstrates another mode of looking, of a visibility that escapes the viewer. The relation between the two aspects of the painting, like the relation between the two dimensions of fantasy, constitutes each other: the effect of the skull is supported by looking at the ambassadors and the other way around. The skull, which does not adhere to the Albertian laws of perspective, demonstrates the possibility of another perspective while also confronting the viewer with the laws of geometric perspective by its very disobedience of them. This painting is not a unique phenomenon, rather, as Lacan argues, it underscores what already exists in every painting, "a trap for the gaze".[51]

As I showed above, this conceptualization also articulates the complex process of looking. Here, too, there are two opposite aspects that exist within a specific act of looking. Moreover, this concept of painting is different from existing practices of analyzing narrative painting, specifically in two ways. First, it undermines narrativity as unity. A narrative reading of a painting in its an traditional sense or iconological analysis are interpretive practices that assume the painting has a single and fixed meaning. A conceptualization that rests on the supposition that looking at a painting contains two opposed aspects that exist simultaneously would negate these traditional practices, or at least see them as a partial way to interpret a picture. Second, this conceptualization undermines narrativity as universal. The positions that interpret narrative painting as drawing from a text or a framework of knowledge that precedes it, assume that this understanding is valid for different viewers. According to Lacan, looking at a painting includes the particular activity of a singular viewer, which is not given in advance and cannot be reached through a research tool that is valid for other viewers as well.

Moreover, this demonstrates Lacan's claim that painting is not merely about representation.[52] One of the ways to understand this claim is to treat painting as a representation of the impossibility of representing, that is, as a representation of the lack in painting. However, the example of the envious gaze in Augustine's text expresses something even more extreme: the power of the image and its relation to desire beyond being that which represents what cannot be represented, the quilting point between an image and its meaning, like the quilting in the fabric that connects two sides of a pillow. Lacan argues that in language there is a constant movement between signifiers. However, there is also a state in language in which the signifier and the signified are united and, for a moment, the constant movement of signifiers stops. The stopping point of the movement creates the illusion that Lacan calls "the quilting point" (*point de capiton*), like a fabric's quilting point.[53] In the envious gaze, or the painting as looked at by the evil eye, for a split second, there is a state of affairs similar to the connection between the image and the thing that represents it, without the mediating gap between them. However, this is a flickering moment in which the evil eye comes to undermine the illusion of a single meaning constituted by the good eye.

It should be noted that Žižek makes use of concepts relating to different aspects of sight to describe the unstable dimension of fantasy, and not necessarily optical sight. Thus, for instance, he speaks of: "images that haunt me about what he or she is doing when out of my sight, about how he or she deceives me and plots against me".[54] That is, I see phantasmatic sights of what is taking place when I do not see. I believe that this is not a mere metaphor, but that something from the very nature of fantasy is articulated through visual means and, at the same time, is related to sight and the inability to see, or sight that stems from it. This way of thinking is significant when approaching the question of looking at a painting, since it raises an aspect of sight, which, unlike theories that conceive of sight as a physiognomic act of the eye, treats a sight that also includes what cannot be seen, a sight of what exists beyond my field of vision.

Fantasy involves an impossible gaze

According to Žižek, the phantasmatic narrative posits an impossible gaze, since the subject is present in the very same act in which he is perceived as the one who is outside it. Žižek gives as an example a fairy tale by Joze Snoj, a Slovene right-wing nationalist poet, who preaches against abortion. The plot describes an island of children who were not born because their ambitious parents preferred successful careers over them. The unborn children, who miss parental love, reproach their parents with an accusatory yet impossible gaze, since they were never born.[55]

Žižek claims that the gaze of an innocent outside viewer is impossible, since it is the gaze of someone who falsely excuses himself from concrete historical existence.[56] The question we need to ask in such cases is which narrative should the viewer's gaze support. As an example, he cites the plethora of Western news coverage of Mother Teresa's activity in Calcutta. In these reports, which draw on the West's fantasy about the Third World, Calcutta is described as hell, a place of poverty and corruption that is also plagued by the apathy of the locals. Mother Teresa is seen as the one who brings light to the miserable inhabitants by making them understand that their poverty will bring about redemption, that their way toward redemption must pass through their sufferings, and that they are, in fact, recreating the path of Christ. The ideological gain from such a fantasy is twofold: by preaching to seek redemption through suffering, Mother Teresa impedes the people from doing anything to change their state. At the same time, she offers the rich people of the West a kind of alternative redemption if they contribute to her charity organization. All this, in the backdrop of the phantasmatic perception of Calcutta as "Hell on Earth", in which the only hope for change is not through political activity, but only through the work of charity and pity.[57]

Žižek clarifies the phantasmatic nature of an "objective" analysis, in which the interpreter does not take into consideration his own existence as someone with a certain interest in the position to which he relates. Regarding the visual field, we can claim that there is no possibility of an "innocent eye" when looking at a painting, from the very fact that looking at a painting involves a double gaze, in which the viewer is both outside the picture and within it. Gombrich claims that there is no innocent eye, in the sense that looking at a visual image always involves the use of schemes of representation, and that both the artist and the viewer share this process.[58] However, Žižek's argument offers a much more complex state of affairs, in which it is not only complex sight that encapsulates the use of prior frameworks of knowledge, but in which looking, by its very definition, includes an impossible gaze.

When we deal with sight, we do not separate the mode of looking from the object of the gaze. Models of looking at paintings, such as the Albertian perspective, demonstrate the manner in which the subject believes that he possesses sight. That is, Albertian perspective presents, to a great extent, not only "what we see" but also the distance between this articulation and sight itself. Hence, we may conclude that the same impossible gaze that is attributed to fantasy is also true of looking at a painting. However, in relation to the field of vision, this point raises something unique to the visual field that distinguishes it from other media. In the field of vision, certain situations of looking confront the viewer with his own sight, thus creating a separation between what he sees and the mode of seeing or at least pointing to the difference between the two. The anamorphic skull in Holbein's painting is one of the examples in which the effect of the painting also stems from the manner in which the perspective distortion calls the viewer's attention to the existence of perspective representation itself, as an imaginary object. Žižek argues that fantasy enfolds an impossible gaze and that the subject who takes part in it does not see this impossibility. However, in the visual field, this impossibility, which stems from simultaneously being in the situation and outside it, is immanent to the structure and can even sometimes receive visual representation. The manner in which this impossibility is revealed in certain moments is responsible for one of the possible effects of sight.

Fantasy is radically intersubjective

In the beginning of his teaching, Lacan believed that the psychoanalytic experience was not subjective or objective but intersubjective. Later in his teaching, Lacan abandoned the idea of intersubjectivity and, with it, the idea of the relation between the subject and the other, and, in its stead, articulated a perception of a subject who is split between the ego and the unconscious. According to Žižek, the way to distinguish between the fluctuations in the various Lacanian perceptions is to focus on the object's changing status. For the early Lacan, the object is devalued up to its inherent traits. It is conceptualized only in the intersubjective struggle for recognition and love. Thus, for instance, milk is reduced to a mark of love from the mother to the child. The demand for love is a demand to receive a mark of love. In the next stage of Lacan's teaching, the focus moves to the object, the very same object that is part of the subject himself.[59]

Desire in fantasy is not of the subject but of the Other. Fantasy is an answer to the question, "What do you want? What do you really want through a certain statement beyond what is said in it?" This assertion leads the subject to constitute himself through what he believes the Other sees in him, the thing the Other wants from him.[60]

The transition from intersubjectivity to the split subject is analogous to the transition from concepts of sight that attribute to the gaze power and control, such as Mulvey's assertions presented in the previous chapter, and a conception according to which the exchange of gazes between the viewer and the depicted characters deals with the subject himself.[61] While feminist theory supposes a relation of sight that exists between two entities, the development that Lacan offers relates to one: the split subject. This position shows that the relation between the viewer and the picture revolves around questions of the constitution of the looking subject through his own gaze, which returns to him from an unexpected place within the painting. These Lacanian perspectives suppose a different state of affairs between the viewer and the painting: now the subject is no longer constituted by another subject but finds his own gaze returned to him from within the painting. This state of affairs indicates that the viewer must be located both from without and from within the painting, because of the very nature of looking, and not necessarily because of the painted content.

Fantasy creates a multitude of subject-positions

This veil of fantasy, according to Žižek, relates to the way the subject is inscribed in the phantasmatic narrative. This means that the place of identification of the subject in the narrative does not necessarily correlate with the place where he is located as a persona. That is, the subject does not necessarily identify with the character that manifests him in the phantasmatic narrative but can fashion many different identificatory positions.[62] The most common situation is the identification of the subject with the ego ideal, from which the subject "appears in a likeable way".[63] However, there are many possible subject-positions with which the subject may identify; for instance, with a pure gaze looking at a scene without getting involved in it, or with a gaze in which the subject identifies with each of the characters. Identification, according to Lacan, is reflexive and not direct.

This veil of fantasy raises several issues that are relevant to narrativity. First, it enables us to rethink certain concepts of literary theory, such as focalization. Second, this veil makes it possible to reexamine the manner in which art theories formulate perspective in painting. Third, it points to a certain affinity between the subject's position in fantasy and the subject looking at a painting.

A poetic analysis of a literary text outlines the differences between the various focal points from which a literary text is narrated so as to show its complexities. A focal point can be the position of the narrator, such as a character participating in the fiction as one of the protagonists. The information this protagonist provides will, hence, be limited because of his own limitation in the fictional time and space. Moreover, the information can also be "biased" as a result of its function within the fictional world. For instance, William Faulkner's *A Rose for Emily* is narrated from the vantage point of one of the town's inhabitants, and so the order of the events, their comprehension, the worldview and the values related to the characters are all given to the reader as the character in the fictional world experiences them.[64] However, even though the narrator of *A Rose for Emily* knows the end from the very beginning of the story, he does not expose his knowledge and, in his delivery of the information, stays with what he and the other members of the town knew in the past, during the unfolding of the events. That is, the seeing narrator is distinguished from the speaking narrator. As I stated in the first chapter, the term "focalization" enables us to theorize complex states in which there is a separation between the voice of the narrator and the delivered content. Thus, for instance, a man can narrate a story in the voice and language of the infant he once was. The infant, in this case, will be the focalizer.[65] There is a distinction between the focalizer, which is the point from which the elements are seen, and the focalized. The sight of the focalized object is influenced by the focalizer. The focalizer can be an external vantage point of the situation, or the internal gaze of one of the characters, and can even shift between different characters.[66] Focalization is subjugated to the global structure of narrative and follows its logic. The trend in this kind of analysis is to highlight aspects that are unique to the structure of a given literary text. However, this is an articulation of a general characteristic that is detached from a particular reading.

The equivalent of focalization in the visual field is perspective.[67] Thus, the point of view of the painter is articulated in Albertian perspective as a defined place that can be reconstructed and is external to the painting. That is, even though there are many ways to interpret the concept of perspective, which is multifaceted, many interpretations see perspective as an objective articulation of a subjective point of view, from which the painting is organized.

Žižek relates to the possibility for different subjective positions. The principle is that the subject of fantasy does not necessarily identify with his manifestations in the phantasmatic space, and he can move between these different positions. He is free to transfer his identification from one place to the next.[68] He brings a short scene from David Lynch's film *Blue Velvet* (1986) as an example. The film is about a boy who is tempted to solve an enigmatic and bizarre crime mystery that takes place in an American town. Žižek refers to a sadomasochistic scene in which we see the criminal acting violently toward his victim, a bar singer, and the protagonist, who sneaks into the apartment, peers at the scene through his hiding place in the closet. Žižek asks for whom this scene is presented and answers that there are three possible subject positions here: in the first position, the event is perceived from the point of view of the boy who is hiding in the closet. This position is supported by the fact that in the presented scene, the bar singer shoves a piece of cloth into the criminal's mouth, and he breathes through an oxygen mask. As a result, the criminal breathes heavily, and his speech is incoherent since his mouth is full of fabric. These two characteristics of heavy breathing and a low voice are the manner in which the boy perceives his parents when he hears them in sexual act. In this sense, we can see in the scene a visual demonstration of the way the boy imagines what he hears, so the scene is represented from the point of view of the peeping boy. Another possibility is to see the event from the point of view of the violent man, who is striving to reflect his masculine abilities. In this case, this is not a voyeuristic look, like before, but an exhibitionist event in which the criminal presents, in an exaggerated manner, a sexual activity that is meant to veil his impotence. According to the third possibility, the scene is meant for the eyes of the female character, whose depressive state is not a result of the violence she is subjected to but was present from the very beginning. The violence done to her, according to this possibility, is an attempt to extract her from her depressive state and make her act.[69] The three positions of the subject relate to the same sequence of events, but each one gives it a different meaning.

The fundamental difference between the position of the subject in the narrative, as Žižek conceptualizes it, and the point of view of focalization is that Žižek articulates different possibilities in accordance with the different viewers and not a single meta-structure. In other words, Žižek shows that fantasy makes possible the existence of different subjective positions and does not hinge on one possible position that provides narratological unity. Unlike theories of narratology, in which the focalizer or focalizers, in different degrees of complexity, constitute an integral and essential part of a unified whole, Žižek offers a state in which the entire structure of meaning changes in accordance with the focalizer, and the subject moves between these positions. It should be noted that this kind of reading does not suggest that the narrative is fragmented and does not constitute a coherent structure or that its broad scope empties its meaning, but rather that there are several possibilities that the subject may constitute, since the subject himself is not exhausted in his persona.

The many subjective positions, as Žižek articulates them, also relate to what I described in the previous chapter, in which narrativity in painting is constituted by expanding the pictorial arena. At first glance, it seems as though there is an affinity in the logic I presented through Diderot, Riegl and Mulvey, in which the viewer is perceived as part of the scene, and the multiple positions of the subject that Žižek presents here. However, the logic that Žižek presents is fundamentally different: Diderot, Riegl and Mulvey may broaden the pictorial arena, but their notion of the viewer as part of the image supposes, in the end, a fixed structure of meaning, which they all articulate, each in his own fashion. However, like in fantasy, in the process of looking at a painting, there are multiple subjective positions from which the viewer may situate his identification. Thus, the viewer may formulate different positions of identification or alienation from different painterly positions, in accordance with his own particular way of looking, without relating to previous meta-narrative, and without having his point of view, be it external or internal, fixed in advance. Moreover, the viewer of a painting, like the subject of fantasy, does not necessarily identify with one painterly character. That is, the place of the viewer in relation to the painting is not external to it; rather, the act of looking at the painting supposes the gaze that returns from the painting. In both the multiple subjective positions which fantasy creates and in the state in which the viewer's gaze is returned to him from an unpredictable place in the painting, a relation is formed between the viewer and the painting that fashions its meaning. This is a meaning that cannot be given in advance since it is constructed through the very act of looking.

The supposition regarding the disjoining between the subject's identificatory position and his position within the phantasmatic narrative indicates, then, that the subject's position of identification does not necessarily coincide with the place in which he is situated in the fantasy. The split between the subject's identification and his position in the narrative is somewhat analogous to the split between the eye and the gaze that is returned to the subject from the painting. In both cases, both in the case of the subject's position in fantasy and in the case of the subject's position as looking at a painting, we suppose a particular gaze. This way of looking offers a different kind of narrativity, one which is the result of a particular act of looking. Shedding light on the veils of fantasy and comparing them to looking at a painting opens the possibility to reexamine various aspects of this kind of looking. Moreover, the veils of fantasy make it possible to articulate a critical stance toward various art theories, which interpret paintings and expose their phantasmatic aspects in the imaginary relations that they fashion with the painting. The analysis of the veil of fantasy as a narrative makes it possible to think anew about narrative structure and its relation to painting. As I will show in the next chapter, the visual field raises here another possibility, in which visuality makes the existence of a complex structure of meaning possible, which does not necessarily adhere to a confining logic. The veil of fantasy as staging castration exposes imaginary relations that exist between interpretative practices and paintings, which sometimes force a given narrative interpretation on the painting. The other veils of fantasy describe the relations between the viewer and the painting, characterize the gaze that is relevant to looking at a painting and the place of the subject in relation to it. Thus, in the veil of fantasy as a transcendental schematism, I related to the aspect of particularity when looking at a painting; an aspect which does not obey broad interpretive practices. The veil of the two dimensions of fantasy points toward another aspect of looking at a painting, in which the act of looking at a painting can be conceived as a dual act constructed by oppositional forces that operate simultaneously. I used the veil of fantasy as involving an impossible gaze to describe an aspect of looking that is unique to the visual field. This aspect of looking cannot be described in terms of language and representation and relates to the process of looking. The veil of fantasy as intersubjective exposes the reflexive aspect of the split subject looking at a painting. Through the last veil, which relates to the multiple subject positions in fantasy, I examined the position of the viewer in the painting in comparison to the way vantage point and perspective are traditionally conceptualized.

Removing these veils of fantasy exposes the places to which traditional theories do not provide an answer: states of contradiction, of simultaneous existence in different manners, of simultaneous points of view and of a particular process of looking. These are complex and contradictory states, without a theoretical explanation even in theories that relate to the complexities of the literary text. The veils of fantasy show that there is no single universal model of looking. They also help articulate a complex aspect of looking, which makes possible different kinds of narrativity in painting.

The discussion of the characteristics of fantasy raises various topics that are relevant to the processes of looking at a painting, and which will be discussed in the next chapters: narrative, the gaze and the positions of the subject.

Notes

1 Brilliant, Richard. 1986. *Visual Narratives: Storytelling in Etruscan and Roman Art*. Ithaca and London: Cornell University Press, pp. 76–77.
2 Laplanche, Jean, and Jean-Bertrand Pontalis. 1988 [1973]. *The Language of Psychoanalysis*. Trans. Donald Nicholson-Smith. London: Karnac Books, p. 314.
3 Laplanche and Pontalis, 1988, p. 318.
4 Žižek, Slavoj. 1998. "The Seven Veils of Fantasy". In *Key Concepts of Lacanian Psychoanalysis*. Edited by Danny Nobus. London: Rebus Press, pp.190–218.
5 Evans, Dylan. 1996. *An Introductory Dictionary of Lacanian Psychoanalysis*. London and New York: Routledge, pp. 59–60.
6 Žižek, 1998, p. 197.
7 Žižek, 1998, p. 199.
8 Žižek, 1998, p. 199.
9 Žižek, 1998, p.198.
10 Žižek, 1998, p.198.
11 Žižek, 1998, p.198.
12 Žižek, 1998, p. 199.
13 Žižek, 1998, pp. 202–203.
14 Žižek, 1998, p. 203.
15 Fried, Michael. 1987. *Realism, Writing and Disfiguration: on Thomas Eakins and Stephen Crane*. Chicago: University of Chicago Press.
16 Fried, 1987, p. 38.
17 Fried, 1987, p. 40.
18 Fried, 1987, pp. 66–67.
19 Fried, 1987, p. 68.
20 Fried, 1987, pp. 68–69.
21 Žižek, 1998, p. 191.
22 Lacan, Jacques. 2019 [1958–1959]. *The Seminar of Jacques Lacan, Book VI: Desire and its Interpretations*. Trans. Bruce Fink. Cambridge: Polity Press, p. 8.
23 Evans, 1996, pp. 36–37.
24 Kant, Immanuel. 1966 [1781]. *Critique of Pure Reason*. Trans. F. Max Müller. New York: Anchor Books, Doubleday & Company, pp. 121–122.
25 Žižek, 1998, p. 191.
26 This is somewhat similar to Kant's articulation of the judgment of taste, which takes place every time there is a particular encounter between the subject and the object. Kant, Immanuel. 1952 [1790]. *The Critique of Judgment*. Trans. James creed Meredith. Oxford: Clarendon Press.
27 Lacan, Jacques. 1988 [1953–1954]. *The Seminar of Jacques Lacan, Book I: Freud's Papers on Technique 1953–1954*. Trans. John Forrester. New York and London: W.W. Norton and Company, p. 158.
28 Lacan, 1988, p. 158.
29 Lacan, Jacques. 1981 [1964–1965]. *The Four Fundamental Concepts of Psychoanalysis: The Seminar of Jacques Lacan, Book XI*. Trans. Alan Sheridan. New York and London: W.W. Norton and Company, p. 217.

30 Žižek, Slavoj. 1991. "The Truth Arises from Misrecognition". In *Lacan and the Subject of Language*. Edited by Ellie Ragland-Sullivan and Mark Bracher. London: Routledge, p. 188.
31 Žižek, 1991, p.188.
32 Žižek, 1991, p.188.
33 Žižek, 1991, p.190.
34 Žižek, 1991, p.191.
35 Žižek, 1998, p. 192.
36 Žižek, 1998, p. 192.
37 Lacan XI, p. 73
38 For the diagrams see Lacan XI, pp. 91, 106.
39 Lacan XI, pp. 86–87.
40 Lacan XI, p. 96.
41 For further explanation of Lacan's three diagrams see: de Bolla, Peter. 1996. "The Visibility of Visuality". In *Vision in Context: Historical and Contemporary Perspectives on Sight*. Edited by Teresa Brennan and Martin Jay. New York and London: Routledge, p. 68.
42 This point will be further clarified through the description of the wolf man's dream. The sight of the wolves looking at the dreaming child is a paradigmatic case of the manner in which the subject encounters his gaze returning to him from within the image.
43 Lacan XI, p. 101.
44 Lacan XI, p. 116.
45 Lacan XI, p. 103.
46 That is, to Northern still life paintings from the Baroque, which are usually understood as allegories for the transitory nature of life.
47 Lacan XI, pp. 88–89.
48 For more of Lacan on anamorphosis, see: Lacan, Jacques. 1986 [1959–1960]. *The Ethics of Psychoanalysis 1959–1960: The Seminar of Jacques Lacan, Book VII*. Trans. Dennis Porter. New York and London: W.W. Norton and Company, p. 135; p. 140.
49 Božovič, Miran, 1992. "The Man Behind His Own Retina". In *Everything You always Wanted to Know about Lacan but Were Afraid to Ask Hitchcock*. Edited by Slavoj Žižek. Trans. Martin Thom. London and New York: Verso, p. 171.
50 Božovič, 1992, p.171.
51 Lacan XI, p. 89.
52 Lacan XI, p.108.
53 Evans, 1996, p. 146.
54 Žižek, 1998, p. 192.
55 Žižek, 1998, p. 200.
56 Žižek, 1998, p. 202.
57 Žižek, 1998, p. 202.
58 Gombrich, Ernst. 1972 [1960]. *Art and Illusion: A Study in the Psychology of Pictorial Representation*. Princeton: Princeton University Press, pp. 296–300.
59 Žižek, 1998, p. 194.
60 Žižek, 1998, p. 194. The Lacanian discourse distinguishes between "other" as fellowman and which belongs to the imaginary order, and "Other" that relates to the subject as determined by language and which belongs to the symbolic order.
61 Lacan XI, p. 80.
62 Žižek, 1998, p. 193.
63 Žižek, 1998, p. 193. See also: Lacan XI, p. 268. In his first seminar, Lacan distinguishes between Ideal Ego and Ego Ideal. While the former relates to the imaginary mirror image, the second relates to the symbolic order and an ideal that the subject aspires to himself. Lacan I, pp. 138–142.

64 Faulkner, William. 1977 [1930]. "A Rose for Emily". *Collected Stories by William Faulkner*. New York: Vintage Books, pp. 119–130.
65 Rimmon Kenan, Shlomit. 1983. *Narrative Fiction: Contemporary Poetics*. London and New York: Methuen, pp. 72–73.
66 Bal, Mieke. 1985. Narratology: introduction to the theory of narrative. Trans. Christine van Boheemen. Toronto, Buffalo, London: University of Toronto Press, pp. 100–114.
67 For a discussion on perspective and its relation to narrativity, see Chapter 7.
68 Žižek, 1998, p. 193.
69 Žižek, 1998, p. 193.

4 The split image

Constituting visual narrativity

Narrative, according to Lacan, is an essential path toward understanding, yet it fails to describe what it invents. The very existence of the narrative testifies to a repression that it is supposed to veil. That is, in its relations with the object of its own description, the narrative structure shows that it is a means to create unity and significance in the place where it is lacking.[1] Narrative is a kind of package deal in which the payment for the attempt to gain meaning is an adherence to temporal order, coherence and unity. The very existence of this package deal testifies to its status as a veil for something repressed.

Žižek, following Lacan, does not articulate anew the concept of narrative but treats it, like others before him, as a temporal, unified and coherent structure. However, he exposes its hidden sides by showing that narrative is a subjective product and not a coherent description of an object. He does not view narrative as a primal master-structure that is inherent and anterior to the object. Rather, narrative, in this framework, is a product of a senseless chain and is designed to justify this senselessness. This assertion is meaningful for the current discussion since the inter-medial debate is founded on the belief that narrativity and its salient characteristics, such as temporal and causal order, are imminent and inherent traits of the narrative structure, and not an imaginary structure that we retroactively ascribe to the object.

The concept of narrativity as an outcome and not as a preexisting trait that determines the object undermines the very distinction between time and space as the foundation for mediumal differentiation, since this distinction views narrativity as a derivative of the object's immanent qualities. This conception, then, raises the question of how we may now think of narrative painting. Can we, through the supposition of the phantasmatic character of narrative, think of narrativity as a visual characteristic that is unique to the visual field? I would like to argue that a visual image fashions a paradox in which contradictory states exist simultaneously. Hence, the image is constructed from something that contradicts it. That is, the image is also constituted by another narrative that the viewer reconstructs beyond the visible narrative that emanates from the painting. This means that the paradoxicality of the narrative can be expressed through the visual medium. While a verbal narrative resolves the paradox through a narrative description that conceals

DOI: 10.4324/9781003516446-5

all contradictions, painting allows this paradoxicality to appear. That is, by virtue of its immanent characteristics, narrative constitutes a product of the attempt to gain meaning in the visual field, much like in the verbal field. However, at the same time, in the case of painting, the paradoxicality of the narrative structure comes to the surface.

I will show how interpretations of paintings can point toward a certain process of their reading, according to which the image makes possible a dialectical relation between two levels of meaning, and I will call this image "the split image". I will use the split image to demonstrate the Lacanian concept of looking, which I discussed in the previous chapter. It should be noted that it is not my intent to point toward certain painterly elements that constitute the split; rather, I wish to trace the split image through an interpretation that testifies to the fact that it is split. That is, the way to point at the split image is not through its formal analysis but rather through its reflections in the interpretations of its viewers. Nevertheless, I claim that the split is in the structure of the image and is not exhausted merely in the way it is understood.

When Gombrich discusses visual perception, he gives as an example the rabbit-duck case. The image originates in a book on visual anecdotes from the end of the nineteenth century and can be interpreted as both a rabbit and a duck. Gombrich argues that the two images are not seen simultaneously; rather, the same image may be seen once as a rabbit and once as a duck.[2] I argue that unlike the case of the rabbit-duck image, painting constitutes a meaning that simultaneously contains its own inversion or contradiction. However, the two senses do not share an identical status. Rather, they are two different operations of meaning construction with different traits and different statuses, which appear simultaneously. Thus, painting does not necessarily obey narratological logic in two ways. First, painting does not obey a narratological logic that dictates unity, and, as a result, the image makes the existence of paradoxical states possible. Second, the paradoxical image does not necessarily adhere to the narratological demand to represent a progressive sequence of time. As Žižek's examples show, the way to gain coherent meanings passes through a distortion of a certain worldview so as to adjust it to a progressive temporal order. An image that sustains within itself a paradox or simultaneously opposing structures of meaning is hence "liberated" from this demand of narrativity. What is, then, the relation between the image and the narrative in this new sense?

The term paradox in the visual field has been defined in the past in various ways. John Searle called the impossibility of interpreting Diego Velázquez's painting *Las Meninas* through the laws of Albertian perspective a "paradox of pictorial representation".[3] While Joel Snyder argued that perspective distortions, representations that cannot be settled with reality, and mazes that cannot be actualized in a three-dimensional space may be termed complex or weird images, they do not necessarily constitute an example of a visual paradox.[4] Snyder even argues against what he believed to be an unjust overuse of the term paradox in the context of the visual medium, and one of the examples he gives for this overuse is the case of the rabbit-duck.[5] According to Snyder, an image with a double meaning or an image that represents a fantasy still does not necessarily constitute a visual paradox; rather, it can be understood as a fantastic or multi-meaning image.

The aim here is not to present paradoxical images but to point toward an interpretive process that makes a place for this image. This kind of visual paradox takes place when an image is interpreted in a certain way, and, at the same time, another sense arises that inverts the first meaning. The inversion of sense is not exhausted by the new meaning that is given to the image. The two modes of understanding depend on one another and stem from one another. These two modes of observation exist simultaneously; however, they also have different statuses and characteristics. I would like to claim that we can find examples of the construction of this kind of split image in Norman Bryson's discussion of Greuze's *Girl* paintings from the mid-eighteenth century, and in a similar vein, in Charles Bernheimer's analysis of Edouard Manet's *Olympia* from 1863.[6]

Bryson on the Greuze girls

In his analysis of Greuze's paintings, Bryson underscores the complex link between painting and discursivity, or between the different levels of interpretation in the paintings. According to Bryson, Greuze's paintings contain two frequencies, one overt and the other hidden.[7] Bryson relates this duality to two components that stem from each other: the topics or moments that Greuze chooses to present and Greuze's own personality. I believe that beyond the articulation of the cause that propelled Greuze to paint his conflicted images, Bryson's analysis of these paintings brings to the fore a unique aspect of the visual medium – the possibility of the visual image to contain within itself its own contradiction.

Bryson points toward the double-frequency image, which exists in the two types of Greuze's paintings. He believes that they are different expressions of the same painterly phenomenon: family paintings and paintings of girls.[8] In his family paintings, Greuze paints human figures that are presented in a closed and hermetic inner space. The figures, in most cases, are family members and their servants. Greuze seemingly deals with class and age differences, which are emphasized by isolating the characters within the closed space without additional external participants. However, Bryson argues that Greuze attempts to move beyond these restrictive categories. He achieves this by focusing on the transitional moment from one status to another, as the character is either in two places or in neither. For example, the painting *Filial Piety* (1763) of an old man in the transitional moment from life to death, or the painting *L'Accordée de village*(1761), which depicts a transitional moment from youth to marriage.[9] The duplicity of the image in these examples stems from the painting's explicit topic.

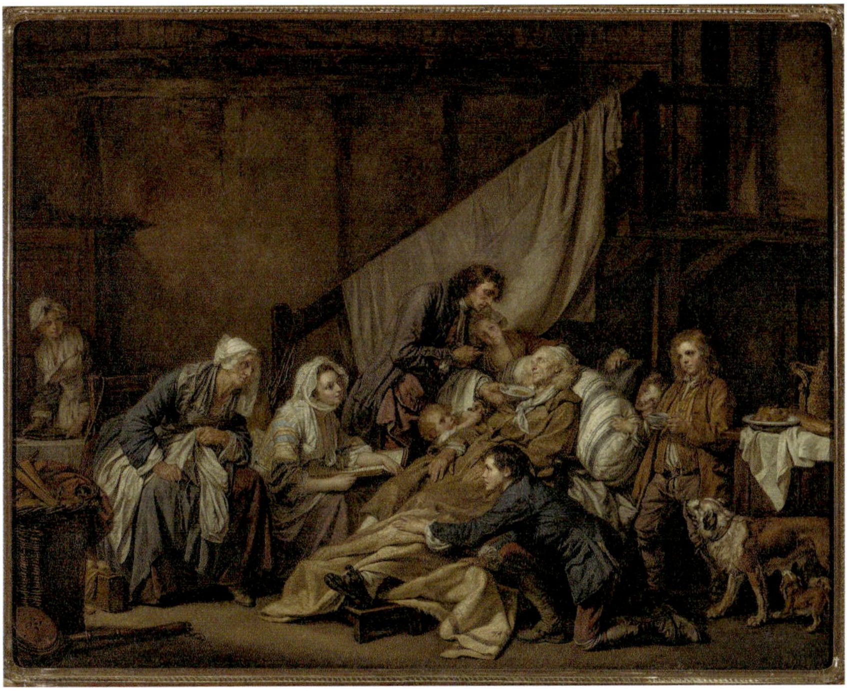

Figure 4.1 Jean-Baptiste Greuze, *Filial Piety (The Paralytic)*, 1763.

The painting *Filial Piety* depicts a more complex state of ambivalence than a mere representation of a moment with two possible states. Bryson argues that these complex states of ambivalence can be found in Greuze's most perplexing images, which he calls "Greuze girls". One of the starkest examples is *The Broken Pitcher* from 1785, which depicts a young girl who embodies both childish innocence and seductive femininity. According to Bryson, just as the moment of death and the moment of marriage fashion a point of entry in which categories that usually cancel each other out can exist simultaneously, in this painting, the female character is simultaneously a woman and a child, naïve and seductive. The two stereotypes, which are usually distinct, are conjoined into a single image.[10]

Bryson argues that although Greuze's paintings are overtly narratological and he is viewed as a discursive painter, which also explains Greuze's astounding success in his period, his paintings show something that cannot be articulated through an explicit narrative level.[11] That is, Greuze's paintings explicitly deal with narratological topics and are like blueprints for verbal ideas, with a clear affinity to the verbal text. However, at the same time, something different emerges from the visuality of the images, which cannot be articulated on a verbal level. I would like to claim that this supplement is what makes possible the existence of the image that strives against itself.

Despite Greuze's commitment to rational narrativity, a different textuality emerges from these paintings. This textuality is bound to emotion and makes the painting nondiscursive.[12] It is precisely Greuze's insistence on painting narratives that makes it possible for the other text, which undermines the initial understanding of the image, to unconsciously infiltrate the image. Bryson attributes this infiltration to Greuze's psychic biography and his lack of consciousness. This fact also explains Greuze's later failure as a historical painter. When he painted domestic scenes, there was a place for his unconscious message that was simultaneously transmitted with the "proper" message of the paintings. However, when he painted historical paintings, the critics revolted against the messages that did not comply with mainstream understanding and denied him the status of a historical painter. According to Bryson, the real power in Greuze's paintings lies in their ability to flirt with obscenity, to confront us with libidinal powers, which Greuze himself disavowed, and which undermine all moralistic categories.[13]

Bryson finds a disturbingly incompatible image in Greuze's painting *La Mère Bien-aimée*, from 1765. The painting portrays a mother and a father surrounded by many children of various ages. The mother is painted as an archetypal mother figure, with her children hanging on to her. This is why Diderot stated that the painting "preached population".[14] However, the parents are also presented as a man and woman with a sexuality of their own. The discarded garment at the forefront of the painting, the father's disheveled clothes, and the mother's open arms indicate that the parents are about to fall into each other's arms.[15] Critics such as Diderot or the Goncourt brothers identified in the painting a disturbing or perverse element. However, as Bryson states, Greuze believed this was simply a depiction of an abundance of happiness; he was unaware that he had become, like in the case of the Greuze girls, the Humbert Humbert of painting.[16]

The additional meaning, which contradicts the initial meaning conveyed by the image, constitutes the foundation for criticism of the narrative. Bryson points here to a painterly phenomenon, which is not, as he tries to claim, a product of the poetics of the artist or the genre and is not dependent on cultural perception. Rather, it constitutes a possible characteristic of the visual image, which is unique to the visual field. Bryson presents the visual image that enables an "anti-narrative" state in the sense that Žižek gives it, of conveying a certain sense of coherency while simultaneously undermining this coherency. This state of affairs is not exhausted by an ambivalence or a subversive sense that works against the canonical structure of meaning. It testifies, rather, to the fact that the image cannot be fixed under a unified and coherent structure since this very coherent and unified structure produces an additional antagonistic frequency.

The interpretations of paintings such as *La Mère Bien-aimée* are important since they show that the initial and coherent understanding is exactly what produces the antagonistic sense. In other words, this is not a deconstruction of the pictorial meaning but a state of vision that does not adhere to a narratological logic, in the sense that it makes possible a state of affairs that is fundamentally incoherent. The paradoxicality of the split image stems from the structure of the image itself. Not only can the image not be fixed, but the attempt to fix the image brings the inverse meaning to the surface. It is not that meaning becomes impossible; rather, the image offers itself to a unified narratological reading while also refusing to remain fixed to it. Unlike ambivalence, which allows for two contradictory meanings to exist simultaneously, here, the structure itself aspires to veil an inverse meaning, where the very attempt to hide it makes it possible to appear.

Bernheimer on Manet's *Olympia*

Bernheimer's analysis of Manet's *Olympia* and the various interpretations given to this painting discloses a similar logic. Bernheimer argues that this painting produces a female character as an object of consumption in a patriarchal society while simultaneously exposing the mechanism of this kind of production.[17] I would like to claim that much like Bryson, Bernheimer also points toward a visual image that fashions its own contradiction. However, while Bryson relates to two inverse images that exist simultaneously, Bernheimer presents a simultaneous operation of certain dynamics and the exposure of this mechanism and argues that the exposure cancels the operation. Both scholars discuss images that have been the focus of much debate and many interpretations (the Greuze girls and Manet's *Olympia*). The similarity between the cases does not lie in the fact that the painting challenges certain social norms, but in the manner in which the painting simultaneously produces a certain conception and undermines it, while the relation between the two generates the complexity of the image.

Olympia caused a stir in public opinion from its very first exhibition. The painting was perceived as a disturbing and problematic image that did not comply with the mainstream representational frameworks. Bernheimer claims that *Olympia* is constructed from a series of details that produce the effect of ambivalence. On the one hand, the painterly surfaces are divided in a rigid fashion, for instance, the black ribbon on Olympia's neck that seems to decapitate her. On the other hand, other areas in the painting are painted softly and fluidly; for instance, her body is painted with a unified tonality. Thus, *Olympia* generates a simultaneous sense of fragmentation and wholeness for the viewer. This is also true for the angle from which the figure is painted. *Olympia* is placed in the painting higher than the viewer, but she also looks straight at him. She does not look down at the viewer, as her heightened position on the pillows would dictate. The scales of the paintings also generate this ambivalence: the figure is big compared to the bed and tiny compared to the servant and the flowers. The same is true with painterly surfaces. The surfaces are made of carefully treated spaces alongside painterly areas in which the technique of covering the surface declares itself. Olympia's hand covers her pubic area in a tense and self-conscious manner. Bernheimer

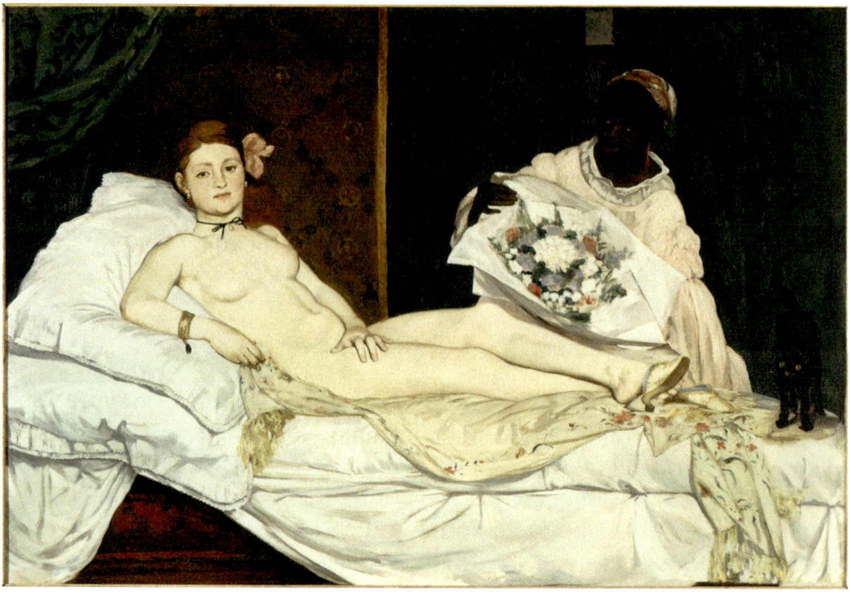

Figure 4.2 Edouard Manet, *Olympia*, 1863.

contrasts this gesture with the paintings of Venus, such as Titian's painting, in which the gesture of the hand is seen as somewhat inviting. This hand, combined with the ambivalence of her gaze, creates, in the viewer, a sense of resistance as well as a sense of invitation. The viewer confronts the question of what is being concealed and what is suppressed here.[18]

Bernheimer refers to Mulvey, who argues that the woman, who is presented to the male gaze by her lack of a penis, evokes the anxiety of the male viewer and threatens him. However, Bernheimer is not interested in reducing the effect of the painting only to the anxiety of castration that it evokes. He argues that the hand does not merely undermine the conventions of female nudity, but "puts her in possession of her own sexuality precisely to the extent that the identity of her sexuality is thrown into doubt".[19] This is why critics were so enraged by the hand and saw it as the source of the scandal. The painting evokes contradictory signs of sexuality, and the meeting point of these signs is in the tense hand. The representation of the hand generates unconscious anxiety concerning the sexual difference that the male viewer is certain he has already overcome. This anxiety stems from the fact that the painting presents the process of displacement and substitution that leads to the construction of the female as a fetish.[20] That is, the painting exposes the way in which the woman becomes an object of enjoyment for the male gaze.[21]

The painting raises unanswered questions, which enhances the uncanny effect on the viewer.[22] While fetishism, according to Freud, offers the viewer a substitute for anxiety, the painting does not offer a substitute but rather awakens castration anxiety and sexual uncertainty over and over again.[23] The painting, with its copious contradictions, offers no solution, only new contradictions. The male viewer sees the woman as a fetishistic object that is given for his consumption. However, the act is not fulfilled, since the process itself is exposed, as the initial lack that generated the passion for a fetish reignites the phantasmatic content.

Bernheimer's complex analysis of the painting exposes states of contradiction, a seeming solution and its simultaneous undoing. *Olympia* is a complex net of internal contradictions that cannot be resolved, and the different modes of understanding it do not compose stages of a linear process at the end of which lies a unified understanding of the image. Rather, the image itself is the contradictions that it sustains. In this sense, I find a relation between Bryson's analysis of the Greuze girls and Bernheimer's interpretation of *Olympia*. Bryson's and Bernheimer's analyses do not attempt to resolve the conflict but rather point toward it. Despite the vast differences in their interpretations, both Bryson and Bernheimer articulate in their analyses a visuality that sustains contradictory states and refuses to obey narratological logic, while also not excluding narrativity.

It should be noted that both Bryson and Bernheimer point toward different aspects of contradiction that exist in the paintings. It is important to distinguish between thematic contradictions, such as the choice to paint the moment of transition in the case of Greuze, according to Bryson, and formalistic contradictions, such as the uneven treatment of the surface in the case of *Olympia*, according to Bernheimer, and contradictions of a constitution of meaning that emerge from the image and cannot be articulated univocally. While the first contradictions relate to the complexity of the artistic expressions and have always been subject to interpretations, the contradictory image offers a dialectical state in the relations between the painting and the viewer. These are relations that do not offer a guarantee of a single coherent understanding at the end of the process since the image at stake is not merely a complex image that is difficult to decipher; rather, this is more extreme: the image undermines the very possibility of fixing one stable meaning.

Bal reads Rembrandt

To elaborate and clarify the concept of the split image, I wish to compare this form of interpretation with other complex interpretations of visual images and the way in which the meaning of the image is constituted through them. For this, I will relate to Mieke Bal's analysis of Rembrandt's paintings.[24] Bal focuses on an array of questions that relate to the constitution of the pictorial content, such as the narrative in the painting or the relation between the pictorial narrative and a prior canonical verbal representation. Bal deals with the same aspects of the visual image as Bryson and Bernheimer. However, as I will show, in most cases, despite the similar nature of the questions, Bal's analysis of the paintings is vastly different from Bernheimer's and Bryson's analyses. Although Bal eventually extrapolates a new and complex construction of meaning from the painting, it is still a complete and unified construction. That is, if we return to Žižek's criticism of narrative, then Bryson and Bernheimer's debates demonstrate how visuality can bypass the limitations of the narrative structure, while Bal's analysis leads to a conception of the painting as an alternative narrative structure that continues to comply with the limitations of the structure.

Bal, as stated, analyzes Rembrandt's paintings. Like many other narrative paintings, these paintings refer to an anteceding verbal, canonical, mythical or biblical text. Bal argues that there is a complex relation between visual and textual representations. The image constitutes a new narrative alongside the familiar story. The tension between the two stories, the visual and the textual, creates another narrative in itself. The added narrative can offer a new and different story from the previous one. In other cases, the narrative essence is preserved in the new version, but the focalization is different. Thus, the visual image, in these cases, constitutes a different structure of meaning than the one of the verbal text and it may even contradict it. However, it is still a unified and coherent structure. This can be seen in Bal's analysis of the painting *Danaë* from 1636.[25] The painting shows a woman sprawled on a bed, above her flies an angel with his hands clasped together, and in the background, there is an aura of light. The textual story revolves around Danaë, whose cruel father does not love her. Zeus comes to her in the form of a golden shower and successfully lifts the taboo her father placed on her. This is the story of the visuality of Western culture: the male is the voyeur, and the woman constitutes the object and erotization of visuality. The gender roles are fixed, and through them, gender itself is built.[26]

Between the text, which is the story of the entrance of Zeus into Danaë's bedroom, and the image, in which the woman is presented before the consuming male gaze, Bal finds another narrative: the product of the painting. The third narrative does not adhere to the other two narratives, the verbal or the visual. The primary text functions as a kind of framework for the visual text. The existence of the anterior text makes it possible to separate the two stories and create a new narrative that is constructed from the tension between them.[27] The two stories collide and interact within the textuality of the painting. There is tension between them, yet they do not contradict each other. They generate a new narrative in which Danaë's text sustains a relation between the painting and the viewer. The female figure is transformed from an object to a subject, and she controls both the viewer and her lover.

Bal proves another example from two paintings entitled *Lucretia*, one from 1664 and the other from 1666. In the verbal text, Lucretia is raped and then commits suicide by plunging a dagger into her body before the eyes of her husband and father. The two paintings that address this subject show a female character holding a dagger, with her head tilted to the side. Bal offers a visual interpretation of the paintings and shows throughout her debate how the

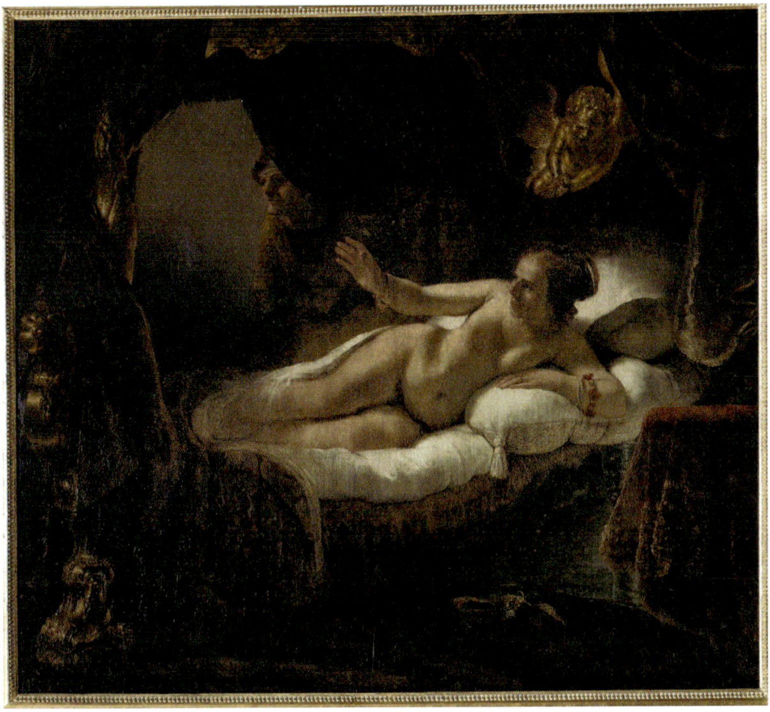

Figure 4.3 Rembrandt van Rijn, *Danaë*, 1636.

different interpretations not only constitute layers of meaning but, through their own interactions, also fashion a new and complex story.[28]

Bal argues that rape is identified with suicide rather than murder. Lucretia kills herself not only because her chastity was taken away but also because a victim of rape was seen as someone who committed a crime against herself. Rape is represented as suicide since rape cannot be represented visually, both because it is internal and hence exists only as an experience and a memory and also because the rapist hides the victim, both physically and metaphorically. The metaphorical veiling takes place since, through the act of rape, the rapist destroys his victim's subjectivity. By turning her head away, Lucretia gestures to the external spectator. As Bal states: "Lucretia turns her head away in order to break contact with the spectators, preferring isolation to remaining an object of their voyeuristic gaze".[29] The dagger casts a double shadow. Bal interprets this as a doubling of the act of rape. After the victim is completely destroyed, the only way for her to act as a subject is to repeat the act of rape so as to regain her lost subjectivity.[30]

The paintings of *Lucretia* refer to the same verbal text, but unlike the verbal story, the paintings deal only with empathy toward the ruin of the woman by presenting her, and her point of view, at the center. That is, the text and the image describe the same plot and their difference lies in focalization.

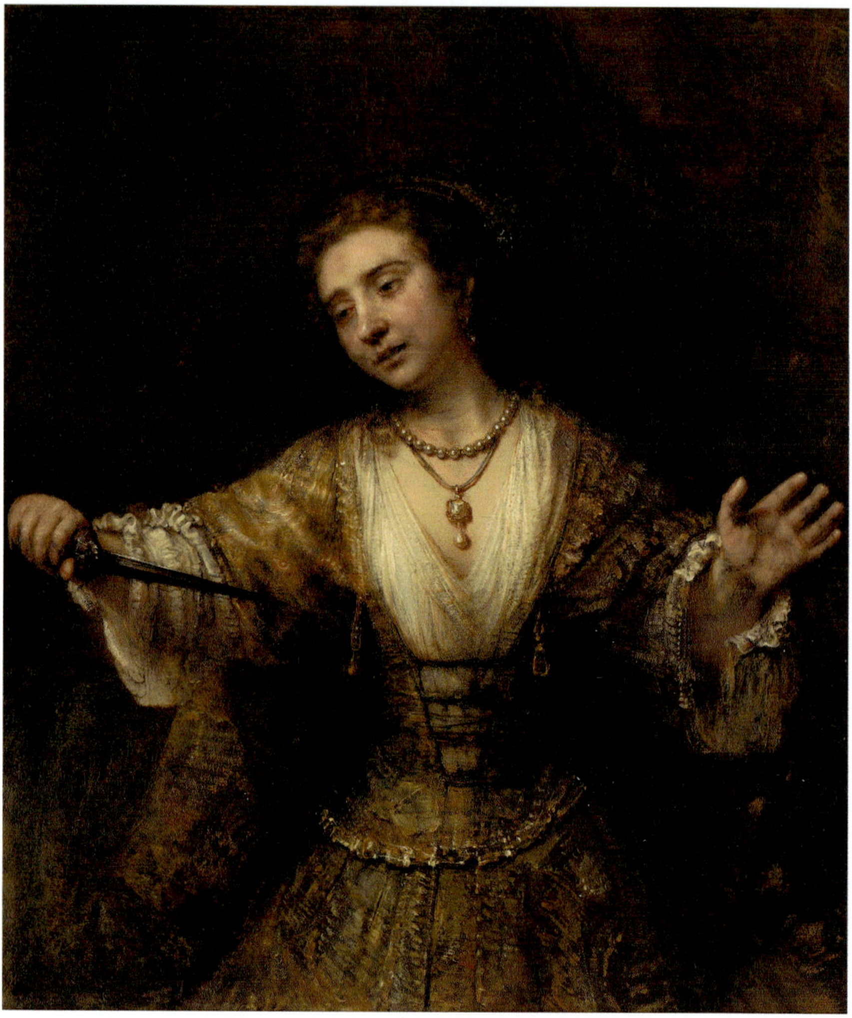

Figure 4.4 Rembrandt van Rijn, *Lucretia*, 1664.

However, while the semantic structure that Bal extrapolates from Lucretia's paintings fashions an alternative narrative to the original narrative, even if the "visual representation", as she defines it, is different from the verbal representation, it is still a coherent and unified semantic structure.

The only painting in which Bal's interpretation lets the split image emerge is *Susannah and the Elders* from 1645. Bal, here, addresses a similar phenomenon to the one I discussed, in which the image includes within itself a critical stance toward itself or criticism of the meaning that is attributed to it.[31] The topic of the painting is Susannah walking alone in a garden while the two elders look at her in secret, desire her and even attack her when

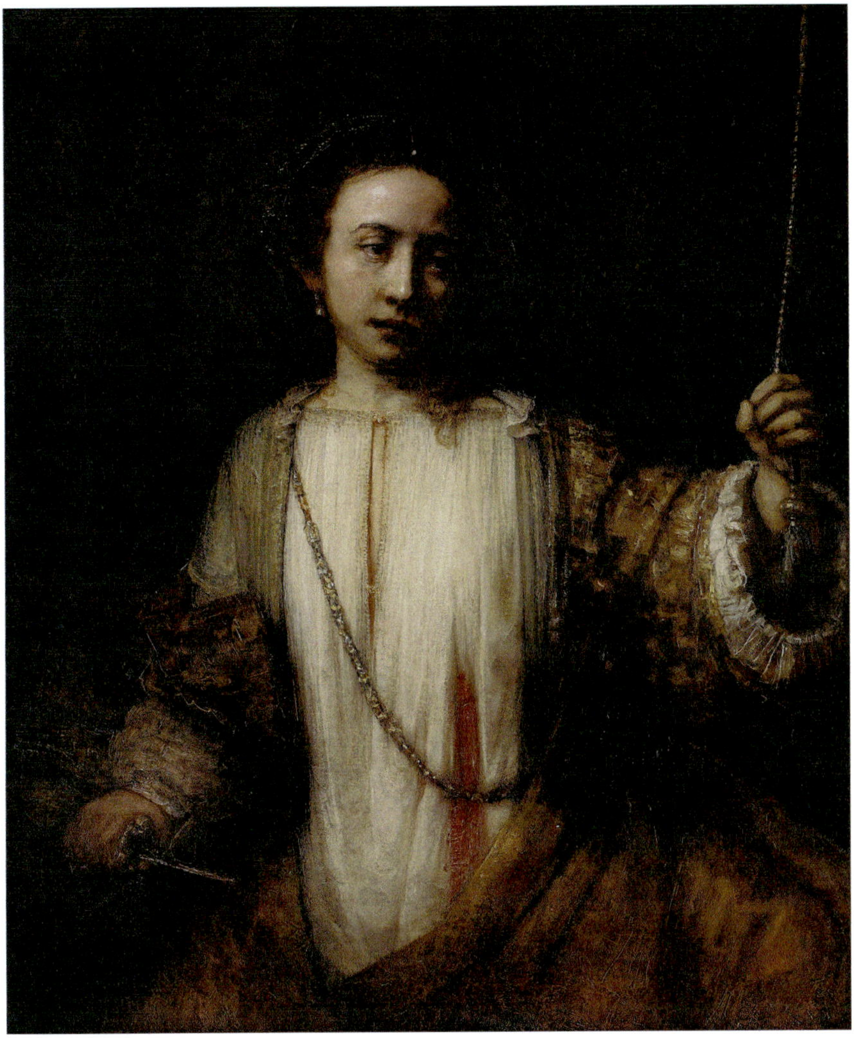

Figure 4.5 Rembrandt van Rijn, *Lucretia*, 1666.

she bathes. Rembrandt's painting depicts a half-naked woman with two male figures standing behind her. Bal focuses on the way the hands are represented. Susannah is conventionally represented in the pose of Venus, with her hand extended to the side as if showing her beautiful body, thus representing Susannah as a provocateur. Rembrandt breaks with this tradition by representing Susannah trying to hide her body with her hand. She does not provoke but is presented as an innocent victim. The change in the position of the hand has a narratological meaning in the attempt to resist the rape.[32]

Bal relates to the representation of the elders in the painting. She focuses on the relation between gestures of the hands and acts of seeing. The men in

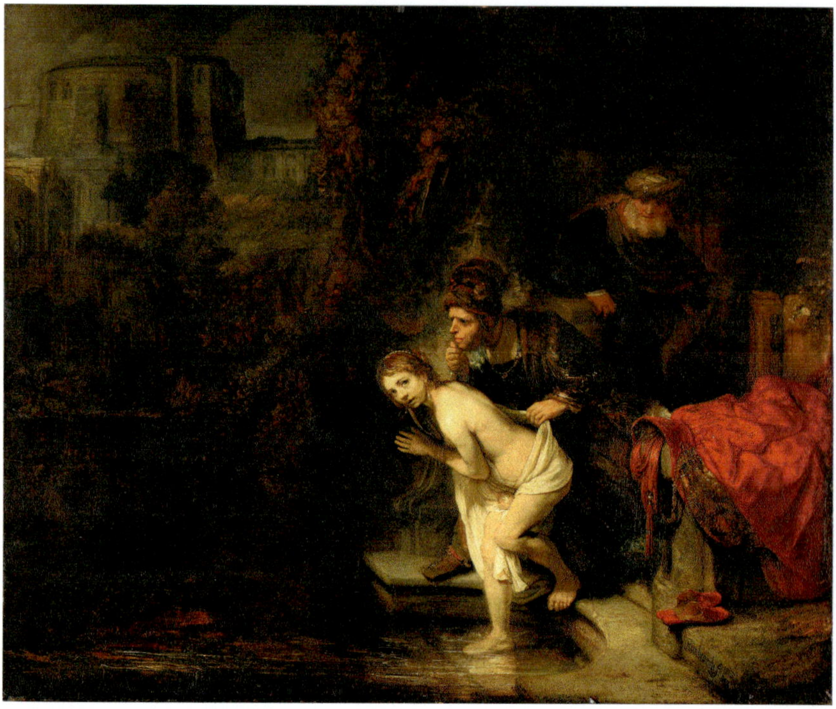

Figure 4.6 Rembrandt van Rijn, *Susannah and the Elders*, 1647.

this pictorial scene are "spectators by definition, whose acts of seeing actually lead to the use of their hands".[33] The man next to Susannah holds her and seems to be attempting to disrobe her with one of his hands, while his other hand is strangely clenched into a fist next to his face. His look is focused on a specific point on Susannah's hair. This is strange, since while the hand that disrobes her follows the textual version of the apocryphal section of the *Book of Daniel*, the other hand does not complete this story. This is seemingly a painting of rape, and the spectator participates in the sadistic situation. However, according to Bal, this painting can also be read differently. The painting can also be interpreted as criticizing the status quo, and the image does not present a monolithic position but also critiques itself. The look of the rapist is directed to the same pictorial place that is meticulously done, to the pearls braided into Susannah's hair, while the rest of the image is not so meticulously painted. Thus, Rembrandt fashions a parallel between the look of the elder and the look of the voyeuristic spectator peeping into the pornographic situation, thus making a criticism from within the painting to the outside world possible.[34]

It seems that Bal points toward a unique aspect of the visual image, to which I referred through Bryson and Bernheimer's analyses. In this case, the painting, which, through a certain painterly detail, criticizes the represented scene, contains an internal contradiction, a negation of meaning while simultaneously constituting it. This is similar to the contradictions that we have isolated in Bryson's debate of the Greuze girls and Bernheimer's analysis of *Olympia*.

The split image and the dimension of time

The double frequency transmitted by the Greuze girls, and the way in which *Olympia* simultaneously sustains within itself both a mechanism and its exposure, are examples that demonstrate a similar principle, according to which the visual image contains not only a single direct meaning but also the inversion of this meaning, or, as in the case of *Olympia*, a criticism of the way in which this meaning is constituted. However, is the characteristic of visuality derived from the simultaneous way in which the painting unfolds before the viewer, or is it related to the temporal aspect of the process of seeing the painting?

The analysis of processes of sight and visibility conceptualizes sight through two different stages that take place one after the other.[35] These kinds of analyses link the process of sight to a certain periodic continuity; they assume that there exists a form of initial sight and a later understanding or sight that follows it. Unlike these conceptualizations, the split image articulated here is not composed of a continuum of two subsequent images or a substitution of one understanding for another. This is a structure in which the painting generates two ways to understand it, and this duality is inevitable. Reading 1 is necessary so that reading 2 will take place, while reading 2 undermines or inverts the meaning of reading 1. The transitions between the two readings are difficult to articulate since it is not a linear and progressive sequence. Once one reading is articulated, the other reading appears, and the first option is a condition for the existence of the second. Both readings constitute each other, and each reading is at the backdrop of the other.

As noted above, while textual narrativity attempts to resolve a contradictory structure, visual narrativity makes it possible to preserve the paradox in the image. To answer the question of how visuality preserves the paradox, I would like to turn to a certain aspect of the question of time in psychoanalysis.[36] As part of a discussion of the subject and the Other, Colette Soler, following Lacan, argues that when one speaks, the question of what the speaker wants makes itself present beyond what is said. The answer to the question moves in two dimensions: in the dimension of the Other, it is formulated in a desire that escapes language and cannot be articulated in language. Soler argues that the question is also what the subject is beyond signifiers, and the answer to this lies in the drive. The signifier and the drive suppose different temporal conceptions: the time of the signifier and the time of the drive.[37] The time of the signifier is the time of anticipation and retroactive time. That is, the time of the signifier is organized between the anticipation of what will be spoken and the retroactive organization of the things that were spoken.

Thus, for instance, when someone speaks, the listener anticipates the end of the sentence and then retroactively organizes what was said. The two actions suppose two times, and in both cases, this is not an "objective" or measurable time. The time of the drive is very different from the time of the signifier. This time is constructed as an accidental encounter and takes place in the blink of an eye. This time of the drive operates as a cut that disturbs and fragments the continuity of the time of the signifier. Thus, we can understand that the sense of the discourse is constructed by two operations that are also distinguished by the periods in which they operate, and there is a gap between their duration and their occurrence.

Soler claims, then, that speech sustains a certain relation between three times: the time of anticipation, the time of retroactive organization and the time of the drive that splits them like a cut. I believe that the relation between these three times operates differently when we look at a painting. The image appears before the viewer at once. However, this does not cancel the gap between the time of anticipation and retroactive organization since, even in this case, the process of perception takes the duration of processing; the gap is no longer derived from the duration of time in which the act of speaking and listening takes place. As a result, the relation between the time of the signifier and the time of the drive changes: they act simultaneously. The relation between the two times in the visual image can hence explain the phenomenon of the split image, in which the time of the signifier is isomorphic to the initial understanding of the image, to the surface meaning, whereas the time of the drive is isomorphic to the second, contradictory interpretation that stems from the first meaning.

The split image and the cinematic gaze

To explain the relations between the parts of the split image, I would like to turn to a cinematic operation that Žižek describes, in which a foreign element infiltrates the cinematic frame. I will now examine if we can compare the articulation of the split image through Bryson's and Bernheimer's debates and the cinematic operation that Žižek ascribes to Hitchcock's films.[38] Žižek makes use of these films to explain the "victory of the gaze over the eye", concerning the way Lacan describes sight in his eleventh seminar. He describes two cinematic procedures that exemplify opposite states: a surplus of the symbolic over the real and a surplus of the real over the symbolic.

Žižek refers to the three orders of psychoanalytic discourse as Lacan articulated them: the imaginary order, the symbolic order and the real. The imaginary order belongs to the constitution of the ego, and relates to the way in which the subject grasps himself through his specular image.

The symbolic order relates to the way in which the subject is constituted through language. As Lacan states, "If the subject is...determined by language and speech, it follows that the subject, *in initio*, begins in the locus of the

Other, in so far as it is there that the first signifier emerges".[39] Bruce Fink explains this through the fact that the infant is born into a language that predates him. The needs of the infant are interpreted and articulated through the language of his parents, which is not his own, and here also lies the relation between the subject of language and alienation.[40]

The real, according to Lacan, is a product of the symbolic order in the sense of that which cannot be articulated or represented. To a certain extent, it is Kant's "thing in itself", as that which we cannot access. These three orders are not separate; Lacan describes the link between them as a Borromean knot made of three intertwined rings – if we cut one of them, the entire structure collapses.[41] As Žižek states: "The elementary feature of a symbolic order in its relation to 'reality' is that it always contains a surplus-signifier, a signifier that is 'empty' in the sense that there is nothing in reality that corresponds to it".[42]

Lacan draws from Claude-Levi-Strauss's structural anthropology and the analogy he makes between language and culture.[43] Levi-Strauss compares the blood-related family unit with the phoneme, a linguistic term that refers to a phonetic unit. According to Levi-Strauss, social structures are not a biological given but represent social symbolism.[44] The family unit takes on its significance the moment it constitutes a part of a general social structure. In a similar vein, the phoneme can only receive its significance as an element within the system of language. In both cases, meaning emerges only when the unit is combined within the system, and in both cases, the systems are constructed unconsciously. Levi-Strauss shows how, in primitive societies, when tribes are divided into sub-tribes, at a certain point, one reaches the name of a tribe that does not exist in reality. Žižek argues that Lacan's master signifier functions in a similar fashion. He relates it to the S1 signifier, which is Lacan's formal expression for a signifier that marks, for the subject, the other signifiers. It is an arbitrary signifier that provides discourse with its sense.[45] The master signifier in and of itself is senseless, and it only receives its meaning through its relation to other signifiers. As Žižek states:

> The asymmetry of these two returns (that of the stain of the Real where the word fails; that of the signifier to fill the void that gapes in the midst of representational reality) is dependent on the split between reality and the real. 'Reality' is a field of symbolically structured representation… yet a surplus or the real eludes the symbolic grasp… a hole in reality that designates the ultimate where 'the word fails'.[46]

Žižek gives a cinematic example of the symbolic surplus on the real from Hitchock's film *The Lady Vanishes* from 1938. In the scene that takes place in the restaurant car of a moving train, the name of a certain person appears on the steam-covered window.[47] The surplus is in the sense of the name that remains empty, a representation that does not represent anything. Žižek gives two cinematic operations as examples of an opposite state, of a surplus of the real over the symbolic. One of these examples can help shed light on the relation between the different parts of the split image.[48]

This cinematic operation, which relates to the surplus of the real over the symbolic, is manifested in dialectics between the cinematic frame and what is outside of it when an alien body penetrates the frame. For instance, in films such as *Psycho* from 1960 and *The Birds* from 1963, when the threatening element, the knife of the murderer or the flock of birds, enters the frame not as part of the fictional world represented within it, but as an element that exists between the external and internal worlds, and invades the frame like a spot. In *The Birds,* this is also literal, since, in some cases, the birds were a later addition planted into the film's reel.

In a scene at Bodega Bay, the birds enter the frame from a back angle to the camera from an all-seeing point of view. This blurs the distinction between fiction and reality as the viewer is no longer external to the scene. Žižek argues that this is like watching a storm from a closed window. We are close to the event, but the window creates a kind of screen. The enjoyment of riding the train lies in the illusion of the subject that he is standing still while the world around him moves. The infiltration of a spot into reality breaks this sense of safety. A foreign object invades our field of vision and creates the feeling that the spot is in our eye, not in the thing that we are seeing.[49] What is important for our purposes is not the extra detail we see – birds, a spot of blood or an anamorphic skull – but the way we see what we see, a vision that includes a disturbance of vision, a vision that can be viewed as a disturbance of vision.

Is there a link between Bryson's and Bernheimer's interpretation and this cinematic operation? Both cases deal with modes of sight, while the second sight undoes or exposes the first sight, pointing to its blind spot. I believe that when Bryson describes the additional frequency that emerges from the painting, or when Bernheimer claims that the painting contains a mechanism that turns the character of the woman into a fetish while also exposing this mechanism, they describe a similar operation of an infiltration of a foreign object into the cinematic frame, as Žižek describes it, an object that constitutes a spot that invades the field of vision.

We can, hence, describe the relation between the parts of the split image or the difference between these two parts, which do not constitute alternative options of understanding, as the dialectic that, according to Žižek, exists between the cinematic frame that describes Bodega Bay and the birds that invade it and create a spot that lies at the eye of the viewer. What is, then, the relation of the split image to narrativity beyond being a demonstration of an alternative narrative? Narrativity is necessary to understand visuality through its inversion: narrativity as a unified structure is needed to make it possible for the "spot", or that meaning that cannot be coherently understood to emerge.

To elaborate on the relations between the parts of the split image, we need to explain the very use of the term "spot". According to Lacan, the spot, or the screen, which he describes in the second diagram of vision, as I showed in the previous chapter, is what mediates between the point of view of the viewer and the painting, not in the optic-geometric sense as what makes vision possible, but in its opacity.[50]

Antonio Quinet explains that while the spot is usually viewed as something that veils, here the spot operates both as what veils and what shows. The spot hides and shows the gaze. This is the sense of the ambivalence of the word "spot", both as a stain and as a source of light. The spot can be a testimony to a crime, like in the case of Lady Macbeth, who tries to erase the blood stain. In this scene, the screen refuses to fulfill its function since Lady Macbeth is not able to erase the spot, and this is a testimony to her madness. Here, too, the spot defines the subject, who encounters anxiety in the act of looking at it.[51] It seems that we can understand the birds in Hitchcock's film in a similar vein: like a spot on a windowpane, they are a disturbance in the field of vision, while at the same time, they are a part of this field. The relations between the parts of the split image are hence analogous to the relations between the field of vision and the spot, which both veils and shows. Narrativity as a unified structure emerges so as to let the spot appear, and the spot disturbs unified vision but makes it possible to see the image, whose paradoxicality is immanent to it.

The case of the Pre-Raphaelites

Žižek's analysis of fantasy as a narrative and the relevance of this analysis to the process of looking at a painting led me to develop the concept of the split image. To conclude this articulation, I will outline Žižek's debate on the Pre-Raphaelite paintings. According to Žižek, the different interpretations that were given to this movement can provide another example of narrative as one of the veils of fantasy. Moreover, Žižek reads these paintings as split images. The case of the Pre-Raphaelites and their changing status throughout the history of art exposes the imaginary aspect of the very act of cataloguing and the seeming evolutionary progress of the history of art. Moreover, Žižek's analysis of one of the painters of this image shows that the Pre-Raphaelite painting itself is a split image. Thus, he shows that in the case of the Pre-Raphaelites, applying narrative structures to the visual medium works in a double fashion, both in the context of the painted fictional world and in the context of the general conception of the school.

The Pre-Raphaelites Brotherhood entered the stage of art history in the mid-nineteenth century. According to historians, their declared purpose was to go against the frivolity of the art of their time by representing subjects taken from nature. Their source of inspiration was fifteenth-century painting, which predated Raphael's painting. The particularity of the Pre-Raphaelites lies in their belief that their art had the power to heal the maladies of society.[52]

Žižek argues that the Pre-Raphaelites are seen in the history of art as a case that is located at the paradoxical limit between avant-garde and kitsch. When they first entered the scene in the mid-nineteenth century, they were seen as revolutionaries in painting who broke the traditions that came before them, from the Renaissance onward. Soon after, though, with the rise of the Impressionist painting in France, the critics' appreciation they received was replaced by harsh criticism that their paintings constituted the epitome of Victorian pseudo-romantic kitsch. This demeaning attitude toward them continued until the 1960s, when, with the rise of postmodernism, they suddenly received a newfound appreciation. Žižek raises the question of what made the Pre-Raphaelites' painting understandable only retroactively, through the postmodern paradigm.[53]

Žižek argues that the main artist in this context is William Holman Hunt. Hunt is usually seen as the first Pre-Raphaelite, who, at a certain point, began to produce saccharine religious paintings, such as *The Triumph of the Innocents*,[54] from 1883 to 1884. A closer look at his paintings confronts the viewer with strange sensations, with a disturbing dimension that creates a sense of unease despite the seeming ideality of the paintings. Thus, for instance, *The Hireling Shepherd*, from 1851 to 1852, depicts a pastoral ideal in which a young shepherd seduces a country girl, and thereby neglects his flock, with all the allegorical meanings that accompany this. The more we look at the painting, claims Žižek, the more we notice Hunt's position toward pleasure and vitality and his sense of disgust toward sexuality. The shepherd is muscular and crude. The girl's devious smile indicates a manipulative use of her own sexuality. The painting's all too colorful jubilance with its red-green colors gives it a disgusting appearance.

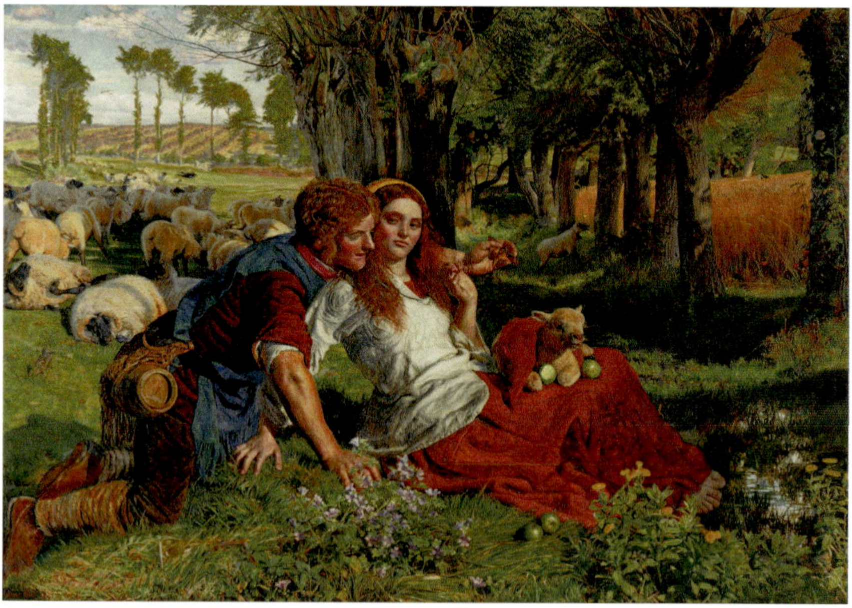

Figure 4.7 William Holman Hunt, *The Hireling Shepherd*, 1851–1852.

Another characteristic of the Pre-Raphaelites relates to their very definition: to show things "as they really are", before they were ruined by Raphael's academic rules of painting. The Pre-Raphaelites believed in a naïve ideology of a "natural" way to paint. The most salient aspect of these paintings is their flatness, which differs from the perspective representation that creates the illusion of three-dimensional space. It is as if these paintings are not trying to trace a realistic reality but a reality constructed as a relief. This is also true of the painted figures, which are puppet-like in the sense that they lack the dimension of depth we usually ascribe to the concept of "subject". The Pre-Raphaelite definition is, in these senses, literal, since they abandon Renaissance perspective and prefer the space that is typical of medieval paintings.[55]

The case of the Pre-Raphaelites, then, exposes the paradoxical aspect of the master narrative of the history of art since this movement is alternately perceived as either groundbreaking avant-garde or decadent kitsch. As stated, the term narrative does not allow for the description of synchronic states or states of internal contradiction. Despite the pretense of narrative to offer the semblance of a "realistic" chain of events, it is a phantasmatic product with an imaginary relation to the object. The Pre-Raphaelites, in this sense, are seen, on the one hand, as naïve, and, on the other hand, the use they make of medieval painterly conventions of representation to return to the "real painting" before Raphael is what makes this painterly style seen as kitsch, as an artificial way of representation. The history of art that alternately accepts and rejects them demonstrates the phantasmatic aspect of narrative since it turns to contradictory models so as to explain the Pre-Raphaelite phenomenon. Thus, the Pre-Raphaelite painting is understood, at a certain historical period, as avant-garde, and in another, as kitsch and outdated, and each reception fixes the Pre-Raphaelites in a master narrative that illuminates only a single aspect of their art. In light of Žižek's interpretation of Hunt's paintings, I would like to interpret the Pre-Raphaelite image as a split image. This interpretation shows a form of painting that embodies within itself two opposites, two contradictory meanings – visuality as the manifestation of paradoxicality. According to Žižek, Hunt's paintings, like Bryson's analysis of Gereuze's paintings, transmit "two frequencies" or make possible "two readings", which are not compatible. Hunt's religious paintings are interpreted as saccharine paintings. However, something different emerges from them, according to which the saccharine relates to decay and disgust. Viewing these paintings as a split image can make it possible to understand them with their complexity and not through their changing reception, which illuminates only certain aspects of these paintings at a time. In this sense, the Pre-Raphaelites are not an exception in the history of art, but they offer a distinct demonstration of a characteristic that exists in different strengths across various painterly styles. The split image, then, does not only demonstrate a characteristic of the visual field but also makes it possible to think anew of the relation between painterly styles and the interpretive-theoretical models that are given to them.

When Lacan describes the split between the eye and the gaze as a split between sight that supposes Albertian perspective and another sight that is projected on the screen, he speaks of a flickering image in constant oscillation between two different modes of sight. I believe that the split image embodies a conception of painting that emerges from Lacan's debate on sight. Moreover, the split image sheds light on the relevance of the narratological principle and its manifestation in the visual field. The visual image is split between the narratological dimension that provides meaning and structure, and a surplus of the real, which marks the function of the visual as a veil to a real that cannot be made whole by a narrative.

In the following chapters, I will discuss two other main components that emerge from Žižek's debate on the veils of fantasy and that make it possible to think anew about the relation of painting to narrativity: the gaze and the positions of the subject.

Notes

1 Žižek, Slavoj. 1998. "The Seven Veils of Fantasy". In *Key Concepts of Lacanian Psychoanalysis*. Edited by Danny Nobus. London: Rebus Press, pp. 196–197.
2 Gombrich, Ernst. 1982 [1960]. *Art and Illusion: A Study in the Psychology of Pictorial Representation*. Oxford: Phaidon Press, p. 5.
3 Searle, John. 1980. "*Las Meninas* and the Paradoxes of Pictorial Representation". *Critical Inquiry* 6: 477–488.
4 Searle argues that the paradox in *Las Meninas* is rooted in the representational manner: the perspective presents itself as Albertian yet does not adhere to the laws of this perspective. Snyder refutes this claim by proving, through geometric drawings, that the painting does indeed adhere to the laws of traditional perspective. I will return to the argument between Searle and Snyder in the seventh chapter in the discussion of *Las Meninas's* perspective representation. (Snyder, 1985, pp. 539–572).
5 Snyder, Joel. 1985. "*Las Meninas* and the Mirror of the Prince". *Critical Inquiry* 11: 539–572, p. 566.
6 Bryson, Norman. 1983. *Word and Image: French Painting of the Ancien Regime*. Cambridge: Cambridge University Press; Bernheimer, Charles. 1989. "Manet's *Olympia*: The Figuration of Scandal". *Art and Literature. Poetics Today* 10: 253–277. We can find another example of an analysis that brings to the forefront the split image in the way Barth articulates the photography in Eisenstein's films (Barthes, Roland. 1977. *Image, Music, Text*. Trans. Stephen Heath. New York: Hill and Wang, pp. 52–68). Barth identifies three levels of meaning in the image: an informational level, a symbolic level and the level that he calls *the obtuse meaning*. This is an identification of a certain visual detail with a double sense, and the two senses cannot necessarily be reconciled.
7 Bryson, 1983, pp. 122–153.
8 The painting *The Girl weeping for her Dead Bird*, which was discussed in the second chapter, is one of Greuze's Girl paintings.
9 Bryson, 1983, p. 131.
10 Bryson, 1983, pp. 131–132.
11 Bryson, 1983, p. 138.
12 Bryson, 1983, pp. 146–147.
13 Bryson, 1983, p. 153.
14 Bryson, 1983, p. 135.

15 Bryson, 1983, p. 136.
16 Bryson, 1983, p. 137. It could be argued that by demonstrating the ambivalence of Grueze's images through a literary reference to Nabokov's protagonist, Bryson indicates that this ambivalence is also possible on the verbal level. However, the uniqueness of the split image lies in the fact that it enables two antagonistic narratives to reside together, and not just describe a complex or conflictual state.
17 Bernheimer, 1989, p. 274.
18 Bernheimer, 1989, p. 268.
19 Bernheimer, 1989, p. 269.
20 It seems that Bernheimer uses the term "fetish" in the sense that the subject is seen as a sexual object and not in the psychoanalytic sense of the word.
21 Bernheimer, 1989, p. 269.
22 It seems that Bernheimer relates to the sense of discomfort or anxiety the image arouses, again, not necessarily to the Freudian sense of the uncanny (*unheimlich*). I will elaborate on the Freudian concept of the uncanny in the fifth chapter.
23 Bernheimer, 1989, p. 273.
24 Bal, Mieke. 1990 "The Point of Narratology". *Narratology Revisited. Poetics Today* 9–10: 727–753; Bal, Mieke. 1991. *Reading Rembrandt: Beyond the Word-Image Opposition*. Cambridge: Cambridge University Press.
25 Bal, 1991, pp. 19–22.
26 Bal, 1991, p. 20.
27 Bal, 1991, p. 21.
28 Bal, 1991, p. 60–93.
29 Bal, 1991, p. 72.
30 Bal, 1991, pp. 72–74.
31 Bal, 1990.
32 Bal, 1990, p. 746.
33 Bal, 1990, p. 746.
34 Bal, 1990, pp. 748–749.
35 See, for instance, the different interpretations given to the way in which Lacan speaks about looking at a painting: Stephen Melville's distinction between recognition and acknowledgment (Melville, Stephen, 1996. "Division of the Gaze, or, Remarks on the Color and Tenor of Contemporary 'Theory'". In *Vision in Context: Historical and Contemporary Perspectives on Sight*. Edited by Teresa Brennan and Martin Jay. London: Routledge, p. 108), or the way in which Stuart Schneiderman describes the difference between Looking and Seeing (Schneiderman, Stuart. 1988. "Art According to Lacan". *Newsletter of the Freudian Field* 2: 17–26.
36 The fifth chapter will discuss the question of time in psychoanalysis that is relevant to the concept of the gaze.
37 Soler, Colette. 1995. "The Subject and the Other (1,2)". In *Reading Seminar XI: Lacan's Four Fundamental Concepts of Psychoanalysis*. Edited by Richard Feldstein, Bruce Fink and Maire Jaanus. Albany: State University of New York Press, p. 52.
38 Žižek, Slavoj. 1992a. "In his Bold Gaze My Ruin Is Writ Large". In *Everything You Always Wanted to Know about Lacan but Were Afraid to Ask Hitchcock*. Edited by Slavoj Žižek. London and New York: Verso, pp. 235–240.
39 Lacan, Jacques. 1981 [1964–1965]. *The Four Fundamental Concepts of Psychoanalysis: The Seminar of Jacques Lacan, Book XI*. Trans. Alan Sheridan. New York and London: W.W. Norton and Company, p. 198.
40 Fink, Bruce. 1995. *The Lacanian Subject: Between Language and Jouissance*. Princeton: Princeton University Press, p. 5.
41 Evans, Dylan. 1996. *An Introductory Dictionary of Lacanian Psychoanalysis*. London and New York: Routledge, pp. 18–20.
42 Žižek, 1992a, p. 236.

43 Levi-Strauss, Claude. 1963 [1958]. *Structural Anthropology*. Trans. Claire Jacobson and Brooke Grundfest Schoepf. New York: Basic Books.
44 Levi-Strauss, 1963, p. 159.
45 Lacan demonstrates this through a description of a man who finds a stone covered in hieroglyphs, which he cannot read. However, it is clear to this man that these are signifiers that someone wrote, and that each signer is related to the other signifiers. Lacan XI, p. 199.
46 Žižek, 1992a, p. 239.
47 Žižek, 1992a, pp. 237–238.
48 I will relate to the second cinematic operation in my eighth chapter.
49 Žižek, 1992a, p. 237.
50 Lacan XI, pp. 96–97.
51 Quinet, Antonio. 1995. "The Gaze as an Object". In *Reading Seminar XI: Lacan's Four Fundamental Concepts of Psychoanalysis*. Edited by Richard Feldstein, Bruce Fink and Maire Jaanus. Albany: State University of New York Press, pp. 144–145.
52 Janson, Horst Woldemar. 1995. *History of Art*. London: Thames and Hudson, p. 712.
53 Žižek, Slavoj. 1994. *The Metastases of Enjoyment*. London and New York: Verso, p. 113.
54 National Museums and galleries on Merseyside, England.
55 Žižek, 1994, p. 114.

5 The gaze and the picture

Temporality, reflexivity and blindness as vision

In the first chapter, I argued that the exchange of gazes between the viewer and the visual object can help us rethink the relation between narrativity and painting. The sixth chapter will explore the position of the subject and outline the logic that makes it possible to think of such narrativity from a psychoanalytic perspective. However, beyond the question of the status of this exchange of gazes lies the question of what exactly the gaze that is relevant for looking at a picture is, what its characteristics are and what the relation between this gaze and the sight supposed by various theories of art is. This chapter offers a conceptualization of that gaze based on the discussions of Lacan, Bryson and Merleau-Ponty.

Throughout history, different theories of art have articulated, each in their own fashion, the relation between the subject and the painting as the object of his gaze, and from this relation a certain process of looking has been extrapolated. Despite the profound differences between these theories, they all share two basic premises. First, they assume that the painting spreads open before the eyes of the viewer and is completely accessible to his sight. This uninterrupted vision leads to an understanding of the painting: the deeper the vision, the deeper the understanding. It is a progressive and accumulative process in which the more details are revealed, the more light is shed on the understanding of the painting. The second assumption is that the viewer of a painting, through his observation, gives the painting its interpretation, in which the meaning of the painting is revealed, whether in the form of a narrative, an allegory or a formalist meaning. Meaning, in this paradigm, precedes the looking process and is revealed through it.

In his eleventh seminar, in his discussion of the split between the eye and the gaze, Lacan discusses sight and the dream, describing the dreamer as caught in a state in which the dream "shows" him various images and leads him through sight. As Lacan states:

> In the field of the dream… what characterizes the images is that *it shows*…. Look up some description of a dream, any one… and you will see that this *it shows* is well to the fore. So much is it to the fore, with the characteristics in which it is coordinated – namely the absence

DOI: 10.4324/9781003516446-6

> of horizon, the enclosure, of the which is contemplated in the waking state, and also, the character of emergence, of contrast, of stain, of its images, the intensification of their colors – that, in the final resort, our position in the dream is profoundly that of someone who does not see. The subject does not see where it is leading, he follows.[1]

If we understand Lacan literally, we might reach the conclusion that he is diminishing the importance of sight or at least points to the way in which dream sight does not relate to sight.[2] However, I believe that Lacan points toward a different manner of vision, one that is relevant to looking at a painting. This is a sight that includes its own point of blindness and considers what it veils and what it cannot see.

The third chapter raised a few claims relating to the gaze. First, I argued that looking is founded on a fixation on an object and that the structure of the object is not the condition of fixation. Rather, the object is grasped as a result of this fixation. I wish to relate this argument to a conception of time that is relevant to the gaze and its point of fixation. Later, I will show the time of the gaze that is relevant to painting via Bryson's conceptualizations of the two terms of the gaze and the glance and the tension between them.[3] Another aspect of the time of the gaze will be shown through Jean Baudrillard's and Bryson's discussions of *trompe l'oeil* (deception of the eye) paintings. The goal is to articulate the temporality of the gaze, which is essentially different from a temporality that is derived from the relation of looking offered by traditional theories of sight and art. Another claim related to the gaze that can be found in the discussion of fantasy is that the mode of looking is particular to the subject and constitutes the act of looking. This claim relates to the reflective aspects of the gaze, that is, to the manner in which sight is founded on the gaze that is returned to the viewer from the object. The third claim is that looking is essentially double-faced, since it is simultaneously founded on two registers: the imaginary, which deals with representing an object, and the real, which relates to an object that escapes representation. On the basis of this claim, I intend to offer a form of sight that contains within itself a point of blindness that constitutes the very condition of this sight.

These three aspects fashion a starting point for a discussion of the gaze that will move on three axes: the time of the gaze, reflexivity and a blindness that is intertwined with vision. This is merely a methodological distinction while, in essence, these three aspects intertwine and intersect. These three aspects of the gaze will bring forth a conception of painting that undermines the suppositions I outlined above and makes it possible to think in a different way about the process of interpreting a painting, which is not necessarily accumulative and progressive.

The time of the gaze

The discussion of painting as fantasy showed that the act of looking presupposes a fixation on an object, whose structure is grasped as a result of that fixation and not as its condition, while the function of fantasy is to justify the fixation on the subject's particular object of desire.[4] This logic contains a particular temporal order in which the fixation, the lingering on the object, takes place first, and the fantasy, which explains the reason for the fixation on the object, takes place afterward. The supposition is that the act of looking begins with a fixation that is directed at an object, with no relation to its structure, and that the narrative structure is the result and explanation of this fixation. This supposition undermines canonical theories of narrativity, according to which narrative structure is supposed to be the source and cause of the fixation, not its result. That is, narrative theories postulate that the narrative structure upholds a necessary relation with a sequence of time since the appearance of any period of time is a fundamental condition for any narrative. A narrative, which is constructed from a sequence of events, opens with a causal event, which leads to a chain of events that, in turn, are connected through temporality and causality.[5] This fundamental conception has led theories dealing with the possibility of narrative in painting to suppose that in the process of looking at a painting, the viewer constructs a sort of temporal and causal sequence that adheres to a narrative structure based on the painted details. However, the unintentional fixation on the painting and the looking process that stems from this fixation presuppose a radically different conception of time from the temporal sequence which is seen as the necessary condition for a narrative structure.

Bryson's discussion of the gaze offers a conception of time that is relevant for painting, which does not presuppose a linear sequence. Bryson theorizes the concept of the glance, whose time perception is fragmented, unpredictable and arbitrary.

Another position that encapsulates an alternative temporality in relation to looking at a painting can be found in Baudrillard's and Bryson's arguments on *trompe-l'oeil*.[6] In his analysis of *trompe-l'oeil* paintings, Baudrillard points toward a temporality that is unique to this painterly phenomenon. Yet Baudrillard does not believe that we can extrapolate knowledge about painting in general from these paintings, since, as he states, the *trompe-l'oeil* does not fall under the category of a painterly genre but belongs to the field of metaphysics.[7] However, I would like to claim that the temporality that can be extrapolated from *trompe-l'oeil* is not an exception in the field of painting; it can also be found in paintings or segments of painting that do not fall under this painterly category. The current discussion, then, aims not at a perception of temporality that imposes itself on the visual field but at a kind of alternative perception of temporality that is relevant to this field and adheres to its logic.

What, then, is the time that is relevant to the gaze that characterizes looking at a picture? According to Lacan:

> That which in the identificatory dialectic of the signifier and the spoken will be projected forward as haste, is here [in the field of vision-E.B], on the contrary, the end, that which, at the outset of any new intelligence, will be called the moment of seeing.[8]

In other words, while in the act of speaking the movement between the signifiers is fast, in a picture it is a final and fixed moment. The moment of seeing is the transitional moment between signifiers; however, unlike speech, in which one moves to the next signifier, in painting the movement stops. Lacan then goes on to discuss his earlier conceptualizations of the perception of time:

> What I noticed there was a suture, the pseudo-identification, that exists between what I called the time of terminal arrest of the gesture and what, in another dialectic that I called the dialectic of identificatory haste, I put at the same time, namely, the moment of seeing.[9]

That is, the moment of seeing enfolds within itself the moment of stopping, the choice to stop the movement of haste and stare at a certain thing, for no apparent reason. The second moment of seeing is the glance of identification, in which I refer to what I see.

The fixation of the gaze and the past in the future

In the case of the Wolf Man, one of Freud's famous patients, the patient tells Freud of a nightmare from his early childhood. The terrifying scene takes place when "suddenly the window opened of its own accord" and he confronts a scene of wolves sitting on a tree looking at him with rapt attention.[10] In his dream analysis, Freud reaches the conclusion that the dream consists of a few transpositions: the window does not open on its own accord. What opens are the eyes of the dreamer, and the concentrated gaze attributed to the wolves is the gaze of the dreamer himself, looking at them with rapt attention.[11] Freud connects these two transpositions to a repetition of a scene from the Wolf Man's early childhood. In this scene, he is an infant sleeping in his parents' bedroom. All of a sudden, he wakes from his sleep and witnesses his parents in the act of copulation. The sight remains hidden in his unconscious and resurfaces afterward in his complex relations hip with his father and the fear of castration, embodied in the dream. The moment the look is arrested is the moment of encounter between the gaze, the object and the phantasm. This is the moment the subject sees his own gaze returned to him through the wolves, who are supposedly looking at him. The wolves staring at him fashion a phantasmatic image that substitutes for the sight of his parents engaged in the sexual act – an event that carries with it a portion of anxiety. In a certain sense, we could say that the sight of the wolves staring at him constitutes the impossible sight of his own gaze seeing his parents. The subject does not have access to the real event but only through the phantasm of the wolves on the tree. In other words, sight is a fixation on a certain detail, which constitutes a link between the object of the gaze and something of the real that returns to the subject, while optical vision fashions the cover story for the unconsciously repressed event or object. I argue that the fixation on the object, the staring eyes that do not yet know what they see and the narrative that emerges as a result of this act of looking constitute essential characteristics of every act of looking at a picture. The description of the Wolf Man's gaze coming to a halt is structurally similar to the manner in which the subject pauses on a detail in the picture, while the overall meaning of it, be it in narrative or another form, is a later construction that is designed to give sense to this fixation.

In this manner, looking at a painting relates to Žižek's analysis of Daniel C. Dennett's discussion of the genesis of consciousness and its relation to Lacan's conceptualization of the phantasm.[12] Žižek explains how, according to Dennett, standardized thinking assumes that there exist two processes of understanding. One deals with direct experience and the other with the articulation and understanding of that experience. This is a kind of Cartesian theatre, in which consciousness interprets and organizes the things that appear before it. According to Dennett, the process is, in many ways, the opposite. Dennett gives an example of Bertrand Russell's love letter to Lady Ottoline, in which he writes that the moment he declared his love to her, he realized that he was indeed in love.[13] That is, unlike the assumption that the experience comes first, and the verbal articulation comes later, the order here is reversed. A word or a sentence imposes itself on us and hence fashions a cover of a narrative order for our confused experience. There is no prior existence of a "deep consciousness" that is expressed in the sentence; rather, the sentence itself is what organizes our experience into a "deeper consciousness".[14] In other words, while falling in love is usually described as a gradual process that is first formed and then verbally articulated, here the order is reversed: the verbal articulation conditions reality. In a certain sense, the words do force themselves on us, the way the words are uttered "on their own" is isomorphic with the unintentional fixation of the gaze on the image. This approach connects to Lacan's claim that the dreamer does not see but is led by his dream. The image in the dream, in the sense that it is the thing that leads the dreamer, is homologous to the words that force themselves on him. In both cases, the signifier receives its unconscious value in a manner that asserts itself on the subject.

The time of the gaze relates then to a reversed order of time, which Lacan conceptualizes through the concept of the "past in the future" (*future antérieur* or future perfect in English), a grammatical tense that can be applied to looking at a painting. This notion of time allows us to understand various interpretative models that are given to a painting, a product that retroactively explains the image, and not a means to decipher it. Moreover, the time of the gaze is the inversion of Lessing's fruitful moment, in the sense that it is devoid of duration or sequence. Unlike Lessing, who conceptualized painting as a fruitful moment that includes hints of what took place before and what will take place after, the time of the gaze presupposes an empty conception of time. The meaning of the image is not constructed through deductions and deciphering from which we might construct a sequence of events; rather, it is the image is used as the reason for the construction of the sequence of events.

Bryson's gaze and glance

Another reference to a notion of time relevant to looking at a painting can be found in Bryson's distinction between the two kinds of gazes that exist in painting – the "gaze" and the "glance". The gaze is the official gaze of the viewer, who examines the field of vision from a distance without any involvement with this field. This is a gaze that "belonged to the protocols of the court".[15] The glance, on the other hand, is "furtive or sideways look whose attention is always elsewhere...which is capable of carrying unofficial...messages of hostility, collusion, rebellion, and lust".[16]

Bryson links the two kinds of gazes and the ways in which they operate to different traditions of painting. He claims that Western painting involves different levels of denial. Each thin layer of oil color hides the previous one, every brushstroke erases its tracks. The time of producing the painting is completely expelled from the final result. Hence,

> the logic of the gaze is therefore subject to two great laws: the body (of the painter, of the viewer) is reduced to a single point, the *macula* of the retinal surface; and the moment of the gaze (for the painter, for the viewer) is placed outside duration.[17]

That is, while in Chinese painting the movement of the painter's body remains visible through the brushstrokes, in Western painting the brush strokes do not declare themselves in the final product, so that the physical presence of the painter, and hence the viewer as well, is denied. According to the second law, the moment of the gaze of the painter as the creator of the painting and the moment of the viewer's gaze are expelled from the sequence. The act of viewing is constructed as expelled from the dimension of time and space.[18] This kind of painting officially makes possible only the gaze. The glance operates here in a subversive manner that undermines the gaze. However, as Bryson later shows, the glance and the gaze are in a dialectical relationship, and hence the gaze is instituted only by denying the glance, and vice versa.

Bryson, in fact, shows how the official gaze, which Western painting supposes, is an impossible gaze, one that does not take into account the viewer as a concrete, particular subject, but assumes an abstract vision of a device or nonhuman entity. Bryson shows this by articulating the Albertian perspective, which failed to reduce the subject to a point on the retina and to reconstruct his location.[19]

Unlike the gaze, which is intertwined with denial and the cancellation of the body, and with expelling the dimensions of time and space, the glance, according to Bryson, takes place when the eye crosses over the canvas in a fragmented and unpredictable manner. The trajectory of the glance is hence different from the trajectory of the gaze, which is systematic, organized and consistent. Through its fragmented trajectory, the glance constructs an alternative conceptual version of the compositional structure, which is radically different from the version of the official gaze. The construction of the alternative version does not take place in the act of the gaze, but rather, before and after this act. While the gaze assumes a complete, simultaneous and systematized perception of the painting, the glance assumes a time that is always too early or too late: it is the contingent look that crosses the painting, receives fragmented information and retroactively organizes it. This swift glance sees the things that can only be perceived after the eye moves onward and receives new fragmented information.[20]

Bryson describes the function of the glance in Western painting as an act that undermines the official activity of the gaze. He describes the trajectory of the glance over the canvas as a series of offhanded looks. It is not that the glance receives fragmented information and turns it into a coherent semantic structure; rather, the glance works in such a manner that segments of meaning are erected, shattered and then re-erected. The fragments of information that are transmitted to the viewer through the glance do not necessarily accumulate but can bring about the construction of an inherently divided and ambiguous semantic structure.

The temporality of the gaze in *trompe l'oeil* paintings

Further references to the question of the relation between time and seeing can be found in different debates on *trompe l'oeil* paintings, for instance, in Baudrillard's and Bryson's debates. Baudrillard makes use of these paintings to present his claim that the perception of reality is fashioned through its representations. *Trompe l'oeil* paintings, with their excess visibility, challenge traditional manners of representation. Thus, they undermine the relationship between representation and reality. And this is where Baudrillard locates the effect they have on the viewer. *Trompe l'oeil,* he claims, "is not derived from painting but from metaphysics".[21] This is not a painting since there is no theme, narrative or characters. Space is vertical; there is no sense of gravity. That is to say, these paintings manifest a turning away from the pictorial discourse with its traditional values such as depth and perspective.[22] The conception of space in these paintings is also inverted: instead of a vanishing point that is internal to the painting, which draws the viewer in, the image here casts itself in the reverse direction toward the viewer's face.

The relation between *trompe l'oeil* paintings and the perception of time can be gleaned from the way Baudrillard describes the viewer's sense of *déja vu* when looking at these paintings. As Baudrillard states, the viewer is eventually left with a sense of a negated chronology. It is as if the objects have already existed: time was already present, and the space had already existed. The only thing that is left is anachrony, a complex form of time and space.[23] Bryson adds that these are objects that are devoid of human presence, and hence, this is a dimension of a time of the gaze that has been subtracted or was never present in the first place.[24] It seems that Baudrillard wishes to demonstrate how these paintings do not represent but rather expose the prevailing

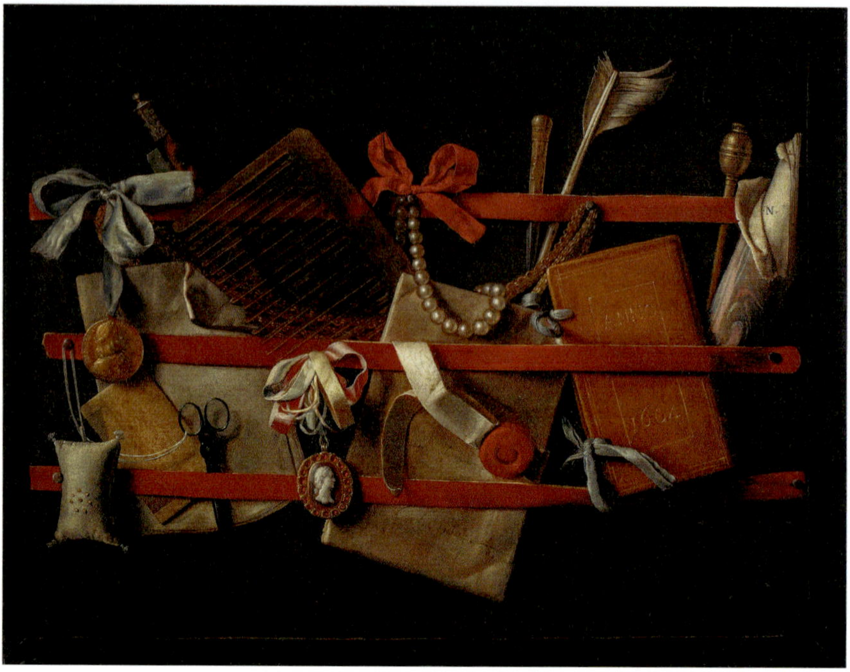

Figure 5.1 Samuel van Hoogstraten, *Trompe-l'oeil Still Life*, 1664.

belief that painting represents, that it is a transparent object to a reality that supposedly lies beyond it. *Trompe l'oeil* paintings are the exact opposite: they are opaque, an image that does not represent.[25] The manner in which these paintings "show visibility", which constitutes reality for us makes it possible to think of them as existing in a twilight zone, one that supposedly lies beyond Kantian intuitions, beyond the perception of human time. According to Baudrillard, if these pictures demonstrate any fantastic sight, the wonder does not stem from excess realism but from the fact that it seems like a real object, from the way these paintings expose simulacrum.[26]

According to Baudrillard, *trompe l'oeil* paintings present us with a time that is unique to these paintings, a negative temporality that is inherently inhuman. Unlike paintings that present the concept of time through representation, here it is an essentially different temporality.

Despite the immense difference between the conventional interpretations of these paintings and Baudrillard's reading of them, both readings point to a sense of time that is not compatible with the image. It seems that *trompe l'oeil* presents us with an aspect of seeing that might also exist in other paintings, only that in their case, because of the isolation of this aspect, it can be more clearly articulated. That is, in some paintings, a certain pictorial element may cause the viewer the same corporeal effect typical of *trompe-l'oeil* paintings, stemming from the momentary inability to differentiate between seeing

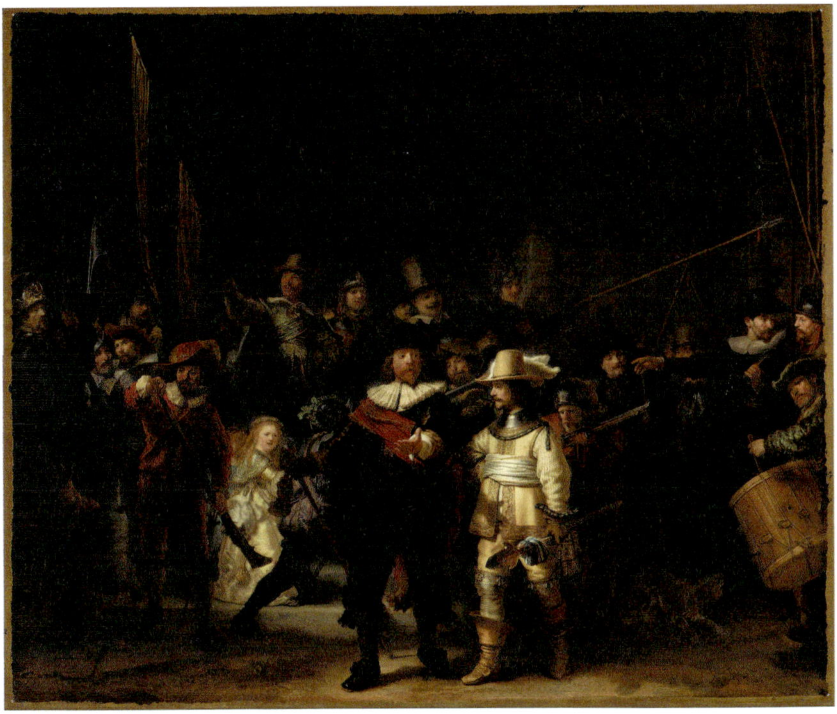

Figure 5.2 Rembrandt van Rijn, *The Night Watch (The Company of Captain Frans Banning Cocq and Lieutenant Willem van Ruytenburch)*, 1642.

a painting and seeing reality, as representation reaches such an extreme saturation that it eliminates itself.

An example of this can be found in Merleau-Ponty's analysis of the play of light and shade on the hand of the captain in Rembrandt's *The Night Watch*.[27] Merleau-Ponty claims that the hand

> pointing towards us is truly there only when we see that its shadow on the captain's body presents it simultaneously in profile. The spatiality of the captain lies at the intersection of the two perspectives which are incompossible and yet together.[28]

He sees in this painting a case in which a disturbance in vision brings about a vision that is closer to human sight. The way in which the hand of the captain appears is similar, in many ways, to the same discordance between time and image that takes place in *trompe l'oeil* paintings. The shadow, which appears on the male figure to the right of the captain, appears suddenly after we see the figure of the captain. That is, this is not a hidden pictorial detail that reveals itself to the viewer after a close observation. This is a pictorial detail that it is possible not to see at all, but when one does notice it, it comes as a surprise, not as an advanced stage of continuous observation, but a sudden appearance that is disconnected from the sequence. Moreover, this pictorial detail does not "add information" for the viewer, but is experienced differently, as if revealing to the viewer something about the very nature of human sight.

Prevailing narratological theories conceive of narrative as a temporal sequence, which the subject reconstructs in relation to an object with which that sequence is compatible. Thus, the subject is the founder of the narrative. However, the temporality of the gaze undermines this concept. It is fashioned from many different and fragmented temporal sequences, which operate simultaneously, and which also include the cutting and breaking of this sequence. These temporal sequences do not follow a chronological or accumulative order, and there is no necessary compatibility between the time of the gaze and the image. This is a sequence that is not dictated by the subject but one that dictates the perception of the subject. This distinction introduces another central aspect of the gaze, that is, its reflexivity, or the returning of the gaze toward the viewer.

Reflexivity

One of the most famous dream descriptions in Freud's *The Interpretation of Dreams* is the dream of the burning child, the dream of the father who has lost his son.[29] The father had cared for his feverish child for many days and nights, until his son passed away. The night after his son's death, the father went to sleep in the adjacent room, leaving the door open so that he could see into the room of his dead son. Tall candles were placed around the son's bed, and an old man was given the task of watching over the child's bed; he sat by the bed and prayed. As Freud writes

> After a few hours of sleep, the father had a dream that *his child was standing beside his bed, caught him by the arm and whispered to him reproachfully: 'Father, don't you see I'm burning?'* He woke up, noticed a bright glare of light from the next room, hurried into it and found that the old watchman had dropped off to sleep and that the wrappings and one of the arms of his beloved child's dead body had been burned by a lighted candle that had fallen on them.[30]

The dream presents a complex exchange of gazes: the look of the dead child, who sees and calls for the attention of his living father, who does not see and reproaches himself that his blindness has brought about the son's demise. Another gaze that is present in the scene is that of the guard, who should have seen but, having fallen asleep, has failed in his role along with it. As I stated earlier, a complex exchange of gazes also takes place in the dream of the Wolf Man, in which the wolves stare at the child after his bedroom window opens of its own accord. Freud, as stated, interprets the dream as a reversal;

that is, it is not the window that opens, but the eyes, and the penetrating gaze is not the gaze of the wolves but of the dreaming child.

These two dreams are mentioned at the beginning of Lacan's discussion on sight and the split between the eye and the gaze.[31] Lacan turns to the dream of the burning child since it demonstrates the presence of the gaze in an encounter with an impossible object that cannot be confronted directly. The two dreams include an inversion of roles between seeing and being seen. Another distinction, which constitutes, to a certain degree, a product of the exchange of roles between seeing and seen, is the significance of the blind spot in the process of seeing. After describing the two dreams, Lacan turns to an intensive debate with Merleau-Ponty's conception of visibility, and the philosophical history of the conceptual connection between seeing and being seen. This self-vision will return later in Bryson's discussion of visuality.

I will turn to reflexive vision to expose another aspect of the gaze which will later connect to the positions of the subject. I find this aspect significant because it makes it possible to describe a complex visuality that undermines the dichotomous distinction between inside and outside, the seer and the seen. This is because reflexivity does not imply a passive mirror reflection. The question that will be raised is how this visual aspect makes the foundation of meaning in painting possible and what its position is in relation to visual narrative.[32]

Reflexive vision constitutes another characteristic of the visual medium. It seems that Lacan agrees with Merleau-Ponty's analysis of this characteristic; however, this characteristic also underscores an essential difference between them. According to Merleau-Ponty, reflexive vision is actually an inverted vision, and the difference between the two conceptions of inversion/reflexivity includes within itself a critical difference between the Lacanian gaze and Merleau-Ponty's conception of visuality. An analysis of Merleau-Ponty's position in conjunction with Lacan's criticism will make it possible to articulate the Lacanian position regarding vision. Merleau-Ponty and Lacan point toward the same phenomena of vision. However, this is where the similarity between their positions ends, since each one of them understands these phenomena in an essentially different manner.[33]

Merleau-Ponty's reversibility

To closely examine Merleau-Ponty's complex perception of vision, which is rooted in phenomenology, we need to understand his conceptualization of the flesh (*chair*). Merleau-Ponty distinguishes between the human body and an entity that is not a distinct subjective being but is made of an intertwined object-subject relation. He describes flesh through negation and claims that it "is not matter. It is the coiling over of the visible upon the seeing body, which is attested in particular when the body sees itself, touches itself seeing and touching the things".[34] The flesh, claims Merleau-Ponty, is, on the one hand, neither a fact nor a sum of facts; yet, on the other hand, it does refer to location and temporality.[35]

According to Merleau-Ponty's theorization of the visible, the relation between the flesh and the object of its vision is founded on a relation of visibility that makes their reversibility possible. Unlike reflexivity in vision, which usually pre supposes a passive mirror reflection of the seer toward the object of his vision, this reversibility is not a mere return to its origin but an active, two-way process. The inversion of the returning gaze to me does not suppose its reflection but constitutes an active sight that turns to me from within the object of my vision.

This reversibility stems from Merleau-Ponty's radical conception of vision. According to this conception, vision is not an asset that belongs solely to the subject: the subject does not simply see the world, but the world shows itself.[36] In other words, vision is not the subject's active optical physiognomic action; rather, it exists in the world and predates the subject's vision. The seeing subject is a product of his encounter with visibility. Merleau-Ponty explains this through a metaphor of two mirrors facing each other, onto which different images are projected. The projected images do not belong to either of the mirrors, since the sight on each is comprised of an amalgamation with the opposite mirror. Thus, real sight is that of the two mirrors together, more than that of each separately.[37]

The relation between body and world is, hence, not a dualistic relation of inside and outside, but an uncertain relation of the internal and external, like a mobius strip.[38] Unlike the Cartesian doctrine, in which the subject looks at and sees a world that is external to him, Merleau-Ponty undermines this dichotomy and claims that visibility is immanent in everything, thus he blurs the boundaries between the seeing subject and the world. The flesh is not defined by abstract empirical means, but by its own reversibility. Reversibility relates to the double status of the subject's body both as the one who perceives and as the object of perception. As one hand touches another, it also becomes the object that is touched. The relations between the two touching hands, simultaneously touching and sensing touch, are isomorphic to the relations of sight. Vision is conditioned by the fact that the one who sees is also himself seen. Since vision can be inverted by its very definition, the seer cannot hold vision unless he also belongs to it, constituting a part of it. The touching hands need to move to the other side and be touched or seen so that they can sense the touch from the inside.[39]

The subversion of the external-internal relations is also manifested in the process of looking at a painting, which Merleau-Ponty describes. Thus, the painting fashions an internal parallelism within the viewer and awakens within him a sensual formula of his presence, not in the sense of a faded copy or an optical illusion. Looking at a painting is not like looking at an object; rather, the gaze that wanders on the surface of the painting looks in accordance with the painting or sees with it. The painter projects things that are visible within himself, which leads to an exchange of roles between seer and seen. This exchange of roles is manifested in a plethora of Dutch paintings in which there is a mirror, and it explains why so many artists painted themselves as painting.[40]

The relation between Lacan's conceptualization of vision and Merleau-Ponty's conceptualization is complex. It appears that there are many meeting points within the extraordinary conceptualization of vision that each of them proposes. They both make use of similar metaphors, connect vision to narcissism and describe a state of affairs in which the limit between seer and seen is blurred. However, the vision that Lacan proposes and its function for the subject differ vastly from Merleau-Ponty's conception of vision. Lacan makes use of optical models and vision to elucidate subjectivity, whereas for Merleau-Ponty, vision itself has a crucial role.

Both Merleau-Ponty and Lacan discuss the gaze that returns to the seer; they both point toward a relation of vision, of mutual looking, within which there is no separation between the active seer and the passive seen. As Lacan states, the manner in which Merleau-Ponty uses the metaphor of a glove turned inside out that sees itself seeing itself is analogous to the external-internal structure of the gaze. That is, the way Merleau-Ponty describes visibility in the world, in which both the seer and the object of his vision exist, has an affinity with the Lacanian gaze that subverts the dualism of a seer who is separated from the object of his vision. However, despite these similarities, Lacan's conception of vision is essentially different from that of Merleau-Ponty. As Lacan goes on to state, the split that he explores, which exists between the eye and the gaze, is not related to the limitations of vision in the phenomenological sense but embodies the drive in the field of vision.[41] While the eye represents the *cogito*, the subject of consciousness and knowledge, the gaze emerges from the side of the unconscious subject and desire.[42] The gaze is not a concrete look of another being. It is a gaze the subject attributes to the desire of an Other that fashions him as a subject.

The return of the gaze that Merleau-Ponty describes stems, as stated, from the phenomenological tradition to which he belongs. His description of vision demonstrates aspects of vision that elude verbal articulation and can be understood only subjectively and intuitively. Moreover, Merleau-Ponty's gaze is, as Lacan claims, a "happy encounter" between the subject and the object of his vision,[43] which is articulated in positivistic expressions. In these two points, Lacan differs immensely from Merleau-Ponty.

As stated above, Lacan and Merleau-Ponty's common starting point is the reflexivity of vision and the mutual vision that they propose, according to which the gaze is returned to the viewer. However, it is in this very common ground that we may locate the crucial difference between them, in the distance between reflexivity and reversibility or in the manner in which each of them conceives of the gaze returning to the viewer from within the picture. The reversibility Merleau-Ponty refers to, unlike reflexivity, is not the passive reflection of the viewer who sees himself reflected but refers to a two-way sight that enfolds within itself the entire process of the inverted sight that is returned to me as an active act. While they both argue against a predictable, passive reflection, and both assume a dependent relation of the seer in being seen, the return of the gaze for each of them is radically different.

For Merleau-Ponty, the gaze returns from within the painting, since the gaze is not owned by the subject but is the property of a vision that is immanent in everything. For Lacan, on the other hand, the gaze that returns to the viewer from within the painting, from an unexpected place in it, stems from the subject's structural split. As Lacan states:

> At the scopic level, we are no longer at the level of demand but of desire, of the desire of the Other....Generally speaking, the relation between the gaze and what one wishes to see involves a lure. The subject is presented as other than he is, and what one shows him is not what he wishes to see. It is in this way that the eye may function as *objet a*, that is to say, at the level of the lack.[44]

Lacan separates the eye and the gaze. The gaze is the object of the act of seeing, or the object of the scopic drive. The gaze is not positioned on the side of the subject but is the gaze of the Other. If, for Jean-Paul Sartre, the gaze constitutes an action that is a product of intersubjective relations that exist between a subject and a concrete other,[45] the Lacanian gaze is the lacking object of the split subject. As Lacan states, the gaze is not a visible gaze but a gaze that the subject imagines in the field of the Other.[46] The subject grasps the gaze as the cause of the desire of the Other. And this is why Lacan claims that the desire of the subject is the desire of the Other. That is, according to Lacan, the gaze is the cause of the Other's desire, which remains unattainable for the subject. While Merleau-Ponty and Sartre, albeit in different ways, presuppose a vision in which there are mutual relations between "seeing the other" and "being seen by him", Lacan presupposes a paradoxical relation between the eye and the gaze. The eye is of the subject, while the gaze is on the side of the object, and the two are not congruent, since "you never look at me from the place from which I see you".[47] When the subject looks at an object, the object returns his gaze, but from a point which the subject cannot see. The split between the eye and the gaze is the split of the subject himself, which is expressed in the field of vision.[48]

If, according to Merleau-Ponty, the gaze is reversible and returns to me in the same way in which it came out of me, then for Lacan, the gaze is fashioned from a different reflection. This is a reflection that relates to its blind spot, which is not a result of excess visibility but of the limitations of the seeing subject. While reversibility supposes the return of an active gaze in the same manner as its active source, the return of the gaze in the Lacanian discussion supposes an asymmetry, that is, the gaze that returns to me is not isomorphic or similar to its source. The gaze returns to the viewer, since the viewer sees in the object something of himself. The object of the gaze is not neutral, because the moment the subject chooses to look at it, something in the object looks back at him. Thus, in everything I look at, I necessarily am also reflected. However, this is not a harmonious, complete subject but a split subject, and the gaze that returns will always exist as what Lacan calls a "strange contingency".[49]

We may ask, then, how this reflexivity is relevant to the processes of looking at a painting? In what sense does the gaze that returns from the painting establish the act of looking, the looking subject and the pictorial object? The Lacanian position knots the three elements together and postulates that the relations of looking are particular and unpredictable. Looking at a picture cannot be exhausted by thinking of representations. Hence, iconological, allegorical or formalist interpretation, which is *a priori* and set, cannot fully describe them.

Blindness as sight

Martin Jay argues that Lacan follows Freud's footsteps since both are representatives of a position that dethrones the central place of vision. Jay turns to Lacan's use of the term "scotoma". According to Lacan, when one is about to see something that is too threatening, the blind spot will appear in place of the object of anxiety. Jay makes use of this argument to support his claim on the relation between psychoanalysis and an anti-ocular position.[50]

I would like to argue that, even if we assume that the Lacanian debate on vision and the gaze is meant to demonstrate the relation between the subject and the object of the drive, we can extrapolate from it a conception according to which the blindness involved in vision is the signifier that takes the place of the object that cannot be represented. That is, this discussion points toward a structure of vision that is intertwined with blindness and disturbances of vision. Thus, the blind spots of this vision constitute an inseparable part of it. The question, then, is not to what extent Lacan places vision at the center or dethrones it from its hegemonic status, but whether we may understand here the ambivalent nature of vision and the blindness that it enfolds as an immanent part of it. I would like to argue that the blind spot is not necessarily anti-vision, but we may think through it regarding the characteristics of human sight and its relevance to painting. Here as well, I will draw on Lacan, Bryson and Merleau-Ponty.

Vision, according to Merleau-Ponty, includes within itself, by its very nature, a string of internal contradictions, which also makes it possible. The links between the optic nerves and parts of the brain are crossed in the shape of an X. The diagonal connection between each eye and the opposite part of the brain is the chiasm. This chiasm is an essential structure for the physiology of sight and constitutes a foundational means of seeing a stereoscopic image. Merleau-Ponty makes use of these biological facts to support his exploration of sensory vision. As Cathryn Vasseleu explains: "The chiasm is flesh in its intertwining, reversibility and its divergence or non-coincidence with itself".[51] The chiasm causes a certain incongruity, and the lack opened up by this incongruity has a visual value. Hence, the chiasm makes it possible for an inner and sensual meaning to emerge, and this meaning, paradoxically, is both present and absent in sight. That is, the chiasm is a disturbance in vision that makes vision possible, while also negating it or constituting a kind of disturbance in vision through which we may see something further. Moreover, according to Merleau-Ponty, a vision that is free of disturbance is completely hypothetical, since, due to the character and structure of sight, any vision is necessarily disturbed.

Another disturbance in vision that makes vision possible, like the chiastic incongruity, is the constant movement of the body.[52] Unlike the movement that blurs vision, the movement of the seeing body does not constitute a disturbance; on the contrary, it constitutes a condition for sight. The way in which these disturbances make sight possible can be found in Merleau-Ponty's example of looking at the bottom of the pool through the water:

> When through the water's thickness I see the tiled bottom of the pool, I do not see it *despite* the water and the reflections; I see it through them and because of them. If there were no distortions, no ripples of sunlight, if it were without that flesh that I saw the geometry of the tiles, then I would cease to see it *as* it is and where it is.[53]

Merleau-Ponty turns to Rembrandt's *Night Watch*, as a pictorial example that demonstrates vision. Merleau-Ponty, as stated, refers to the way in which the pointing hand of the captain is painted. He claims that the hand that points toward us only exists when it is seen in profile through the shadow it casts on the body of the figure standing next to the captain. The hand painted in perspective casts a shadow that is different from it, and this gap between the two different yet simultaneous perspectives is what creates the sense of depth in the painting, since any seeing human being has seen a similar situation, in which a play of shadows makes it possible to see an object in space. This is a visibility that operates through the shadows cast upon it, and sight is achieved through veiling or disturbances.[54]

This description is similar, to an extent, to Lacan's story of the sardine can. In his discussion of vision in his eleventh seminar, Lacan recounts a story from his youth, when he spent time with fishermen in Brittany. These were hardworking fishermen who risked their lives, and among them was a young man named Petit-Jean:

> One day, then, as we were waiting for the moment to pull in the nets.... Petit-Jean pointed out to me something floating on the surface of the waves. It was a small can, a sardine can. It floated there in the sun, a witness to the canning industry, which we, in fact, were supposed to supply. It glittered in the sun, And Petit-Jean said to me – *You see that can? Do you see it? Well it doesn't see you!* He found this incident highly amusing – I less so...If what Petit-Jean said to me, namely, that the can did not see me, had any meaning, it was because in a sense, it was looking at me all the same.[55]

The sardine can glitters in a manner that demonstrates the split between the gaze and the eye. The return of the light hides the can itself, even though the flash of light is only possible because of its presence. The can and the flash of light hold a paradoxical relation of making possible through disturbance and vice versa. The can makes the gleam of light possible, and the gleam of light does not allow one to see the can as a can. A similar relationship between sight and blindness, although to a lesser degree, exists in Merleau-Ponty's description of the hand of the captain in *The Night Watch*.

As stated, like the reflective/reversible relations of vision, here, too, Lacan and Merleau-Ponty seem to be taking seemingly parallel, yet essentially different, paths. Vision that enfolds its disturbances, as Merleau-Ponty articulates it, is a vision whose progress is not linear. Trying to sharpen this vision would not necessarily yield a better result. However, like adjusting the focus in a slide projector, we need to find the optimal relation between vision and blindness to make sight possible.

The vision Lacan proposes involves its own blind spot. This supposition can also be demonstrated in Lacan's seminar on *The Purloined Letter*. Although this text does not ostensibly deal with vision and visibility, the conception of vision is very much present there.[56] The seminar analyzes Edgar Allan Poe's short story "The Purloined Letter". In the story, the Prefect of the Parisian police tries to locate a letter with sensitive and secret content, which was stolen from a member of the royal family by a minister. The Prefect was given the task of returning the letter to its owner, without the minister having sensed anything. The police search every corner of the minister's quarters, and yet find nothing. While trying to help the Prefect, Detective Dupin finds the letter. He goes into the Minister's quarters and extracts the purloined letter, which, during the entire time, was hanging on a somewhat conspicuous place on the wall of the Minister's quarters.[57] The plot unfolds various versions of this story, as described by different narrators, and this is, in many ways, also the subject of the seminar that analyzes Poe's story. Lacan demonstrates through the story how the subject is duped by the signifier, which is the letter, and shows, through the various versions of the story, the different positions of the subject with the same signifier.[58] As stated, this seminar does not explicitly deal with vision but with language in its intersubjective aspects and with questions relating to the crux of the analytic situation. Nonetheless, problems of vision and visibility can be explicitly and tacitly found in the story and the seminar. The purloined letter constitutes, in actuality, a painting: Nothing of its content is revealed; however, its shape, folds, size and color are given in great detail. The letter is identified through these details, and through them it is hidden and discovered anew. It is not expelled from the field of vision when it is hidden; on the contrary, it remains present yet remains concealed by its very exposure. This concealment is similar to the zoological examples Lacan brings when he discusses camouflage, for instance, the tiny animal that sits on the back of a crab and looks like a part of it, or the image of the giant eyes that appear on the wings of butterflies to protect them against their predators.[59]

The purloined letter demonstrates vision that is similar to the anamorphic skull in Holbein's painting of *The Ambassadors*. It is not expelled from the field of vision, but it becomes inaccessible to vision, placed on another register in such a way that seeing it requires a different mode of looking after the methodical search fails. Another practice of looking needs to be employed to notice that the old piece of paper is the stolen letter, which was present before the eyes of the seekers throughout their thorough searches.

The purloined letter and the way in which it escapes vision also relate to Bryson's debate on the pictorial phenomenon of *trompe l'oeil,* which I discussed in relation to the time of the gaze. In these paintings, Bryson claims, objects that are devoid of human attention appear. By erasing human attention, these objects reveal their autonomy: "It is as though it is the objects that make the world, and the unconscious force stored in their outwardly humble forms – not their human users".[60] And here also lies the threatening dimension of the *trompe l'oeil*: In their hyper-realism, these paintings mimic the sense of reality and parody it to the extent that they cast doubt on the place of the human subject in the world, and ask if such a place even exists for this subject.[61] Usually, states Bryson, painting controls the visual field via the authoritarian gaze that dominates the entire scene in favor of its human viewers. However, in the case of *trompe l'oeil,* it is as if this gaze was removed or was never present: what we see are the objects in and of themselves – not as they are with people around, but as they really are, left to their own devices. Bryson quotes Lacan, who claims that the visual experience is organized by the ego, claiming that "there is always an excess in vision over and beyond what the subject can master in sight".[62] *Trompe l'oeil* paintings are an example of such a case. Rather than obeying the authoritarian gaze, they escape it and forcefully occupy the visual field. They "look back" at the viewer, as "though there were no right by which human observation takes command of its surrounding world and imposes its own order upon it from a position of visual center".[63]

In *trompe l'oeil* paintings, representation reaches its saturation, its maximum possible point. Representation is so complete and extreme that it does not bring about visibility; on the contrary, it produces blindness. A similar principle is described in the seminar on *The Purloined Letter,* which demonstrates how the eye refuses to see the letter that is present in its field of vision. The *trompe l'oeil* paintings to which Bryson refers, which depict everyday objects, demonstrate Lacan's claim when he refers to the difference between Zeuxis deceiving birds and Parrhasios deceiving man. This is the story of the two Greek painters who competed to discover which one of them was the better painter. Zeuxis, according to the myth, painted grapes so convincingly that birds came to peck at his fresco. Later, Parrhasios invited Zeuxis to look at his painting, and Zeuxis tried to move the curtain to see the painting he believed was behind it, only to discover that the curtain itself was the painting. As Lacan claims, the birds who picked at Zeuxis's painting were tempted to what was a sign for them of grapes. These birds would not have pecked Caravaggio's grapes, which look like real grapes; they would only peck grapes that signal to them as real grapes. Man, on the contrary, is tempted by the screen and what is behind it.[64] The *trompe l'oeil* paintings expose this principle in reverse: The viewer believes that he encounters the object, only to find that he is standing before the representation.

Lacan's ultimate example of the relation between sight and blindness, that is, sight that encounters its own impossibility, can be found in his description of the gaze present in the expressions of anxiety, in his tenth seminar. The apex of anxiety is the moment Oedipus understands what he did and then plucks out his eyes. This is a prototypical case in which the subject is seen by his own eyes, which are dismembered yet continue to look at him. This is an excess and impossible sight. These eyes were the cause of his downfall, since, in his desire to know what happened, he eventually saw something that he could not bear.[65]

Notes

1 Lacan, Jacques. 1981 [1964–1965]. *The Four Fundamental Concepts of Psychoanalysis: The Seminar of Jacques Lacan, Book XI*. Trans. Alan Sheridan. New York and London: W.W. Norton and Company, p. 75.
2 Martin Jay reaches a similar conclusion and connects Lacan's position with a conception of crises in the central place of sight (Jay, Martin. 1997. "Lacan and the Crisis of Ocularcentrism". In *Image, Word and Self*. Edited by Maria Letizia Proietti. New York, Washington D.C., Baltimore: Peter Lang, pp. 169–198).
3 Bryson, Norman. 1983. *Vision and Painting: The Logic of the Gaze*. New Haven: Yale University Press.
4 Žižek, Slavoj. 1998. "The Seven Veils of Fantasy". In *Key Concepts of Lacanian Psychoanalysis*. Edited by Danny Nobus. London: Rebus Press, p. 191.
5 van Dijk, Teun. 1975. "Recalling and Summarizing Complex Discourse". University of Amsterdam. Mimeograph, p. 61.
6 Baudrillard, Jean. 1988. "The Trompe-L'Oeil". In *Calligram: Essays in New Art History from France*. Edited by Norman Bryson. Cambridge: Cambridge University Press; Bryson, Norman. 1990. *Looking at the Overlooked: Four Essays on Still Life Painting*. Cambridge: Harvard University Press.
7 Baudrillard, 1988, p. 53.
8 Lacan XI, p. 114.
9 Lacan XI, p. 117.
10 Freud, Sigmund. [1918]. "From the History of an Infantile Neurosis". *S.E.* 17: 7–122, p. 29.
11 Freud, [1918], p. 34.
12 Žižek, Slavoj. (ed.). 1998a. *Cogito and the Unconscious*. Durham and London: Duke University Press, p. 247. It is important to note that though the two processes seem to follow a similar logic, Denett's discussion, which is rooted in the field of cognitive science and processes of understanding and information organization, is essentially different from psychoanalytic thinking. As can be seen later in Žižek's discussion, while both cases presuppose the word as prior to the experience, the reason for its precedence is different in each field: while the starting point of cognitive science is in the subject's consciousness, the source of this precedence in psychoanalysis is rooted in its intrinsically anti-dualistic position.
13 Žižek, 1998a, p. 252.
14 Žižek, 1998a, p. 252.
15 Bryson, 1983, pp. 93–94.
16 Bryson, 1983, p. 94.
17 Bryson, 1983, p. 96.
18 Bryson, 1983, p. 96.
19 For a discussion on Bryson's conceptualization of perspective see Chapter 7.

20 Bryson, 1983, pp. 120–121.
21 Bryson, 1983, p. 53.
22 Bryson, 1983, p. 54.
23 Bryson, 1983, p. 55.
24 Bryson, 1990, p. 143.
25 Baudrillard, 1988, p. 54.
26 Baudrillard, 1988, p. 59.
27 Merleau-Ponty, Maurice. 1993 [1961]. "Eye and Mind". In *The Merleau-Ponty Aesthetic Reader: Philosophy and Painting*. Edited by Galen A. Johnson. Trans. Michael B. Smith. Evanston: Northwestern University Press.
28 Merleau-Ponty, 1993, p. 128.
29 Freud, Sigmund. 2001 [1900]. "The Psychology of the Dream-Processes". *S.E.* 5: 509–511.
30 Freud, 2001, p. 509.
31 Lacan XI, pp. 68–70.
32 Jean-Paul Sartre's discussion on the gaze also raises the idea of mutual constitution through gazes. Sartre connects the gaze of the other with the sense of shame he makes me feel. However, the Sartrean gaze is, to a large extent, intersubjective, while the reflexive gaze concerns only the observing subject and the object of his observation. (Sartre, Jean-Paul. 1992 [1956]. *Being and Nothingness: A Phenomenological Essay on Ontology*. Trans. Hazel E. Barnes. New York: Washington Square Press, pp. 340–400).
33 In this regard I do not agree with Melville, who sketches an opposition of conceptualizations of vison, in which Merleau-Ponty and Lacan are situated on the same side while Sartre is located on the opposing side. According to him, Lacan and Merleau-Ponty suppose a similar structure of vision, they simply use different terms. (Melville, Stephen. 1996. "Division of the Gaze, or, Remarks on the Color and Tenor of Contemporary 'Theory'". In *Vision in Context: Historical and Contemporary Perspectives on Sight*. Edited by Teresa Brennan and Martin Jay. London: Routledge, p. 109).
34 Merleau-Ponty, Maurice. 1997 [1968]. *The Visible and the Invisible*. Trans. A. Lingis. Evanston: Northwestern University Press, p. 146.
35 Merleau-Ponty, 1997, pp. 139–140.
36 Melvile, 1996, p. 108.
37 Merleau-Ponty, 1997, p. 139.
38 Vasseleu, Cathryn. 1998. *Textures of Light: Vision and Touch in Irigaray, Levinas and Merleau-Ponty*. London: Routledge, pp. 26–27.
39 Vasseleu, 1998, p. 52.
40 Merleau-Ponty, 1993, p. 129.
41 Lacan XI, pp. 82–83.
42 Berressem, Henjo. 1995. "The 'Evil Eye' of Painting: Jacques Lacan and Witold Gombrowicz on the Gaze". In *Reading Seminar XI: Lacan's Four Fundamental Concepts of Psychoanalysis*. Edited by Richard Feldstein, Bruce Fink and Maire Jaanus. Albany: State University of New York Press, p. 175.
43 Lacan XI, p. 79.
44 Lacan XI, p.104.
45 Sartre, Jean-Paul. 1992 [1956]. *Being and Nothingness: A Phenomenological Essay on Ontology*. Trans. Hazel E. Barnes. New York: Washington Square Press, pp. 340–400.
46 Lacan XI, p. 115.
47 Lacan XI, p. 103.
48 Evans, Dylan. 1996. *An Introductory Dictionary of Lacanian Psychoanalysis*. London and New York: Routledge, p. 72.

49 Lacan XI, p. 72.
50 Jay, 1997, pp.169–198.
51 Vasseleu, p. 29.
52 Merleau-Ponty, 1993, p. 124.
53 Merleau-Ponty, 1993, p. 142.
54 Merleau-Ponty, 1993, p. 128.
55 Lacan XI, p. 95.
56 Lacan, Jacques. 1988 [1957]. "Seminar on *The Purloined Letter*". Trans. Jeffrey Mehlman. In *The Purloined Poe: Lacan, Derrida, and Psychoanalytic Reading*. Edited by John P. Muller and William J. Richardson. Baltimore and London: Johns Hopkins University Press, pp. 28–54.
57 Poe, Edgar Allan. 1988 [1844]. "The Purloined Letter". In *The Purloined Poe: Lacan, Derrida, and Psychoanalytic Reading*. Edited by John P. Muller and William J. Richardson. Baltimore and London: Johns Hopkins University Press, pp. 6–27.
58 Lacan P.L, p. 29.
59 Lacan XI, p. 73; Lacan E, p. 3. I elaborate on the subject of vision and concealment in the sixth chapter.
60 Bryson, 1990, p. 142.
61 Bryson, 1990, pp. 142–143.
62 Bryson, 1990, p. 143.
63 Bryson, 1990, p. 144.
64 Lacan XI, pp. 103, 111–112.
65 Lacan, Jacques. 2014 [1962–1963]. *The Seminar of Jacques Lacan, Book X: Anxiety*. Trans. Adrian Price. Cambridge: Polity Press, p. 162.

6 The subject position of the viewer

The case of self-portraiture

In this chapter, I will develop the psychoanalytic conceptualization of the term "subject positions", so as to explain the logic unfolded in previous chapters, according to which the subject is not separated from the aesthetic object. This logic subverts the distinction between subject and object and hence exposes the way in which the "expanded arena" actually takes place.

In what follows I will show that the subject, in its Lacanian articulation, is not an autonomous, unified entity, but a split subject, constituted by lack, while the object is an inseparable part of him. The discussion of subject positions will serve here to describe the complex relationship between the picture and the looking subject. This relationship radically differs from the determinate mode of looking, which traditional theories of art assume. When describing the picture-viewer relationship through the term "subject position", it is no longer possible to separate the painting and viewer. These relationships, however, are not harmonic in nature, but are characterized by incongruence.

The previous discussion on the seven veils of fantasy included two arguments on subject positions: the first was that, like fantasy, looking at a painting consists of a multiplicity of subject positions, which do not result from an *a priori* structure and do not necessarily overlap with the fictional characters present in the painted world. The second was that looking at a painting involves an impossible gaze, since the subject positions may be situated in an impossible manner according to any reality criteria.

These two arguments, which Žižek articulated in his essay as part of what characterizes fantasy, touch upon Lacan's principal notion of the subject and his positions. The subject is split, and the split is essential for him. This subject does not have a single, unified position; rather, his position emerges out of the discourse of the Other. Thus, the positions of the subject are multiple and emerge only as flickers.

First, I will examine various psychoanalytic fundamental concepts so as to clarify the context of the term "subject positions". I will then demonstrate how these conceptualizations can be used to examine self-portraits as a test case of subject positions in painting. Self-portraits are a genre that is usually conceived as non-narrative. I would like to claim that it is for this very reason that they make it possible to underscore the nature of the connection between

DOI: 10.4324/9781003516446-7

the subject and the object of his gaze. Since these paintings do not explicitly represent any narrative, but are meant simply to represent the painter himself, they expose the structure of the relationship between the painting and the viewer.

On subject positions

The term "object relations" originates in Freud's theory of the drives. According to Freud, the object is the aim of the drive, and it can be an external object, a body part of the subject himself or another subject.[1] Object relations denote relations which are not restricted to the way in which the subject constitutes his object, but also to the reverse procedure, in which the object takes part in the constitution of the subject.[2] According to Lacan, the object with which the subject conceives of himself as worthy of the Other's desire is part of the subject himself. Thus, the desire of the subject is the Other's desire, since it stems from a response to the question regarding what the Other wants from me. This is a question which the subject avoids answering, but his desire, perceived as the Other's desire, is directed toward the answer to this question. In other words, the subject is not only a subject for himself, but part of him is invested in an object that is seemingly external to him. In this way, the subject is simultaneously a subject and an object.

What is, then, the Lacanian subject, and what is the function of the visual field in his constitution? In his early essay "The Mirror Stage", Lacan describes the encounter of an infant, at the age of 6–18 months, with his specular image.[3] The infant, whose motor ability is still restricted, identifies himself at a certain stage with his own mirror reflection, which provides him with a unified and coherent self-image. This image stands in contrast to the fragmentary experience of his non-distinctive excitations. Unlike an animal, which abandons its interest in the image, once it recognizes that it is only a reflection, the infant lingers before his reflected image which gives him a sense of joy.[4] This joy stems from the fact that the infant gains imaginary corporeal control by identifying his complete and symmetrical reflection with himself, while this wholeness radically differs from his experience of motor insufficiency. This identification constitutes the infant's first alienation between an external symmetric and coherent form, and an internal sense of motor insufficiency.

As Lacan states, the specular form would be called the "Ideal Ego". Lacan refers to terms Freud coined in his essay on narcissism, Ego Ideal and Ideal Ego.[5] The ideal ego is the target of self-love, which, at a primal stage in childhood, was part of the ego. For instance, the infant's own reflection as projected to him through the loving eyes of the one who took care of him. As the subject grows up in light of his own judgment as well as the judgments of his surroundings, he can no longer retain this childish perfection. As in many other cases involving libido, here also the subject refuses to cede the satisfaction he once had and hence seeks a new ego ideal. He imposes on himself an ego ideal which is supposed to substitute the lost narcissism of his childhood and to adhere to his current ideal.[6] By using the term ego ideal Freud explains why one person finds pleasure in certain experiences that another rejects:

> the one man has set up an *ideal* in himself by which he measures his actual ego, while the other has formed no such ideal. For the ego the formation of an ideal would be the conditioning factor of repression.[7]

In his first seminar, Lacan distinguishes between ego ideal and ideal ego:

> The ideal ego governs the interplay of relations on which all relations with others depend…the ego-ideal is the other as speaking, the other in so far as he has symbolic relation to me…which…is both similar to and different from the imaginary libido.[8]

In contrast to the ego-ideal, which belongs to the symbolic order, the ideal-ego is an imaginary reflection. The ideal-ego is a promise of an illusory unity upon which the ego is built. Moreover, it is distinct from the ego-ideal, which is a signifier that functions as an ideal, orienting and governing the position of the subject in the symbolic order.[9]

According to Lacan, the mirror stage shows that the external self-image, which is by definition prism-inverted and unequal in its size, is the very same image that constitutes the ego.[10] In other words, a great extent of self-perception, a major part of the way in which one sees oneself, is constituted by an external, distorted image. Lacan underscores the status of the image for animals and humans. For animals, there is a correlation between image and object. Looking at a female image is enough for the male to begin his sexual activity. In humans, however, the situation is much more complex, since there is a gap between the image and his experience of his own body, and at the same time, an external image constitutes the sense of self. That is, the same self-alienation constituted at the mirror stage, in which the subject first encounters the appearance of his own body, which does not coincide with the way he experiences himself, characterizes the human subject as such and will accompany him throughout his whole life.

The mirror stage, says Lacan,

> is a drama whose internal thrust is precipitated from insufficiency to anticipation – and which manufactures for the subject, caught up in a lure of spatial identification the succession of phantasies that extends from a fragmented body-image to a form of its totality.[11]

In other words, this seemingly complete image, which is granted to the subject in the mirror stage, constitutes a kind of promise of future wholeness, but at the same time, this very image alienates the subject from that completeness.

As Lacan states: "The mirror-stage would seem to be the threshold of the visible world, if we go by the mirror disposition that the *imago of one's own body* presents in hallucinations or dreams".[12] That is, the relation between identity and image is fundamental to the structure of the subject. Furthermore, this relation demonstrates the subject's false autonomy throughout his life.

In his eleventh seminar, Lacan presents this split as part of the subject, not as stemming from an encounter with an external image. In this seminar, Lacan relates to another crucial aspect of sight: that which is not given to any specular reflection, that is, the *objet petit a*, presented in this seminar in the scopic field as the gaze. Although the split of the subject is still related to an external image, it is perceived as part of the split between ego and unconscious.

The concept of the split subject does not include a subject qua biological organism. As Lacan states:

> in the term *subject* ... I am not designating the living substratum needed by this phenomenon of the subject, nor any sort of substance, nor any being possessing knowledge in his *phatos*, his suffering, whether primal or secondary, nor even some incarnated logos, but the Cartesian subject, who appears at the moment when doubt is recognized as certainty – except that, through my approach, the basis of that subject prove to be wider, but, at the same time much more amenable to the certainty that eludes it.[13]

Lacan, then, relates to the Cartesian subject, whose certainty is attained through thinking. Lacan goes on to show that while the Cartesian subject is present through his thinking, the subject Lacan articulates is presented through a signifier:

> The signifier, producing itself in the field of the Other, makes manifest the subject of its signification. But it functions as a signifier only to reduce the subject in question to being no more of a signifier, to petrify the subject in the same movement in which it calls the subject to function, to speak, as subject.[14]

To elucidate how the Lacanian subject is present through a signifier, we can turn to the subject's encounter with language. The infant is born into a preexisting language, which precedes him. The external helpers, be they the mother or someone else, interpret the infant's cry as an expression of a need, and they try to address this need in the way they understand it. Hence, fulfilling the infant's demand is designated by someone external to the subject, who takes the place of the Other. Thus, language, by definition, involves alienation: needs are articulated not by the one who demands them but through their interpretation. The subject, hence, emerges from the discourse of the Other.

As Lacan states: "The Other is the locus in which is situated the chain of the signifier which governs whatever may be made present of the subject – it is the field of that living being in which the subject has to appear".[15]

The Lacanian split subject is, hence, made present by language, by the symbolic order. The split of the subject is also present in language in the gap between the subject of the statement and the subject of enunciation. The ego, or the I, which relates to the thinking subject, is not the Lacanian subject, but is only the subject of statement (*énoncé*). This is an imaginary image of the speaker, presented by the conscious subject of the statement. The subject of the unconscious, however, emerges from a chiasm stemming from a discrepancy between the imaginary "I" of the uttered content, as the subject of discourse, and the speaking subject embodied by the signifier, as the subject of enunciation (*énonciation*). Lacan explains the gap between these two levels of discourse by turning to the paradox of the liar, in which the speaking subject is not congruent with the subject of the enunciation, and the gap between the two creates the famous paradox.[16] Lacan describes this as two parallel chains of signifiers: one is that of speech, and the other is that of the unconscious. The unconscious manifests itself in its formations, like slips of the tongue, stimulated by something that allegedly has no apparent relation to what is stated consciously.

The relevant question at this point is the position of the split subject in relation to the act of looking at paintings. "Where the subject sees himself, namely, where that real, inverted image of his own body that is given in the schema of the ego is forged, it is not from there that he looks at himself", says Lacan.[17] That is, the subject sees his imaginary specular reflection from a different position in relation to the one from which he is looking. Lacan implies that when the viewer looks at himself, his gaze, which turns back to him, does not take the same route. This seemingly single look is actually constituted by two gazes, which do not intersect. The act of seeing, as a perceptual ocular act, and the act of gazing, as directing someone's gaze toward something, appear as two separate, incongruent acts. This is a seeing that contains seeing sight itself, and the distance between these two acts is a gap that constitutes the subject as seeing. In other words, the same split that takes place in language is also manifested in the visual field and can be articulated according to terms of visuality. There is a gap between the way in which the subject sees, in the sense of perceiving himself qua ego in relation to the painting, and the way in which the subject encounters the gaze that returns to him from the picture, the gaze as *object petit a*, screening something of the real. That is, sight itself is split between the imaginary seeing of the eye and the gaze, which is of the order of the real. The gaze that returns to the looking subject emanates from this split. As stated above, Lacan claims that the gaze, as object, is part of the subject himself, but a part that the subject perceives as coming from the Other. This complex state of affairs can be exemplified as something in the painting that seizes the subject, embodying for him what cannot be represented, and which can only be manifested through its veils.

As I have shown in the third chapter, the gap between the eye and the gaze is demonstrated by the three diagrams in *Seminar XI*. The diagrams show how, alongside the imaginary seeing characterized by the subject's illusory sense of control of the visual field, there is another form of seeing in which the subject's gaze looks back at him from the painting. This reflexive look is intricate, since the supposed subject is a split subject who is, in a way, the Other. This split explains why relations of looking stemming from the concept of a split subject may assume several different subject positions, from possible and impossible points of view.

I would, hence, turn back to Žižek's discussion about fantasy in order to demonstrate how his articulation of the multiple subject positions stems from the Lacanian concept of subject. Žižek claims that the subject's point of identification in the narrative does not necessarily correlate with his appearance there. The subject may identify with the ego ideal, the gaze or the perspective from which he appears in the phantasmatic narrative. As Lacan states:

> Interpretation cannot be bent to any meaning. It designates only a single series of signifiers. But the subject may in effect occupy various places, depending on whether one places him under one or other of these signifiers.[18]

Yet Žižek points to another aspect in the subject positions. As mentioned in the third chapter, Žižek argues that since the narrative fantasy involves an impossible gaze, as the subject is present in the act which he perceives, there is no possible external innocent viewer, "since this gaze is the impossible neutral gaze of someone who falsely exempts himself from his concrete historical existence".[19] The significance of this argument lies in paving the way for multiple possible and impossible subject positions alike. Yet, this does not mean that any possible subject position is relevant since the position chosen by a particular subject is never by chance: the object of observation has a relation of necessity to the subject on which it imposes itself.

The self as other: self-portraiture and subject positions

In his articulation of the mirror stage, Lacan argues that the subject is constituted through the act of looking at his own image. This mundane experience is embodied in the genre of self-portraiture, which I will explore so as to analyze the Lacanian subject in relation to looking at paintings as a visual case of subject positions.

Art historians propose several kinds of self-portraiture; among them is that in which the painter paints himself painting. Though other self-portraits do not describe the painter in his act of painting, they still strive to embody his external appearance "as is", to capture something essential of the painter's image. I define this kind of self-portrait, in which the painter is congruent with his mirror reflection, as "the specular model". Another model of self-portraits is "the theatrical model", in which the painter paints himself as another character. A paradigmatic example of the theatrical model, though not unique to self-portraits, can be found in Svetlana Alpers's research on Rembrandt.[20]

These two categories, the specular model and the theatrical model, suggest two different views of self-representation: the first proposes the representation of the self as other, that is, as a separate self-entity from the one that paints, while the second attempts to achieve maximum congruence between the self that paints and the painted image. I will discuss several problematic issues these models raise, and then turn to the psychoanalytic discourse and show how Freud's concept of the *uncanny* addresses these problems, as demonstrated in Mladen Dolar's discussion.[21] I will then show how Lacan's concept of the gaze and his conceptualization of the object of observation as part and parcel of the subject himself undermines the distinction between the self as other and the self as a specular image.[22] I would like to argue that the self-portrait is the painter's endeavor to cope with his own image. Embarking upon this enterprise of painting a self-portrait, in the end, underscores the impossibility of the enterprise. It is a paradoxical task in which the very decision to paint an image that would be congruent with the self inevitably dooms it to failure, despite the declaration of the act itself.

The "theatrical model", according to Alpers, who coined the term, can be seen in Rembrandt's paintings. Rembrandt, whose major work was conducted indoors, created a kind of "inner world" in his paintings, a world that was inhabited by dozens of students, models and assistants.[23] Rembrandt planned complicated scenes that he directed and painted, while the sketches he made are reminiscent of the work of a stage director.[24] Similarly, one can comprehend the way Rembrandt paints or directs himself. In *Self-portrait with Bittern*, from 1639, Rembrandt holds the legs of a big bittern in front of him, casting a shadow on his face.

Here, according to Alpers, "Rembrandt identified with both the slayer and the slain".[25] In his examination of Albrecht Dürer's self-portraits Joseph L. Koerner offers another example of the theatrical model.[26] Koerner claims that the similarity between Dürer's *Self-portrait* of 1500 and visual representations of Christ is not coincidental and that Dürer depicts himself as God so as to make a statement about the status of the artist and the position of his art.[27]

The specular model is a mode in which self-portraits aim to create the perfect specular reflection, an accurate embodiment of the appearance of the painter as viewed in the mirror in front of him.[28] In his analysis of Courbet's early self-portraits, Michael Fried presents a complicated development of this model.[29] According to Fried, Courbet's self-portraits are characterized by "a physical proximity of the painted image to the surface of the painting and, beyond that surface, to the beholder".[30] Fried, it seems, assumes a kind of imaginary surface in painting that separates the picture from the viewer. In Courbet's early self-portraits, the distance between this imaginary surface and the viewer is reduced to a minimum. As a result, Courbet's self-portraits, such as *The Wounded Man* from 1844 to 1845, question both the ontological status of the picture plane and the impermeability of the border which

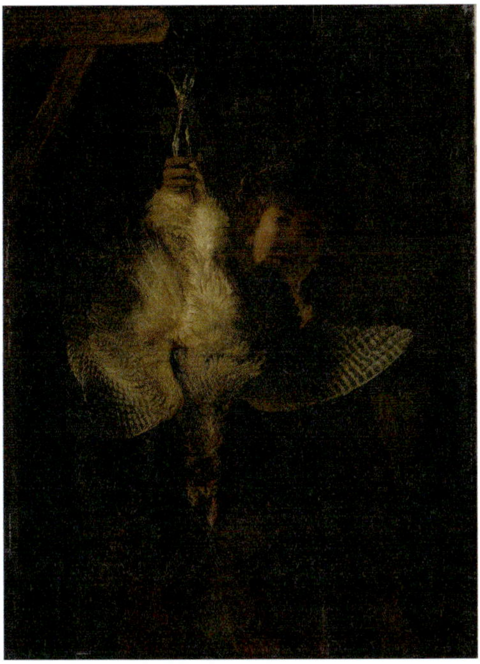

Figure 6.1 Rembrandt van Rijn, *Self-Portrait with Bittern*, 1639.

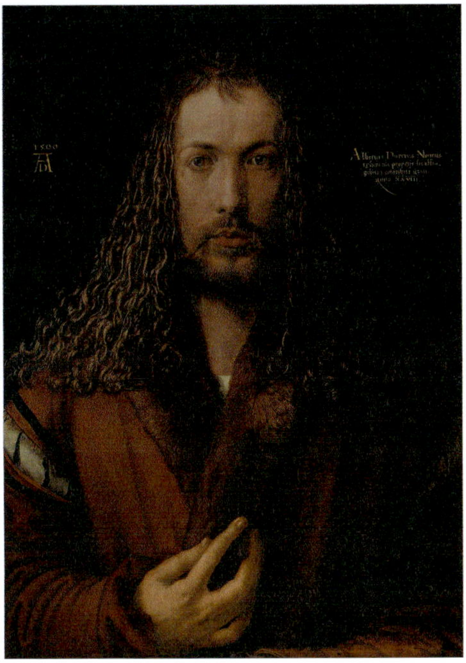

Figure 6.2 Albrecht Dürer, *Self-Portrait*, 1500.

ostensibly exists between the painted surface and the world beyond it. Courbet challenges the idea of the two-dimensionality in painting and reexamines its relation to the viewer.

According to Fried, this sense of nearness is heightened by the figure's compositional location on the canvas and its extreme foreshortening. Fried attributes these pictorial characteristics to Courbet's ambition "to express in and through the medium of the self-portrait a sense or intuition or conviction of his own embodiedness that he could not expound in words". To support this claim, Fried suggests that Courbet depicts his own body in a different way from the other painted elements. Thus, Fried argues that Courbet made use of compositional and perspectival devices to reduce the gap between the painted image and the viewer. Fried, then, shows Courbet's preoccupation with both the nature and status of self-portraiture in his attempt to achieve a perfect congruence between the painter and the painted object.

The problem at this point is that neither of the two models, the theatrical and the specular model, provides a solution to the relationship between the subject and his painted image. In an attempt to reach congruence between image and object, Courbet tries to "overcome" the pictorial arena, and to undermine its two-imensionality. He undermines the two dimensions of the painting by foreshortening the painted figures while also trying to depict

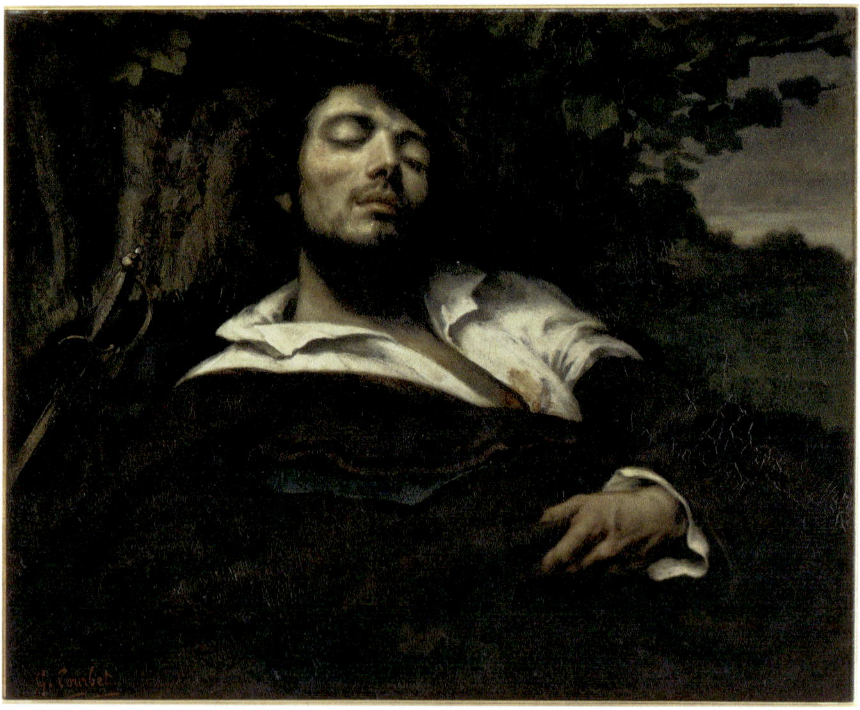

Figure 6.3 Gustave Courbet, *The Wounded Man*, 1844–1845.

himself as closely as possible to how he perceives his inner self, by painting himself with his eyes closed. That is to say, the specular model contains a dialectical relationship between two ostensibly contradictory concepts. On the one hand, there is a wish to create the ultimate copy by erasing the boundary between painter and painted image, while on the other hand, to reach the same goal, an opposing act takes place in which the painter closes his eyes so as to embody this subjectivity from the inside. That is, by painting himself with his eyes closed, Courbet shows his refusal to identify his visual appearance with the embodiment of his subjectivity. Fried's interpretation implies that these two contradictory attempts are designed to achieve the same objective of attaining perfect congruence; however, the gap between the image and the self-perception it was supposed to represent, persists.

The theatrical model presents us with an opposite problem. Here, the attempt to formulate self-perception is intended from the outset to embody the gap between the self and the image, and not to bridge it. The painter designates a role for himself and plays it, but this disguise does not make it possible to erase the presence of the ego, which emerges from the very role that the painter chooses to play.

These theories of art do, however, point to the complex nature of self-portraits. This dual view of self-portraits expresses their intricacy and the difficulty they pose.[31] Their difficulty is rooted in the impossibility of deciding the nature of the relationship between self-perception and its image, in which each choice leaves one aspect unsolved. Moreover, each choice ultimately embodies its opposition as well: the theatrical model retains the self-image, while the specular model retains the gap between the self and the image.

Camouflage and duplication

These two perceptions of the self and the tension between them can be seen in Freud's discussion of the uncanny.[32] Freud situates this discussion in the aesthetic realm and claims that although aesthetic discussions usually concern the beautiful, the uncanny relates to an aesthetic matter, which is opposed to the beautiful and sublime emotions.[33] The meaning of the term "uncanny" (*unheimlich*), says Freud, lies in two opposing senses. *Heimlich* in German denotes something domestic and familiar. However, among the diverse ways of interpreting this word, there is one that matches its opposite meaning, namely *unheimlich*, which means frightening and foreign. One of the meanings of the word thus contains an ambiguity, which conflates the significance of the word with its opposite. This antagonistic sense, according to Freud, situates the concept of the uncanny in an intermediate zone.[34]

Freud begins by turning to Jentsch's definition of the uncanny as that which results from an inability to distinguish between a live body and an object. Later, Freud connects the uncanny effect with a repetition of a detail, event, or place, or duplication as manifested in the phenomenon of the double.[35] Freud relates the manifestation of the double and its uncanny effect to a withdrawal to archaic times, "when the ego has not yet marked itself off sharply from the external world and from other people".[36] Freud thus considers the phenomenon of merging in space and the excessive appearance of the double as two of the mainsprings of the uncanny effect.

This tension between merging in the environment, while the particularity of the subject is embedded in the other, and the appearance of someone who looks exactly like me, in which the particularity is duplicated, is implied in the theatrical model and the specular model. In the theatrical model I represent someone other than me; that is, I am absorbed in the image of the other, while in the specular model, I strive to create an identical image of myself and thus create my double.

I suggest reading self-portraits through these two modes of the uncanny: on the one hand, as camouflage, a total merging of the organism with its environment, and on the other hand, as a phenomenon of the double. These are essentially different actions: camouflage is intended to conceal, to assimilate into the environment. Camouflage in this sense is the erasure of the ego, the blurring of its unique characteristics. The double, on the other hand, draws on the unique aspects of the subject to produce another one like it. Unlike disappearance, duplication is about an increased presence and excess.

Ostensibly, we could identify the self-portrait in which the painter embodies a character with the camouflage model, since, like certain animals in nature, the painter wears an image of the other. The self-portrait, on the other hand, in which the painter paints himself as accurately as possible, could be identified with duplication. However, as I have argued, the artist who disguises himself as another character does not ultimately succeed in assimilating himself in to an image that is external to him. Similarly, the painter who paints himself does not create an image that overlaps with the ego, but rather, the painter of the self-portrait ultimately paints the distance between himself and his image. These two procedures of camouflage and duplication correspond with the subject of self-portraiture. This subject is in a state of camouflage, internalizes and domesticates his image, and this relationship is characterized by the ambivalence of the concept of the uncanny. At the same time, the uncanny effect in self-portrait paintings is linked to the anxiety that emerges from the excessiveness of duplication, from the encounter with the one who looks exactly like me. In what follows, I will examine self-portraits through these two manifestations of the uncanny and by relating them to the concept of an inward-outward relationship, in their psychoanalytical articulation.

As stated, in his essay on the mirror stage, Lacan describes how the infant recognizes his specular image for the first time.[37] Henceforth, he will bear the gap between his fragmentary and incoherent experience and the whole and symmetrical image that he attributes to himself.[38] Two distinct relationships exist between the subject and his image: on the one hand, identification and congruency, and on the other, complete alienation. This relationship cannot be understood in terms of inward-outward relationships; rather, it is a process of absorbing something external while simultaneously discharging something internal. This conflation of the inside and outside henceforth characterizes the relationship of the infant with his environment. The infant absorbs materials from the outside, such as milk, while also discharging other materials from the body. That is, something external is absorbed, which, hence, becomes internal, and vice versa. As stated, the subject of Lacanian psychoanalysis is split between the ego and the unconscious. This split embodies the inward-outward relationship, in which the "inside" of the subject comes from the Other, determining the subject as such, while the "outside" is embodied through repression.

A similar procedure takes place in the act of seeing. Unlike the subject in art theory, who views its object from a sovereign viewpoint, the subject in psychoanalysis gazes at a picture that looks back at him and finds in the picture something of himself: the manifestation of his own gaze. The Lacanian concept of the gaze assumes an antinomy between the eye and the gaze, in which the eye is the eye of the subject, and the gaze is the object of looking, of the scopic drive.[39] While the eye expresses the vision related to the imaginary order, the gaze, according to Lacan, is something of the real that eludes articulation and cannot be represented.[40]

Lacan explains this intricacy with reference to Roger Caillois's research into mimicry and camouflage in insects. Caillois argues that camouflage in insects stems from the organism's relation to the space around it.[41] The traditional way of understanding mimicry in insects, claims Caillois, is in human terms. The theories which claim that certain organisms camouflage themselves in order to defend themselves and survive follow this logic. However, Caillois cites contradictory cases, such as insects that camouflage themselves and yet are still killed, or insects that, by camouflaging themselves are exposed to new hazards, which did not threaten them previously.[42] Thus, understanding camouflage as an act of defense is an interpretation of a human viewer, and does not necessarily describe the phenomenon of camouflage itself. The act of camouflage does not belong to the intersubjective realm but relates to the organism and its perception of space.[43]

"Why, then, do organisms camouflage themselves?" asks Caillois. He concludes that camouflage is a temptation to merge within space, while the search for a resemblance to the surroundings is an intermediate phase for the purpose of achieving the final objective of total absorption. Camouflage is an act of absorption that succeeds beyond expectation when the organism completely loses its sense of self.[44] In other words, camouflage, according to Caillois, is not a defensive mechanism but rather an expression of the inseparable relation between the organism and its environment. Lacan adopts Caillois's views to explain the gap between the subject and its specular image. Just as the insect strives to merge with its environment, so too does the subject strive to unite with the ideal ego, which he sees in the mirror, an effort that can never succeed.

In his discussion of the gaze, Lacan again refers to Caillois when he draws an analogy between the insects' act of mimicry and the human act of painting. The absorption of the organism in the environment exemplifies the Lacanian notion of sight in the sense that the object of observation is not separate from, or external to, the subject but is part and parcel of the subject; his own gaze looks back at him. This situation contradicts traditional dualistic Western assumptions of the subject and his distinct, separated field of vision, and similarly contradicts the common notion that regards camouflage as a defensive device. Thus, both Caillois and Lacan, each for his own purposes, articulate an alternative structure of relations, which is not based upon this duality.

Following Caillois, Lacan claims that the butterfly, on whose wing appears what seems to be a huge image of an eye, does not enchant another insect by its resemblance to an actual eye, a phenomenon that is often understood to be a camouflage technique, but rather by the resemblance to the image of an eye.[45] He asks: "Must we not distinguish between the function of the eye and the function of the gaze?"[46] That is, the image of the eye is not charming because one might substitute it with an actual eye, but rather, the image of the eye is charming because it is so similar to an actual eye. Lacan seems to make a similar claim when referring to the competition between the two ancient Greek painters, Zeuxis and Parrhasios, tating that in order to deceive a human, one must show him a painting of a screen, show him something that will tempt him to ask what is behind it. This can be understood in the following way: seeing the image of a large eye on the butterfly's wing as if it were the eye of a huge and intimidating animal belongs to the imaginary order, to the concept of camouflage as a defensive procedure, when the subject is separate from his object of observation. Simultaneously, however, another procedure takes place, which belongs to the real: the large eye is perceived as the gaze of the viewer which turns upon him, confronts him with his act of seeing. This process is not intended to undermine the boundaries between the organism and its surrounding space, but rather this perception rejects this distinction *a priori* and the question as to whether an object is a thing or just a camouflage, an empty image with no substance, remains open. Thus, Lacan claims, the huge eye on the butterfly's wing is enchanting not because of its similarity to a large animal's eye, but because of its resemblance to a representation of an eye, and hence it returns to the subject his own mode of seeing.[47]

What Lacan argues here, in my view, is that the point in the deception of the eye is not that we see something different from what we actually saw, for instance, seeing an owl with round eyes while in fact it is a butterfly with painted wings, but rather in realizing how much the imitation resembles reality. The function of the gaze undermines the distinction between reality and appearance, returning to the subject his own mode of seeing.

This means that the relationship between the organism and the other is not decided: the uncanny image remains threatening, and, at the same time, while imitating it, there is an aspiration to "domesticate" it, to assimilate it in order to neutralize the uncanny effect. However, these are not unequivocal operations, but rather dual operations that take place simultaneously. In this sense, the act of camouflage illustrates the idea of being in an in-between locus, which Freud points to when discussing the twofold nature of the uncanny.

Viewing self-portraits with the camouflage model shows that the image of the self-portrait contains the dialectic between the self-image as familiar, routine and known, and the self-image as the other. This explains the uncanny effect that these portraits create. That is to say, the psychoanalytic position does not separate the object of observation from the viewing subject. Thus, this position undermines the dichotomy between the other and the self, which art theory articulates through the distinction between the theatrical model and the specular model.

At this point we can return to Alpers's reading of Rembrandt's *Self-portrait with Dead Bittern*, in which, as she puts it, the painter is simultaneously the slayer and the slain. In other words, while Alpers perceives the bilaterality of this portrait as a complicated case of the theatrical model, we may interpret it, from a Lacanian position, as an expression of the divided subject, split between the ego and the unconscious. The subject of the self-portrait is simultaneously subject and object, a viewer who is also the object of his own gaze. Similarly, we can re-view the way in which Fried viewed Courbet's portrait with his eyes closed. The tension that Fried attributes to the gap between how Courbet perceives himself from the "inside" and how he perceives his external image can be reconsidered in Lacanian terms as the subject who simultaneously sees himself as himself and as an object.

As stated above, when Freud examines the situations that generate the uncanny effect, he also adds the manifestation of the double to the lack of distinction between living and inanimate beings, which I have associated with camouflage. The phenomenon of the double is rooted in the attempt to protect the ego from destruction through multiplication; hence, it begins with self-love and is connected to narcissism. At a later stage, the phenomenon of the double, which was initially intended to ensure eternal life, is reversed and perceived as threatening. In what follows I will examine the phenomenon of the double through the discussion of Mladen Dolar of the moment of falling in love.

The self-portrait and the double

Mladen Dolar exposes the imaginary aspect of the process of falling in love as it is perceived in Western culture, namely as a crucial moment of free choice. He shows that it is, in fact, a process of a forced choice, in which the subject acts under the illusion of freedom. As I will show, Dolar draws an analogy between love relations and the narcissistic relations between the subject and his double, a procedure that he connects with the Lacanian mirror stage. Dolar's views on love and the concept of the double elucidate the relations between painter, object and image, which are relevant to self-portraiture.

Dolar claims that falling in love is rooted in a paradox caused by the convergence between something that is accidental and external to the subject, and something that is most intimate and of internal concern.[48] The paradox of love, he claims, lies in the imperative to love things that we cannot choose, such as our parents or our homeland. This imperative is *analogous* to the principle of forced choice, in which the subject can ostensibly choose between two things, yet the choice is forced upon him. Lacan's paradigmatic case of a forced choice is the statement "your money or your life", in which the real meaning of that sentence is that you should choose life, since if you choose money, you will relinquish both.[49] A similar principle, according to Dolar, is at work in falling in love. Classical stories incorporate a chance encounter in which the couple's eyes "meet", an encounter that turns out to be fateful. This becomes the fundamental moment that can entirely transform the subjects, who hence take on the contingent as the very essence of their being.[50]

Dolar shows that, paradoxically, in many stories, the moment of recognition, which is supposed to be a moment of a free choice, is, in actuality, a forced choice: "It turns out that the pure chance was actually no chance at all: the intrusion of the unforeseen turned into necessity... The moment of subjectivation is precisely that moment of suspension of subjectivity to the Other..."[51] The solution, he claims, is to accept the forced choice retroactively, which means accepting the Other's decision as your own. The choice is made retroactively, but involves is a strange temporality, since it refers to a past that was never present.[52]

In falling in love, according to Dolar, three things simultaneously take place: something accidental and external to the subject turns out to be an acceptable object; the acceptable object has not changed, but the subject's position toward it has changed; a procedure of forced choice has taken place, in which something that was forced upon the subject is presented as his own choice. The meaning of this forced choice does not lie in the absence of choosing, but rather in the fact that the possibility to choose is offered and rejected at once, and that subjectivity emerges from that empty gesture. The crucial moment in which the lovers' eyes meet is the moment of recognition. They recognize what "has already always been there", and all of their existence is retroactively re-organized around this moment.[53] This moment of discovery organizes everything that preceded it and simultaneously creates a new future to look forward to: "The lack of sense of a contingent fate, the haphazard string of events, was in that moment suddenly filled by the gaze".[54] In other words, if an event is commonly understood as a consequence of a prior event, Dolar relates to a contingent series of events on which the gaze has been focused and which explains the series of events retroactively as a causal sequence. We can understand this in two ways: on the one hand, as a state of awakening, in which for one instant the subject really sees things instead of just looking at them, or, on the other hand, as a sight, which exists only at the price of blindness:

> The gaze comes to fill the lack of sense in that senseless fortune, it also creates it by filling it, for it is only looking backward that one sees the lack, and only as a lack destined to be filled. Life didn't 'make sense' before, but now, suddenly, it does.[55]

The moment of the encounter, described in literature by the words "their eyes met", relates to the domestication of an object that arouses desire, an object through which the subject sees something himself turning back upon him.

I suggest that the same logic of a forced choice, of a retroactive articulation through which it is possible to organize an allegedly objective reality exists between the painting and the viewer in general, and between the self-portrait and its viewer, in particular. If we return to the theatrical and the specular models as interpretive models in art theory, we see that they are based on looking at a painting in which the viewer constructs meaning in accordance with the visual details that he sees. If we apply the logic of the forced choice to the process of looking at a painting, then, meaning is turned from a product of deciphering the pictorial element in to a product of the encounter between the painting and the viewer, who gives it a meaning that retroactively explains it. In other words, traditional interpretations describing the encounter between picture and viewer assume a viewer who uses the correct code to construct the pictorial details to reveal a meaning that was already inherent in it. Yet, understanding this encounter in terms of the logic of the forced choice assumes that it is a contingent encounter, in which the viewer sees something of himself, of his own gaze staring back at him, which leads him to retroactively articulate meaning. Thus, the order of events is reversed: pictorial meaning cannot be attained through meticulous observation; on the contrary, only a contingent gaze retroactively leads to the construction of meaning.

Dolar proceeds to argue that a similar situation takes place in the mirror stage, when the infant suddenly comes face to face with his specular image. In this narcissistic phase, something akin to love emerges, since all love is, in some way, narcissistic.[56] The moment when the infant encounters his specular image has a double meaning. Alongside the narcissistic joy, he also experiences an uncanny effect. Encountering someone who looks exactly like oneself generates fear of an impending disaster, since my reflection is at once both me and the other.[57] This situation has the uncanny effect of seeing the most intimate thing as alien. This point exemplifies the congruence between camouflage and duplication, which Freud illuminates by noting that the double is a regression to an early mental stage when the ego was not yet differentiated from the external world. According to Dolar, the resemblance between the Lacanian mirror stage and the phenomenon of the double is based on the sense that I need my specular image so as to be myself:

> When I recognize myself in the mirror, it is already too late. There is a split: I cannot recognize myself and at the same time be one with myself. With the recognition, I have already lost what one could call the 'self-being'... The rejoicing in the mirror image ... had already to be paid for. The mirror double immediately introduces the dimension of castration.[58]

The Lacanian gaze is precisely that which is missing, the missing organ. Thus, the mirror presents the split between the imaginary and the real. The double is that impossible specular image containing the gaze, a situation of anxiety in which the imaginary exists alongside the real. The double is the ego to which the gaze is added as the unseen part of being, attached to one's image. Lacan uses the gaze as a representative of the missing part: one can see one's eyes in the mirror but not one's gaze, since that is the missing part that eludes any visual embodiment. If it were possible, for instance, to see my own reflection in the mirror with closed or blinking eyes, then it would be the gaze as an object that appears in the mirror. A similar situation exists with the phenomenon of the double. The anxiety that the double causes is proof of the existence of the gaze. The anxiety is not the outcome of a lack or a loss, but rather is caused by an excess, by gaining too much.[59] The very loss of the lack gives rise to the uncanny effect.[60]

According to Dolar, the phenomenon of the double is an embodiment of anxiety-arousing excess. The relevant question for the current discussion is the connection between the self-portrait, as a representation of the appearance of the subject from his specular reflection, and the phenomenon of the double.

I return to Courbet's self-portrait *The Wounded Man*, in which he paints himself with his eyes closed. As I mentioned above, Fried suggested that Courbet was trying to paint himself from the "inside", as opposed to depicting his external appearance. Dolar interprets precisely the same kind of image, the closed-eyed reflection in the mirror, but he gives it a contradictory interpretation. This image does not describe the subject's closest perception of himself; rather, the closed-eyed specular image is perceived as an excess that arouses anxiety, or, in Dolar's words, "gaining something too much".[61] While Fried explained the closed-eyed self-portrait as an attempt to achieve perfect congruence between oneself and one's representation, interpreting the self-portrait in Dolar's terms leads to an opposite result, in which the self-portrait reveals the gap between the image and the self.

Lacan claims that realizing the existence of the gaze does not make it disappear. Painters like Goya succeeded in conserving the gaze.[62] Dolar's description of the mirror reflection as an excess that arouses anxiety elucidates Lacan's conceptualization of the visual experience, namely the way in which a painting can conserve the gaze as an excess beyond the painted image. It is important to recall that Lacan does not explicitly explain how to locate the gaze, which, by definition, cannot be visually embodied, in a painting. The gaze, which is the product of a particular encounter between subject and picture, emerges from a lack, from something that cannot be represented. I suggest that since the gaze is produced through an encounter between the subject and the object, it can also appear, through surplus interpretations given to certain paintings, at points of contradiction or incoherency, or in the recurring attempts to give meaning, to make that which is incoherent coherent.

I began with the various ways in which art theory interprets self-portraiture. The theatrical model and the specular model distinguish between how I paint myself as an other and how I depict my own appearance. Adopting Dolar's analysis to understand self-portraits from a psychoanalytic perspective permits a different reading. The Lacanian concept of the gaze eliminates the dualism in art theories, which is characterized by an active viewer and a passive object of observation. Lacanian relations of looking unfold between a subject and the object as the gaze that looks back at the viewer. In other words, the distinction between seeing myself as the other or seeing myself as my exact reflection is imaginary. The object of observation is never external to me.

Notes

1 Freud, Sigmund. 2001b [1915]. "Instincts and their Vicissitudes". *S.E.* 14: 117–140.
2 Laplanche, Jean, and Jean-Bertrand Pontalis. 1988 [1973]. *The Language of Psychoanalysis*. Trans. D. Nicholson-Smith. London: Karnac Books, p. 278.
3 Lacan, Jacques. 1977 [1949]. "The Mirror Stage as Formative of the Function of the I as Revealed in Psychoanalytic Experience". In *Écrits: A Selection*. Trans. A. Sheridan. New York and London: Norton and Company, pp. 1–7.
4 Lacan, 1977, p. 2.
5 It seems that there is no decisive resolution whether Freud distinguished between these two terms. See: Laplanche and Pontalis, 1988, p. 201.
6 Freud, Sigmund. 2001a [1914]. "On Narcissism: An Introduction". *S.E.* XIV: p. 94.
7 Freud, 2001a, pp. 93–94.
8 Lacan, Jacques. 1988 [1953–1954]. *The Seminar of Jacques Lacan, Book I: Freud's Papers on Technique 1953–1954*. Trans. John Forrester. New York and London: W.W. Norton and Company, pp. 141–142.
9 Evans, Dylan. 1996. *An Introductory Dictionary of Lacanian Psychoanalysis*. London and New York: Routledge, 1996, p. 52.
10 Lacan Mirror stage, p. 2.
11 Lacan Mirror stage, p. 4.
12 Lacan Mirror stage, p. 3.
13 Lacan, Jacques. 1981 [1964–1965]. *The Four Fundamental Concepts of Psychoanalysis: The Seminar of Jacques Lacan, Book XI*. Trans. Alan Sheridan. New York and London: W.W. Norton and Company, p. 126.
14 Lacan, 1981, p. 207.
15 Lacan, 1981, p. 203.
16 Lacan, 1981, pp. 138–139.
17 Lacan, 1981, p. 144.
18 Lacan, 1981, p. 209.
19 Žižek, Slavoj. 1998. "The Seven Veils of Fantasy". In *Key Concepts of Lacanian Psychoanalysis*. Edited by Danny Nobus. London: Rebus Press, p. 202.
20 Alpers, Svetlana. 1988. *Rembrandt's Enterprise: The Studio and the Market*. Chicago: University of Chicago Press.
21 Dolar, Mladen. 1996. "At First Sight". In *Gaze and Voice as Love Objects*. Edited by Slavoj Žižek and Renata Salecl. Durham and London: Duke University Press.
22 Lacan, *Seminar XI*.
23 Lacan, *Seminar XI*, p. 43.
24 Lacan, *Seminar XI*, p. 44.
25 Lacan, *Seminar XI*, p. 81.
26 Koerner, Joseph Leo. 1993. *The Moment of Self-Portraiture in German Renaissance Art*. Chicago and London: University of Chicago Press.
27 Koerner, 1993, pp. 76–79.
28 I do not claim that the distinction of two models of self-portraiture is foolproof. This can be seen in Dürer's *Self-portrait as a child* (1484). That portrait of the young Dürer can be conceived as an example of the specular model. However, in his

later years, Dürer added to the portrait the title: 'Dürer's self-portrait as a boy'. In this case, the act of declaration retroactively sets the theatrical model in motion. That is, young Dürer's self-portrait was transported from the specular to the theatrical model.

29 Fried, Michael. 1992. *Courbet's Realism*. Chicago: University of Chicago Press.
30 Fried, 1992, p. 58.
31 Note that something of this complexity can be seen in the titles of the paintings as well: Rembrandt's paintings, as paradigmatic cases of the theatrical model, are entitled self-portraits, while Courbet's paintings are entitled as if they were not attributed to the painter himself, for instance: The Wounded Man, Man with a Pipe, and so on.
32 Freud, Sigmund. 1962 [1919]. "The Uncanny". *SE* 17: 219–252. London: Hogarth Press.
33 Freud, 1962, p. 219.
34 Freud, 1962, p. 226.
35 Freud, 1962, p. 234.
36 Freud, 1962, 236.
37 Lacan Mirror stage, pp. 1–7.
38 Lacan Mirror stage, p. 2.
39 Lacan XI.
40 Lacan XI, p. 73.
41 Caillois, Roger. 1984 [1935]. "Mimicry and Legendary Psychastenia". *October* 31: 17–32.
42 Caillois, 1984, p. 25.
43 Caillois, 1984, p. 28.
44 Caillois, 1984, p. 27.
45 Lacan XI, p. 74.
46 Lacan XI, p. 74.
47 Lacan XI, p. 74.
48 Dolar, 1996, p. 129.
49 Lacan XI, p. 212.
50 Dolar, 1996, p. 132.
51 Dolar, 1996, p. 131.
52 Dolar, 1996, p. 132.
53 Dolar, 1996, p. 132.
54 Dolar, 1996, p. 134.
55 Dolar, 1996, p. 134.
56 Freud claimed that love is fundamentally narcissistic and that most men, at a certain point, substitute their early narcissism with a sexual object, while women shift something of their early narcissism towards their love object, so that, in some sense, they continue to love themselves when they love (Freud, 1962 [1914]).
57 Dolar, 1996, p. 136.
58 Dolar, 1996, p. 138.
59 For further discussion on anxiety as a result of losing the lack, see Lacan, Jacques. 2014 [1962–1963]. *Anxiety: The Seminar of Jacques Lacan Book X*. Trans. A. R. Price. Cambridge: Polity Press, p. 42.
60 Dolar, 1996, p. 139.
61 Dolar, 1996, p. 139.
62 Lacan XI, p. 84.

7 Subject positions in perspective

Amplifying or negating narrativity

The discussion on the positions of the subject in its Lacanian articulation sheds light on a way of looking at a picture, in which the object of observation is neither separated from nor external to the subject who is looking at it. I suggest articulating the question of narrative painting through this way of looking, in which the viewer sees himself as an active participant in the painted scene. As a result, narrativity becomes an integral component of the painting and is not perceived as an external supplement to it. The debate on the positions of the subject shows how we may think of the "expanded pictorial arena", defined in the second chapter, as an operation related to narrativity in painting.

This raises the question of the place of perspective in relation to this debate. Perspective, in all its articulations, is viewed as a way of organizing and articulating the pictorial space and the relations between the viewer and the painting. One of the main suppositions of perspective is that it makes it possible to articulate geometrically the distance between the painter, as viewer, and the painting, and that this distance is manifested by the represented scene. In other words, perspective is the solution that the history and theory of art posit to the question of the position of the viewer in relation to the painting. How, then, may we conceptualize the traditional articulation posited by the history and theory of art within the current argument? What is the relation between the position of the viewer and narrativity? Is perspective representation fundamentally anti-narrative, or is it a means of supporting visual narrativity?

Ostensibly, it appears that given that it is based on a distance between the viewer and the painting, perspective is antithetical to the idea of the absorption of the viewer in the painting. However, perspective has become so central to the theoretical discourse on painting that its assumption of a precise distance between viewer and painting does not preclude considering perspectival paintings in which the viewer takes an active part in the scene. Therefore, perspectival representation is also present in those paintings interpreted according to the "expanded pictorial arena", such as the French salon paintings from the eighteenth century, on which Fried based his absorption theory. In what sense does perspective indeed allow us to articulate the

DOI: 10.4324/9781003516446-8

distance between the viewer and a painting, and does this entail a rejection of the narrative option? What is the implication of the distance between the viewer and the painting, and how can we understand this distance in light of the Lacanian discussion?

Faced with these questions, I turn to examine how theories of art articulate the subject's position in relation to painting through the concept of perspective. As in the discussion of self-portraiture, I turn to the discussion of perspective as a test case to explain the difference between the understanding of painting as it emerges from different theories of art and the understanding of painting through Lacanian discourse.

The term "perspective" in the visual field relates to the spatial organization of a painting and the representation of three dimensions through the use of a two-dimensional medium.[1] The use of the term "perspective" in its widest sense has been prevalent in different ways since antiquity. The concept of geometrical perspective was established at the beginning of the fifteenth century, in Brunelleschi's work and in Alberti's text *On Painting*. In his text, Alberti articulates the laws of geometrical perspective as a template of instruction for painters to arrive at the "correct" representation of reality.

Geometrical perspective relies on a few fundamental principles: the painter is always at a precise distance from the object; the painter's and the viewer's point of view are fixed, static and mono-focal; a two-dimensional surface on which the painter draws the three-dimensional object lies between the painter and the object; the three-dimensional object is transferred to the painting's surface by stretching an imaginary network of coordinates from the viewing eye to the object. The painted lines converge at a single vanishing point. All of the painted elements are organized according to the network of coordinates. Although the Renaissance definition of perspective was understood in Western culture as unified and coherent, with fixed rules derived from a single theoretical definition, later studies show that the concept of perspective is fundamentally heterogenic. Perspective has been interpreted in a plethora of ways; it does not originate from a single source. Hence, there are different types of perspective, even if we confine ourselves strictly to the Renaissance period.[2]

In its early articulations, perspective offered a formal means to organize the painted space. It is safe to assume, then, that theorists of perspective saw it as an "objective" tool rather than a rhetorical one. Thus, for instance, when Brunelleschi sets up his device, his declared aim is to duplicate the way in which he views in an exact fashion, without accounting for various ideological considerations that underlie his vision. Starting from a specific historical moment attributed to Leonardo da Vinci,[3] both theoreticians and painters began to acknowledge that it is impossible to distinguish perspective, as an organizational device, from perspective as a rhetorical device, thus also pointing toward the relationship between perspective and narrativity. The question, however, of the nature of the structure of sense that can be ascribed to perspectival representation remains unanswered. As will be shown later, theoreticians who address this question answer it in different ways. Some view perspective as a device that assists in narrative structuring, while others argue that perspectival representation empties the painting of its narrative features. The latter posit that in its attempt to define the viewing relations in a painting geometrically, perspective reduces the viewing subject to an abstract point and thereby erases him. Comparing the definition of the viewing subject in perspective to the Lacanian definition will make it possible to show how the subject cannot be erased in this manner and that he is present beyond the place supposedly intended for him by the painting.

I will open with the question of how different theoreticians address the relationship between perspective and the possibility of representing narrative in painting, and the relation they assume between concepts of pictorial space and narrativity. Given these varied and, at times, contradictory approaches, perspective will sometimes emerge as a device that promotes and assists in the construction of narrative in painting, and sometimes as a formal device that empties a painting of all narrative meaning. I will then show how different interpretations of a given painting do not help in solving the question of perspective and narrativity. The interpretations of the canonical paintings that are seen as explicitly narratological will show that the perspectival representation in these paintings does not necessarily follow the principles of perspective and often even subverts or violates them. Subsequently, I will show that perspective serves as a sense-generating mechanism that works in reverse: the failure of perspectival representation, or the impediment they encounter in their attempt to construct coherent sense as a result of this failure, is the "added value" of perspectival representation. An examination of these interpretations reveals that the generation of sense springs from the contradictions and failures in the perspectival structure, and not necessarily from the attempt to adhere to its principles.

I wish, therefore, to ground this claim from two directions: the theoretical debate about perspective, on the one hand, and interpretations of paintings, on the other. I will address the various contradictory theoretical claims regarding the possible relation between perspectival representation and narrativity, alongside interpretations of canonical paintings where a failure of perspective is apparent. The two directions constitute two sides of the same coin – an internal failure inherent to the use of perspective, which stems from the inability to ascribe a definable sense to the schematic use of perspective.

It is customary to view Alberti's *On Painting* as one of the cornerstones of the Renaissance theory of painting and the discussion of perspective as one of its main achievements. Alberti writes:

> I like to see someone who admonishes and points out to us what is happening there; or beckons with his hands to see; or menaces with an angry face and with flashing eyes, so that no one should come near; or shows some danger or marvelous thing there; or invites us to weep or to laugh together with them. Thus, whatever the painted persons do among themselves or with the beholder, all is ornamenting or teaching the *istoria*.[4]

This quote specifies some of the requirements Alberti posits for a desired painting: it should awaken the viewer to look at it, inform him what is happening, supply the viewer with "instructions for observation", draw him to or away from the painting. The painting is supposed, then, to stimulate an emotional response in the viewer, in order to promote the *istoria*,[5] a response that would situate him in two alternative positions regarding the painting: as an external viewer looking at a scene enacted before him, "whatever the painted persons do among themselves", and/or as a viewer who takes an active part in the depicted scene, while the painted figures respond to this presence accordingly.

The key idea that emerges here is the connection Alberti draws between the painterly action and the relations between the viewer and the painting. Thus, Alberti tacitly suggests that the articulation of the relations between the viewer and the painting constitutes part of the narrative. That is, Alberti's quotation enfolds within it two approaches to narrativity in a painting: internal narrative, represented through the painted characters, and a narrative that is constructed as a result of the emerging relations between the viewer and the painting. This assumption, implied in Alberti's book, is significant since it relates to different ways of conceptualizing visual narrativity: narrativity that is based on a representation of a sequence of temporal events or a part of such a sequence in a painting, as opposed to a concept of painterly narrative that is based on the relations between the viewer and the painting. Note that Riegl's terms of internal and external coherences in painting, which I discussed in the second chapter, offer a similar state of affairs.

Perspective received a wide range of responses. Yet, only a few studies have ever addressed its narratological aspects and those that did treated it as a secondary topic or as a casual reference. It is possible to analyze the relationship between perspective and narrativity in different ways: as a hierarchical device that supports the formation of plot and can, therefore, highlight certain elements against others; as a device that structures the relations between foreground and background and as an attempt to control, or at least moderate, the duration and order of the act of viewing. Moreover, as Alberti already argues, it is possible to analyze the relation between narrativity and perspective on the basis of the way in which something in the painting "draws" the viewers into the painted field or "draws them out."

In the following pages, I will present the relationship between narrativity and perspective as it emerges from the writings of key art scholars. I intend to show the wide gamut in the opinions about the relationship between perspective and narrativity. Some scholars point toward a direct relationship between perspectival representation and narrative structure, while others argue that perspective works as a formal device that denies narrativity and empties a painting of all meaning apart from its formal aspects. However, even among those who find a connection between perspective and narrativity, there are conflicting voices that ascribe this connection to different aspects of the painting.

Perspective as a narrative support

As part of her discussion of Dutch Baroque painting, Svetlana Alpers compares Dutch and Italian modes of painting. She compares the spatial organization of Italian painting of the Renaissance to that of Dutch painting.[6] Italian paintings, she claims, obey the strict requirements of Albertian perspective, and due to their perspectival spatial organization, are narrative in nature. They render narrativity since they represent hierarchical spatial organization. The figures are placed in the center, like stage actors; there is a clear and distinct hierarchy among the elements depicted in the painting: figures are differentiated according to their role in the represented scene. The protagonist gains a more salient position than other characters; the main event is represented in the foreground and so on. The painting's main interest lies in the story it tells, and all the pictorial elements are calculated in order to achieve this goal.[7]

Although Alpers's main interest is not narrative painting, she implicitly suggests an overall opposition between a geometrical narrative perspective and other modes of spatial organization, such as the model of the camera obscura, which are basically descriptive. Italian painting, hence, can represent a narrative plot, which entails a time sequence and temporal ordering.

E.H. Gombrich also associates geometrical perspective with narrativity. He claims that perspective is a scheme of representation which, much like other schemes common in a certain culture, determines modes of representation.[8] Perspective, according to Gombrich, challenges the viewer to perceive a two-dimensional surface as a representation of a three-dimensional object.[9] Gombrich argues that Alberti first invented perspective so as to fulfill the narrative needs of painting. Until the fourteenth century, the prevalent model for painting was religious and paintings would depict biblical scenes through a cluster of symbols known to both painter and viewers. Then, at a certain point in the early Renaissance, there was a demand to replace religious paintings with a new model, designed to describe scenes as they "really occurred", to produce paintings that would describe a fiction to which the painter was allegedly a witness. Hence, geometrical perspective is positioned beyond a conventional form of spatial organization, the consequence of a paradigm shift from religious paintings that made use of shared symbols to a narrative painting representing a plot. Thus, perspective functions as a narrative device in two ways. First, it makes it possible to represent a narrative as a situation occurring in a certain specific space, as opposed to a representation of a narrative by a cluster of symbols. Second, these scenes are supposed to represent a real documentation, i.e. perspectival representation meant to contribute the image's truth-value.[10]

Gombrich, like Alpers, connects perspective to the ideological-cultural needs of a culture at a definite historical moment. He also connects narrativity with perspectival spatial organization. But while Alpers compares the perspectival model with the model of the camera obscura, Gombrich compares it with a painting based on a series of symbols.

He adds the documentary value, or the need to assert a painterly "truth", to the relation between narrativity and perspective. This raises a problem: does pictorial truth document a given reality, or does it imply an adherence to presupposed laws of perspective? Alberti indeed believed, as his writings imply, that perspective is a tool that traces vision and can, therefore, have the value of truth in some sense. The model of viewing attributed to Brunelleschi indicates that Brunelleschi held a similar position. As I will show in the next chapter in the discussion of *Las Meninas*, despite the naivety of these early Renaissance positions, critics still ascribe these values to perspective in their search for the "perfect solution", especially when they discuss a painting where perspective appears to be complex or fraught.

Whereas Alpers and Gombrich see perspective as a support to narrativity, Erwin Panofsky presents a less unequivocal position. In his *Perspective as a symbolic form,* he grasps perspective as a universal mode of spatial organization, meant to unify a painting by making all its represented pictorial elements commensurable.[11]

Panofsky's essential contribution to perspective lies in his definition of perspective as an interpretive tool for spatial representation, unlike earlier naive approaches that regarded perspective as an objective description of three-dimensional space by two-dimensional means. That is, whereas Alberti and his followers consider perspective to be a scientific, geometrical tool for spatial organization, Panofsky sees perspective "as a symbolic form", i.e. a form subordinated to changing cultural demands.

Panofsky shows that perspective is not an invention but a procedure adequate for a certain historical period, while other periods, such as antiquity, for example, made use of other perspective methods with several vanishing points, which may have created an illusion of depth but did not unify all the pictorial elements. Giotto and Duccio later developed the concept of a perspectivally unified space.

Panofsky's outlook implies that perspectival representation in the Renaissance manifests a shift from the concept of painting as a combination of separate elements, to a concept of painting as a unified space. Perspectival paintings, he claims, include their interpretive position, presented through perspectival representation itself. Although Panofsky does not address the question of the connection between perspective and narrativity, his point of view on perspective raises the following supposition: if perspective is regarded as a vehicle through which a painting made of separate elements becomes part of a fictional reality, perspective can be seen as promoting narrativity in painting.

Later, Panofsky claims that perspective seals off religious art from the realm of the magical and introduces it to a new domain, that of vision, in which magic is a direct by-product of the viewer's experience. By representing miraculous events in an apparently "natural" space, perspective makes it possible for the viewer to absorb these supernatural scenes. Prior to the emergence of perspective, paintings represented the supernatural by means of arbitrary symbols displayed in unnatural, magical space.[12] Perspectival paintings, on the other hand, represent unnatural events as part of a familiar spatial organization, and hence, in a way, "domesticate" these events. Panofsky concludes that "perspective, in transforming the *ousia* (reality) into the phenomenon (appearance), seems to reduce the divine to a mere subject matter for human consciousness; but for that very reason, conversely, it expands human consciousness into a vessel for the divine".[13] In other words, perspective functions as a filter that transforms the divine into the familiar and ordinary. Here again, one can draw an implicit connection between perspective and narrativity, although this connection is weaker than the one suggested by Alpers. Perspective, as such, does not transform a non-narrative scene into a narrative but supports the viewer's ability to recognize and comprehend the depicted scene as part of a narrative.

Unlike Alpers and Gombrich, who present an unequivocal position regarding perspective, Panofsky points to the ambiguous nature of perspective. In his view, perspective consists of complex dialectical relations between the particular and the universal, and between a subjective impression and an objective articulation. The question I would like to address is: how should the ambiguous character of perspective be perceived regarding narrativity? What is the meaning of that ambiguity, and how does it affect the narrativity of paintings?

Panofsky, Gombrich and Alpers point to a connection between perspective as a pictorial spatial organization and a narrative structure attributed to a painting that obeys perspectival rules. While each of these theoreticians posits different claims, they all agree that perspectival representation endows painting with narrative abilities, to varying degrees and intensity.

Perspective and narrativity: contradiction or negation

Contrary to Alpers, Gombrich and Panofsky, some theoreticians deny any connection between perspective and narrativity. Martin Jay and James Elkins, for instance, argue that perspective is anti-erotic and anti-narrative.[14] Anti-erotic, since it offers an objective point in the form of a stable, indifferent and abstract eye. Anti-narrative, since perspective precedes the modernist move of reducing painting to its formalist characteristics alone and implies that designating sight and vision through geometrical means replaces discursive content of the painting.

Thus, Jay argues that perspectival order entails repressing desire, with which concepts of sight prior to perspective, were engaged.[15] Besides its anti-erotic aspect, Jay continues, perspective also engenders an anti-narrative effect:

> Alberti, to be sure, had emphasized the use of perspective to depict *istoria*, ennobling stories, but in time they seemed less important than the visual skill shown in depicting them. Thus, the abstraction of artistic form from any substantive content, which is part of the clichéd history of

> twentieth-century modernism, was already prepared by the perspectival revolution five centuries earlier.[16]

That is, perspective follows a scientific worldview, which does not interpret the world as a divine text but sees in it a spatial-temporal order filled with objects, which can be observed with the dispassionate eye of a researcher. Jay, hence, sees perspective as a formal tool with imperial tendencies, taking control not only of the pictorial space but also of the meaning of painting itself. Perspective, according to Jay, signifies a broader shift in painting from its narrative functions toward a formalist attitude, reducing it to its painterly values alone, of forms devoid of any content.

It is interesting to note that like Jay, both Panofsky and Gombrich bind perspective with a secular mode of representation, when compared to an earlier religious model. But whereas Panofsky and Gombrich attributed narrative competence to perspective, Jay points to the same characteristics, such as the spatial-temporal order, to make the argument that perspective is anti-narrative.

Yet Jay's discussion raises a more crucial point concerning the contradiction between perspective and narrativity and their relation to desire. Perspective, according to his view, assumes an indifferent, neutral point of view, devoid of desire; and this impassionate look neutralizes the narrative aspects of the painting. This insight will gain new meaning when, in what follows, I discuss Lacan's reading of both perspective and desire in the visual field. At this point, if we examine Jay's discussion in light of Alberti's definition of the relations between picture and viewer, we can see that Jay confounds two aspects of narrative. That is, while Alberti refers to "whatever the painted persons do among themselves or with the beholder", thus referring to two notions of narrative, Jay relates to these two aspects interchangeably.

Elkins also relates to the effects of the vanishing point. As he states, "It is characteristic of perspective to interrupt a narrative with a 'meaningless' comment. Perspective has this non-narrative impetus: it has to be forcibly put to narrative use".[17] In other words, Elkins implicitly suggests that perspective spatial organization necessarily posits a certain structure of meaning, which contradicts the narrative meaning of the painting as a whole.

Just as in the case of the theoreticians mentioned above, Jay's and Elkins's discussions of perspective and narrativity constitute only a marginal part of a broader discussion. In all these cases (with the exception of Panofsky's ambiguous position), over and above their radically different positions, they argue in similar terms. That is, whereas Alpers and Gombrich saw perspective as supporting narrativity, Jay and Elkins assumed the opposite. However, they all share an unambiguous attitude toward the relations between perspective and narrativity.

Norman Bryson's discussion of perspective presents a different relationship.[18] According to Bryson, the relationship between perspective and narrativity is complex: perspective supports narrativity in the sense that perspectival paintings organize the pictorial information into a unified space, creating a hierarchy among the various details of the painting. However, Bryson also describes another procedure in which, as a result of perspectival representation, the viewer is reduced to an abstract point and, at the same time, returns to the pictorial arena as a corporeal presence. That is, perspectival rules both organize the pictorial details hierarchically and lead to the embodiment of the viewer as a physical entity in the painting. The architectural elements of the painting relate to the viewer as one of its depicted elements. He argues that perspectival paintings succeed in representing narrative, but the viewer becomes part of the pictorial scene. Bryson thus refers to the internal and the external narratives, which, according to Alberti, can coexist in the same spatial organization. Bryson, however, shows how the internal and external narratives each relate differently to the same spatial organization, which then becomes ambiguous.

In order to explain the ambiguity of the vanishing point, Bryson describes a historical shift in the perception of pictorial representation. Like Panofsky and Gombrich before him, he distinguishes between two fundamental spatial perceptions: An image that consists of several separate pictures and an image organized under a unifying spatial organization.[19] Bryson binds these different modes of painting with the semiotic terms denotation and connotation. He argues that at a particular historical moment, there was a transition from a conception of painting as a denotation to its conception as a connotation.[20]

A denotative painting is a painting that functions like a symbol, standing for a hermetic unit of meaning, which is external to the painting, and which the viewer is supposed to identify. This kind of painting does not assume the corporeal presence of a viewer watching it, nor does it refer to the procedure of looking or to the viewer's speculations. The viewer directly passes from seeing the picture as a symbol to understanding the meaning it stands for. The specific viewer and his particular way of looking are irrelevant since all that is required is activating a minimal a priori scheme. Thus, claims Bryson, the painted episodes are not seen as part of a developing narrative but rather as a circular narrative: a narrative that begins right after it has ended.[21] The gaze assumed by this sort of painting is not human but godly: the viewer does not play a part in establishing the meaning of the painting, he is merely a link between image and signification. There is no room in this scheme for the exchange of gazes between a viewer and any pictorial other, since the viewer is reduced to an entity acting under a supreme gaze.

At a certain historical moment, Bryson continues, there was a crisis in this visual regime, since the image expanded beyond the basic interpretive scheme.[22] Each episode strove to break free of the sequence in a move that can be described as a passage from pictorial *langue* to pictorial *parole*. That is, the same image that previously appeared as a series of episodes now sought to gain an independent status for a particular viewer. Moreover, its specific meaning was activated by an encounter with the viewer that could not be predicted.[23] From now on, the image "creates for the viewer a space and indeed a metaphysic of presence, since the viewer is correspondingly singled out from the liturgical chorus and specified ostensively, as the recipient of this particular narrative segment".[24] That is, the denotative image becomes connotative: the image now functions as a dynamic, independent system of signs, which is activated by the vision of a singular viewer. This mode of looking does not provide the viewer with a direct message but entails deciphering implicit contents that the viewer extricates out of the image. The image no longer functions as a narrative unit that the viewer immediately recognizes. Now, it is conceived as a construct that generates an independent space and presence for the viewer.

Bryson hence distinguishes between denotative painting and connotative painting. Alongside these concepts, he posits perspectival painting as a painting of a unified space. Two questions can be raised at this point. First, what is the relation between these two concepts of painting and narrativity, namely, which one is more narrative than the other? Second, where should perspectival painting be posited within Bryson's distinction between denotative and connotative painting?

The solution to the first question may lead us back to Alberti and his differentiation between the two modes of narrative: denotative painting, which relates to an internal narrative in which the depicted figures are engaged, and connotative painting, which refers to a narrative that unfolds between the depicted figures and the viewer.

Regarding the second question, perspectival painting contains, in a sense, characteristics of both denotative and connotative painting and shows that they cannot be easily consolidated. Despite the Albertian ambition to reduce the viewer to a theoretical point, claims Bryson, the viewer is physically present in the painting: "the vanishing point is the anchor of a system which *incarnates* the viewer, renders him tangible and corporeal, a measurable, and above all a visible object in a world of absolute visibility".[25] Bryson continues to claim that, consequently, the viewer's own gaze turns back at him from the vanishing point:

> the single vanishing point marks the installation within the painting of a principle of radical alterity, since its gaze returns that of the viewer as its own object: something is looking at my looking: a gaze whose position I can never occupy, and whose vista I can imagine only by reversing my own, by inverting the perspective before me, and by imagining my own gaze as the new, palindromic point of disappearance on the horizon.[26]

In this sense, apart from its manifested target of organizing the pictorial space, perspectival painting turns the viewer into a presence embodied in the picture, since the viewer's gaze gains a representation of its own – the vanishing point embodies the viewer's own gaze looking back at him. In other words, Bryson refers to two aspects of the transition between two concepts of painting. The first passage is a transition from denotative painting to connotative painting, from a painting that does not take into account a particular procedure of looking to a painting founded on particular terms of viewing. One aspect of this passage of the "crisis of visual regime" is the way in which the painting, as a structure of meaning, is no longer perceived as a stable a priori structure. The second passage is the transition from a painting that does not relate to the viewer's point of view to a painting that is organized around this very point of view. But it is precisely here that an ambiguity, immanent to any perspectival painting, comes into play. Perspectival painting, by definition, relates, on the one hand, to a specific viewer as a corporeal, physical presence and, on the other hand, strives to reduce this entity to an abstract point. In other words, perspectival painting is supposed to function as an open sign system, in contrast to the hermetic symbol, posited by denotative painting. Regarding the relations between picture and viewer, perspectival painting contains the same ambiguity in which, on the one hand, like denotative painting, the viewer is reduced to an abstract point and is thus paradoxically excluded from the act of looking, and, on the other hand, the painting is organized around his physical presence. Bryson claims that Alberti intended this:

> the eye of the viewer is to take up a position in relation to the scene that is identical to the position originally occupied by the painter as though both painter and viewer looked through the same viewfinder onto a world unified spatially around the centric ray ... unified spatially but also informationally, since all the data presented by the image are to cohere around a core narrative structure. Yet curiously, the construction of a punctual and disembodied subject is precisely what painting organized around a single vanishing point fails to achieve.[27]

What kind of relation between narrativity and perspective can be drawn from Bryson's discussion? Bryson's argument suggests that representing a narrative by perspectival means serves to reduce the presence of the viewer to a theoretical point. This argument seems similar to Jay's claim that the act of reducing the viewer to a theoretical point denies narrativity and draws attention to the formal characteristics of perspectival painting. However, according to Bryson, the viewer's body refuses to disappear. The painting simultaneously becomes a window to a fictional world and an object encountered by a corporeal viewer. This twofold logic described by Bryson gives rise to another problem that touches on the connection between narrativity and painting in general. What is the implication of the physical presence of the viewer in the painting for narrativity? Although Bryson does not address this question directly, the ever-failing attempt to reduce the viewer to a theoretical point means that the painting consists of narrative phases and their denial, which function simultaneously, since the internal and the external viewer alternatively give rise to both an official and a repressed narrative.

Ruth Ronen's discussion about perspective and realism can help clarify the discrepancy between the picture as fiction and the picture as a material object, as epitomized by perspective. Ronen takes the ambiguous nature of perspective a step further. She shows how the vanishing point is impossible. It is a material point on the canvas, designating the position of a specific viewer and relating to a sensual mode of looking.[28] And it is also an abstract point, related to a conceptual mode of looking, according to which all the diagonals of the picture converge at one point. Despite the fact that this deceiving sight, in which parallel lines seem to converge on the horizon, characterizes every act of seeing, perspective goes even further and identifies this point of convergence, the vanishing point, with the eye of the viewer. The vanishing point hence represents two different meanings of seeing: "It is a point conceptually and physically occupied by the observer who, by definition, cannot be part of the picture she is looking at".[29]

Bryson's and Ronen's analyses of the ambiguous nature of perspective can shed light on the connection between perspective and narrativity. Ronen shows that the impossibility of perspective stems from the fact that it is simultaneously both a "description of visibility" and "visibility in itself". The vanishing point, argues Ronen, is an embodiment of a paradoxical object: an object as it is and an object as it is seen.[30] The vanishing point, hence, cannot represent anything specific; it embodies the combination of the looking subject and the subject as looked at. The relation between perspective and narrativity presents us with a similar problem: how can perspective function simultaneously as both a foundation of a represented narrative and a device describing an actual mode of looking?

Perspective and narrativity: interpretations given to canonical paintings

So far, I have examined how theoretical analyses provide diverse and opposing views on the relations between perspective and narrativity. I will now turn to several interpretations of canonical paintings, in which a relation between perspectival space organization and narrativity is implied. These interpretations will show that contrary to its manifest goal as a scientific method for unifying and organizing pictorial space, perspectival representation in fact provides a fertile source of ambiguities and contradictions. However, these contradictions do not rule out narrativity, but in a way support it.

Martin Kemp analyzes the spatial organization in Leonardo da Vinci's *The Last Supper* of 1495–1498. He argues that at first glance, the painting seems to follow perspectival rules.[31] Yet, a closer examination reveals a series of ambiguities and inconsistencies. Kemp meticulously analyzes the construction of the ceiling and walls in the painting and suggests that the ambiguity of the painting results from the indeterminate nature of the painting's architecture, while the question of which architectural element is merely a painted ornament and which represents an architectural component of the painted building remains undetermined. Kemp argues that da Vinci was aware of the fragile nature of perspectival representation and made manipulative use of it, so as to delineate an equivocal space. Another pictorial detail that demonstrates the evasiveness of perspectival representation emerges from the position of the figures around the table. The figures at the back of the table are located in an impossible proximity to each other, while their actual positions remain unclear.

The inconsistencies Kemp points out lead him to claim that da Vinci's space has a logical appearance but cannot be unequivocally translated into an actual space. Kemp argues that da Vinci undermined perspectival rules for two reasons: the perspectival system itself and its distance from physiological optics. Theoretically, a painting should be painted from one point of view, a fact that da Vinci was, no doubt, aware of. The optimal point of view for this painting, one that coheres with the narrative, would be in front of the sitting figures, but this would have required an elevated point of view, far exceeding human proportion. Hence, da Vinci painted the scene from a lower angle, as if the figures were seen from below. As shown in his writings, at that period da Vinci already distinguished between "artificial perspective", which relates to works of art and the painter's projections, which he may shorten as required, and "natural perspective", which relates to the natural perception of objects in space. Da Vinci also made use of a third type: "compound perspective". Hence, according to Kemp, one can surmise that he was well aware of the diverse maneuvers perspective makes possible, despite its strict rules. What, then, were these devices of perspective meant to signify? And can perspective be regarded merely as any other pictorial means made by the painter, or does perspective, from the outset, contain a rapture that it is supposed to disguise?

In his discussion of Masaccio's *Trinity* from 1427 Bryson offers another interpretation that indicates the ambiguous aspect of perspective. Bryson analyzes the spatial organization of the painting and demonstrates the ambiguity of the vanishing point in paintings obeying perspectival laws.[32] This ambiguity stems from the way this painting is organized around two different concepts of space, which makes the position of the subject in the painting unclear. Whereas a painting organized under a single concept of space assumes a single unified point of view, which organizes all the pictorial elements painted from the same height and angle, in Masaccio's *Trinity* the lower part of the picture is painted from a low angle, so the pictorial space extends to a great height, far above the kneeling figures that are adjacent to the sarcophagus.[33] While the arched ceiling is also painted from a low angle, in accordance with the lower part of the painting, the image of God is painted from a different angle, which is completely frontal. Thus, the painting is organized from two different contradictory points of view, which seem to be inconsistent with one another. Bryson attributes this incoherence to a fundamental difficulty characteristic of Albertian perspective. Geometrical perspective has never resolved the conflict between the fictional aspect of the painting, as embodied by the vanishing point, and the physical position of the viewer.

The viewer is positioned in front of the lower part of the painting, while his gaze is directed upward to the kneeling figures. Perspective thus makes the viewer feel inferior to the divinity depicted in the scene. This spatial effect presupposes a real, physical viewer, who stands in relation to the scale of the image. At the same time, however, the image gives rise to an additional conception of a viewing subject, in which the central ray is not empirical but theoretical:

> A *second* vanishing point is included in the image ... it is around this separate, post-Albertian point that the schema of the Crucifixion coheres, *in a zone the body of the viewer cannot occupy*: whereas the head and shoulders of God-the-Father tilt backwards, to be seen in a position in real space, the body of Christ remains in parallel with the picture plane; the foreshortened modeling of Christ's face, legs, arms and torso presumes a viewpoint that is spatially elevated far above the viewer's own body.[34]

Bryson provides another example of a canonical painting that displays an impossible perspective in Jacques-Louis David's *Oath of the Horatii* from 1784. Bryson shows how the organization of space in the painting is not distinct from its subject, which he reads on several levels. He shows how, beyond the original tragedy that the painting alludes to, it is tragic also in that it displays an impossible human point of view shared by both the painter and the viewer. That is, the tragic effect of the painting is not confined to the narrative it displays, as tragedy and despair, but also arises from the way in which the painting dictates a particular manner of viewing where the viewer is placed in a position from which the represented scene is blocked.

According to Bryson, the painting describes the transference of signs. The weakened father transfers his patriarchal power to his sons via the swords. It establishes a chain of place holders – swords, hands, shields – that form a chain of power that neutralizes sight. The sons, whose eyes are blinded because of the power that was transferred to them, will set out in a series of violent acts that will culminate in the murder of their sister. Women, therefore, form the final link in this chain of power: They are speechless, devoid of language and subject to the male gaze that determines them as passive. They do not speak and can barely see since their eyes are cast down.[35] Beyond the painting as an image, this is an image about visuality. Unlike writing on painting, which requires words, painting raises rhetorical arguments about vision and blindness through visual means that are intrinsic to it. Hence, painting cannot escape any locus that is external to it. In Bryson's words: "David is portraying a human visuality, and 'portrayal' seems to require a vantage point, a point of knowledge, outside that which is portrayed: but how can the *image* exit from visuality?".[36] Bryson argues that this complexity is embodied in the spatial organization of the painting.

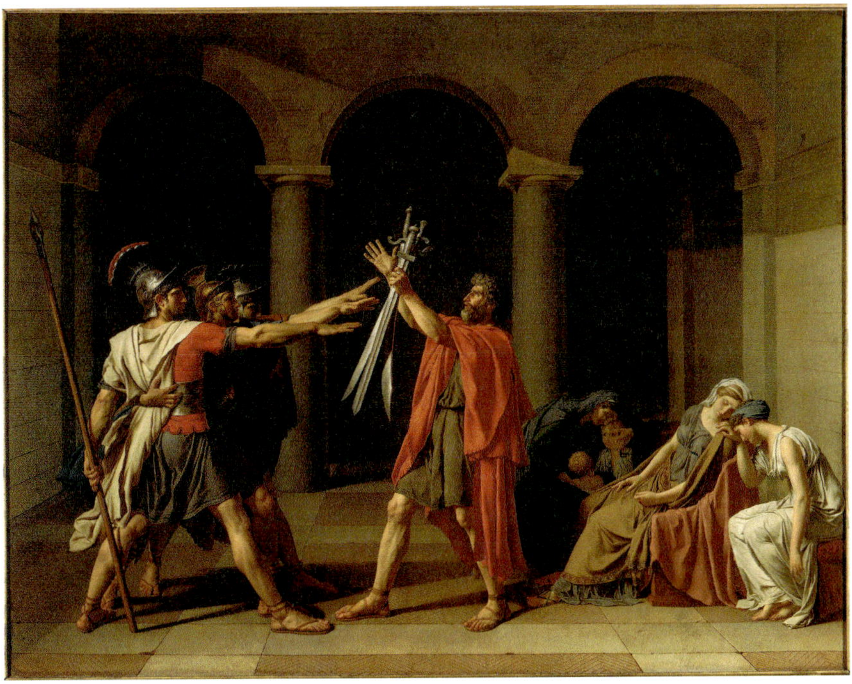

Figure 7.1 Jacques-Louis David, *The Oath of the Horatii*, 1784.

The painting is organized in accordance with an Albertian conception of space in which all the lines converge into a single vanishing point. This spatial organization relates to a single viewer, who is the master of the field of vision and who has complete ownership over what is viewed.[37] But this state of affairs is reversed if the central angle is seen as bidirectional, thereby rendering the vanishing point bidirectional as well. The vanishing point is no longer a point of control for the viewing subject, but also a locus from which he is viewed. And thus, the subject becomes an image himself. In *The Oath of the Horatii,* this process is enhanced since the vanishing point also serves as a narrative focal point, since it is situated at the meeting point between the father and his sons. This means that this point unifies both the viewing of the image itself – i.e. the tormented father passing on the swords – and the act of viewing his point of view. At this point, claims Bryson, the painting ceases to exist on the level of communication, moving from painter to viewer, and creates instead a circular movement of viewing in which the fictional characters, the painter and the viewer are all subject to alienation from what they see.[38] In other words, Bryson shows how the dual function of the painting – an image that we view and an image that analyzes processes of viewing – is entailed in the organization of the painterly space as a locus of impossibility.

However, the complexity of perspective in this painting extends even further than this, since the Albertian perspective does not constitute the only spatial organization in the painting. The frieze of the pillars that appear in the painting in the three arches in the background serves here as a horizontal spatial organization, in addition to the Albertian perspective, which allows for the organization of spatial depth. That is, David posits two concepts of viewing, which function simultaneously: viewing the depth and the horizontal plane at once. He employs two opposing conventions for the representation of space. Their combination renders the painting anamorphic: as if it is possible to view it only from a point that is inaccessible to the viewer. Each of these ways of organizing space, when viewed in isolation, promises the viewer a complete picture, but their simultaneous function causes the image to cohere not from a point the viewer may reach, but precisely from a locus where the viewer is conspicuously absent – that is, the locus where he is excluded from the represented scene.[39] Bryson also shows, therefore, how the perspectival representation in the painting does not reinforce or deny narrativity but serves finally to create an impossible space that does not align with the viewer's position or displays the impossibility of the viewer being part of this space; and this failure operates in correspondence with the painting's main theme about death and blindness.

Michael Fried points to another painting by David containing a violation of perspective, this time in the painting *Belisarius Begging for Alms* from 1781. The painting portrays Belisarius, a renowned army general who fell from grace and became blind, becoming in old age a beggar. Fried claims that in this painting, David shifts the vanishing point to the side. This shift of the vanishing point is designed to place the concrete viewer of the painting in a specific position in front of the figure of the soldier on the left and to the back. The figure of the soldier serves as a surrogate, a mediating figure for the concrete viewer. The flagstones that relate to the shifted vanishing point are represented differently from the way flagstones usually related to a vanishing point are painted.

Fried claims that David undermines the effectiveness of the illusion to enhance the viewing effect. However, the tension that exists between the concrete position of the viewer at the front of the painting and his immersion into the inner space being shifted sideways is not the only tension in the painting. In addition to this, David paints Belisarius in profile, and the inscription on the masonry block next to him is viewed from the side. In a certain sense, it appears as if the painting has been rotated 90 degrees clockwise. This manipulation of perspective lends the impression that the painting does not "reveal itself" to the viewer but, contrarily, conceals from the viewer what is happening. This means that David opens his painting to conflicting points of view that are not available to the viewer standing in front of the painting.[40] This inaccessibility might then relate to the painting's subject in the blindness of the main figure.

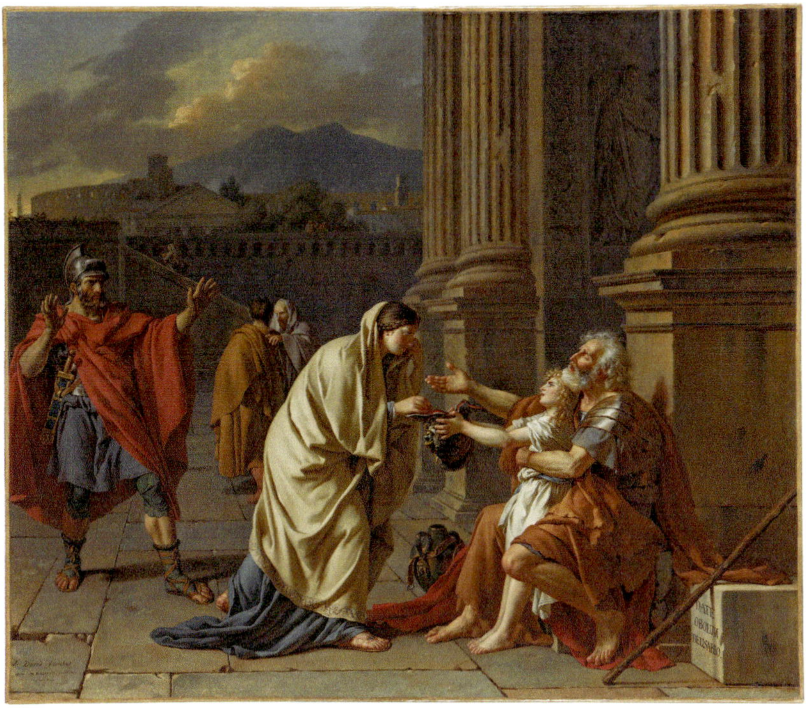

Figure 7.2 Jacques-Louis David, *Bélisaire Begging for Alms*, 1781.

Rudolf Arnheim provides another example of the ambiguity arising from perspective in his interpretation of Tintoretto's painting *The Discovery of the Body of Saint Mark* from 1562 to 1566.[41] Arnheim addresses the failure emerging from the incompatibility between the distortions caused by perspectival representation in the painting and the particular position of the viewer in front of the painting. In this painting, the vanishing point is located in the raised hand of the saint who is standing on the painting's left side. That is, were the painting a photograph, the camera would have to stand on the left side of the frame, in front of the figure of the saint. When a viewer stands in this place, their line of vision aligns with the painted architecture in line with the vanishing point at the left of the painting. According to Arnheim, Tintoretto places the saint outside the painting's center to accentuate "the unexpectedness of the saint's miraculous appearance".[42] Perspective functions here, therefore, as a device that assists narrativity. But what happens when the viewer moves to the right and their vision is no longer aligned with the vanishing point? If it were an actual space, the vanishing point would have shifted with the movement of the viewer. In the painting, however, something else happens as the viewer can move to stand in different positions in front of the painting, but the perspectival distortion remains the same. The result is a paradoxical and impossible space in which the space viewed remains the same, with all of its distortions, even as the viewer changes his vantage point. As Arnheim claims, the viewer looks at an impossible spectacle since they cannot place themselves in a position other than the one afforded by the vanishing point and still see the same perspectival arrangement.[43] That is, the perspective in the painting displays a subjective point of view even as the perspectival device aims to objectify such subjective viewing. What happens in practice is that the viewer, who is not necessarily confined to the vanishing point assumed by the painting, looks at it from different points of view that are not aligned with its specific perspectival design. Tintoretto's painting demonstrates this explicitly, since its vanishing point is not conventional in assuming a specific subject's position. When the viewer takes their traditional place in front of the painting, the pictorial space is revealed as paradoxical, as the viewer is meant to see a picture of an impossible world.[44]

The contradictions that emerge from the different interpretations discussed above relate to several aspects of perspective: the impossible relations established by perspective between the painter and the viewer, as in David's *Oath of the Horatii* or *The Discovery of the Body of Saint Mark* by Tintoretto. The incoherence of the image itself is a point of contradiction and ambiguity, as in da Vinci's *The Last Supper* or Masaccio's *The Holy Trinity*. Do these violations of perspectival representation constitute a mechanism for the generation of sense similar to the way in which perspective itself is understood as bearing sense, or is it perhaps a different matter, where the violation itself allows for pictorial sense to emerge? Is there a deliberate misuse of the laws of perspective out of which sense arises, followed by an attempt to explain the resulting incongruity as veiling something in the painting that precisely escapes sense?

Ostensibly, it is possible to see in perspective the embodiment of the imaginary subject's position in the painting and to assume that this is its primary function. Panofsky's discussion already raises this view by exposing how perspective does not represent truth from a single Archimedean point external to the painting, but rather entails a symbolic form that, from the viewer's point of view, is deemed to represent the truth. However, the importance of perspective in relation to the delineation of subject positions in a painting is not limited to revealing its imaginary aspect. Its importance emerges precisely where its limitations are revealed. As I claim, perspective constitutes a mechanism for generating sense that operates in reverse, and the failure of perspectival representation, or the withholding of coherent meaning as a result of such failure, is precisely the "added value" of perspective. Contradictions in the perspectival structure bring about the generation of sense. As will be shown next, with reference to Lacan's manner of interpreting perspective, the subject that perspective occludes beneath an imaginary point nevertheless reemerges despite the attempt to veil him.

Notes

1 I rely here on Ruth Ronen's discussion of perspective. In the context of a wider discussion about perspective and realism, Ronen surveys key points in the historical development of theories of perspective. Ronen's argument on perspective from a Lacanian position also lies in the background of claims I will later make (Ronen, 2002, pp. 123–163).
2 Elkins, James. 1994. *The Poetics of Perspective*. Ithaca and London: Cornell University Press; Damisch, Hubert. 1994. *The Origin of Perspective*. Trans. John Goodman. Cambridge: MIT Press.
3 Kemp, Martin. 1990. *The Science of Art: Optical Themes in Western Art from Brunelleschi to Seurat*. New Haven and London: Yale University Press, pp. 47–49.
4 Alberti, Leon Battista. 1966 [1435–1436]. *On Painting*. Trans. John R. Spencer. New Haven: Yale University Press, p. 78.
5 Although, as Alberti's English translator, John R. Spencer notes, the term *istoria* could not be identified completely with the term narrative, the term refers to the painting's dramatic content and its effect upon the viewer. Moreover, Spencer himself indicates that according to Alberti "the painter must be capable of employing the perspective construction for the visual, temporal, and spatial unity which it implies" (Spencer, John R. Introduction to *On Painting*, pp. 23–24). This requirement for unity, which alludes to Aristotle's *Poetics*, stresses, I argue, the narrative aspects of painting according to Alberti.
6 Alpers, Svetlana. 1983. *The Art of Describing: Dutch Art in the Seventeenth Century*. Chicago: University of Chicago Press.
7 Alpers, 1983, pp. 41–44.
8 Gombrich, Ernest H. 1960. *Art and Illusion: A Study in the Psychology of Pictorial Representation*. New Jersey: Princeton University Press.
9 Gombrich, 1960, p. 257.
10 Gombrich, Ernest H. 1994. *The Image & the Eye: Further Studies in the Psychology of Pictorial Representation*. London: Phaidon Press Limited, p. 189.
11 Panofsky, Erwin. 1991 [1927]. *Perspective as a Symbolic Form*. Trans. Christopher S. Wood. New York: Zone Books.
12 Panofsky, 1991, p. 72.
13 Panofsky, 1991, p. 72.
14 Jay, Martin. 1988. "Scopic Regimes of Modernity". In *Vision and Visuality*. Edited by Hal Foster. Seattle: Bay Press, pp. 3–23. Elkins, James. 1994. *The Poetics of Perspective*. Ithaca and London: Cornell University Press.
15 Jay, 1988, p. 8.
16 Jay, 1988, pp. 8–9.
17 Elkins, James. 1994. *The Poetics of Perspective*. Ithaca and London: Cornell University Press, pp. 146–147.
18 Bryson, Norman. 1983. *Vision and Painting: The Logic of the Gaze*. New Haven: Yale University Press.
19 A similar distinction was made, as mentioned before, by Panofsky and Gombrich. Yet, as will be shown, Bryson identifies the two painterly models with semiotic terms.
20 Bryson, Norman. 1983. *Vision and Painting: The Logic of the Gaze*. New Haven: Yale University Press, p. 96.
21 Bryson, 1983, pp. 97–98.
22 Bryson, 1983, p. 98.
23 Bryson, 1983, p. 98.
24 Bryson, 1983, p. 98.
25 Bryson, 1983, p. 106.

26 Bryson, 1983, p. 106.
27 Bryson, 1983, p. 104.
28 Ronen, Ruth. 2002. *Representing the Real*. Amsterdam and New York: Rodopi.
29 Ronen, 2002, p. 143.
30 Ronen, 2002, p. 145.
31 Kemp, Martin. 1990. *The Science of Art: Optical Themes in Western Art from Brunelleschi to Seurat*. New Haven and London: Yale University Press, pp. 47–49.
32 Masaccio's *Trinity* is specifically relevant in this context since it is considered as one of the first paintings to demonstrate perspectival rules that would be discussed later by Alberti. See Aiken, Jane Andrews. 1998. "The Perspective Construction of Masaccio's *Trinity* Fresco and Medieval Astronomical Graphics". In *Masaccio's Trinity*. Edited by Rona Goffen. Cambridge: Cambridge University Press.
33 Bryson, 1983, p. 108.
34 Bryson, 1983, pp. 108–110.
35 Bryson, Norman. 1984. *Tradition and Desire: From David to Delacroix*. Cambridge: Cambridge University Press, pp. 70–72.
36 Bryson, 1984, p. 75.
37 Bryson, 1984, p. 77.
38 Bryson, 1984, p. 78.
39 Bryson, 1984, p. 79.
40 Fried, Michael. 1988. *Absorption and Theatricality: Painting and Beholder in the Age of Diderot*. Chicago: University of Chicago Press, p. 158.
41 Pinacoteca di Brera, Milan.
42 Arnheim, Rudolf. 1988. *The Power of the Center: A Study of Composition in the Visual Arts*. Berkeley and Los Angeles: University of California Press, p. 69.
43 Arnheim, 1988, p. 71.
44 Arnheim, 1988, p. 71.

8 *Las Meninas*

The viewer is inscribed in the painting

The previous chapter concluded with the assertion that perspectival paintings promote narrativity by articulating a failure that is inherent to perspectival representation. Indeed, this very failure gives rise to its own particular narrative. Velázquez's painting *Las Meninas*, to which Lacan dedicates four of his lessons during his thirteenth seminar, provides a masterful example of this state of affairs.[1] The various interpretations of the painting provide explanations for a myriad of problems it raises. The purpose of the present discussion is not to take sides in the ongoing debate around the painting, but to examine it from a different position, to explore the gap in sense opened by the painting, without trying to provide interpretations that will fill this gap. Thus, my examination of the painting will adhere to the paradoxicality it presents before us. I would like to claim that the classical representational model provides a sense that stems from the existence of something that escapes this model. This element will come to fashion the foundation for how we can think of narrativity in paintings.

To follow this line of inquiry, I will turn to various interpretations of the painting and compare them to Lacan's reading of the painting. We can extrapolate from Lacan's interpretation three visual aspects that relate to the crisis in the signifier, which lead to the same conclusion: the subject and the object do not stand in and for themselves. This conclusion was articulated in the chapter on self-portraits, in which I demonstrated the way in which the object of the gaze is never external and separate from the gazing subject. Lacan's discussion of *Las Menians* can, therefore, be read as an elaboration of this fundamental supposition and the manner in which the concepts, which I will later attend to – such as the veil, the representative of representation and the gaze – come into play in the act of looking at the painting.

According to Lacan, *Las Meninas* is a unique painting in that it places at its center the gaze, the impossibility of representation, and a system of imaginary projections. Unlike Michel Foucault, who argues that *Las Meninas* demonstrates a crisis in representational relations,[2] Lacan contends that the painting leans on the classical model of representation, but what makes it so unique is that it places at its forefront a fundamental flaw, which is immanent to the representational relations that are manifested in perspective. That

DOI: 10.4324/9781003516446-9

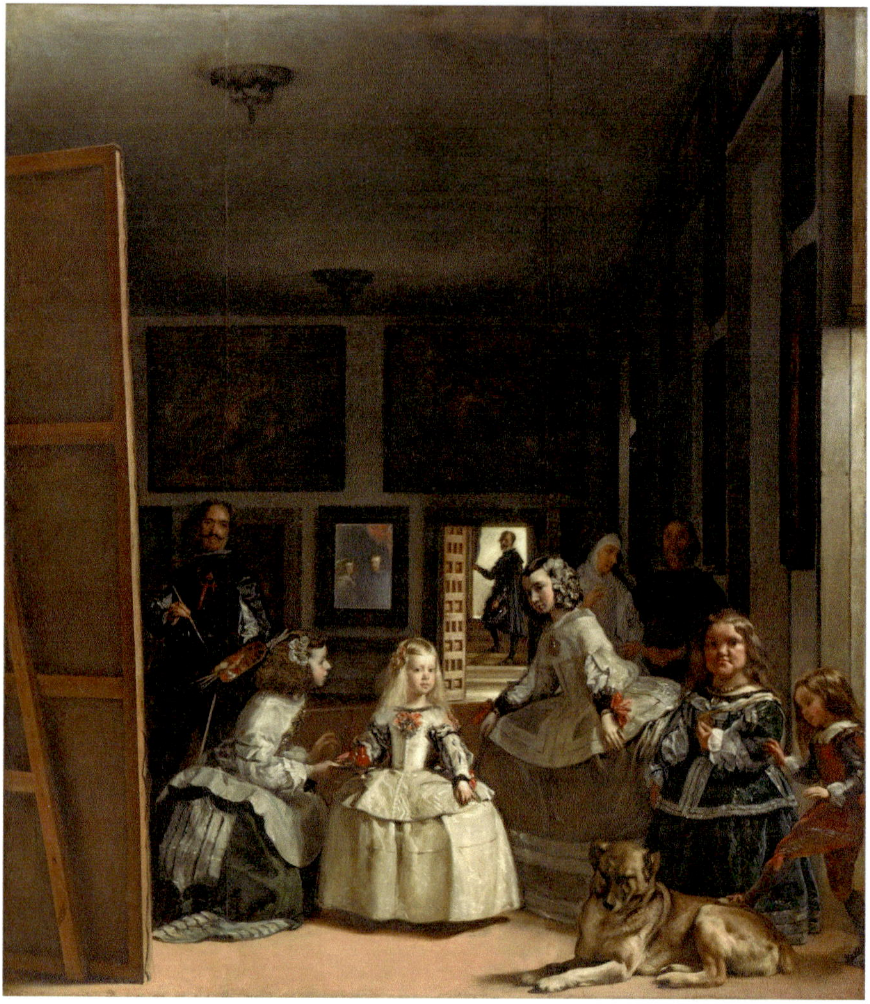

Figure 8.1 Diego Velázquez, *Las Meninas*, 1656.

is, the painting represents operations of sight that exist in every instance of painting; however, in *Las Meninas,* they are turned into the subject of the painting itself. *Las Meninas* is a painting that demonstrates, in an extreme fashion, its own processes of production, representation and viewing. The different interpretations that were given to the painting fell under its spell in the sense that they attempted to extrapolate from it the manner of its production, as if the painting contains a real grain of truth – and by exposing its principles of perspective, it would be possible to reveal this truth. Lacan argues that this is precisely the place in which the painting's spell works. Since it is the place in which we imagine that we are analyzing the painting, but in fact, we are caught in its trap. The impossibility of the painting is manifested in the viewer's interpretative effort, and this is one of the expressions of the painting's Mobius ring structure: the effort to solve the riddle posed by the painting is the painting's subject.

To clarify the Lacanian positions and demonstrate how they address questions raised by the interpreters of the painting, this chapter will follow three aspects I extrapolated from Lacan's interpretation: perspective, representation and the virtual image. These aspects, which help clarify the Lacanian debate, also relate to the topics raised by the other interpretations given to the painting. I intend, then, to address the problems that the critics engaged in, and examine Lacan's discussion of these problems. I will explore the issue of perspective in *Las Meninas* as it is articulated by the various critics and present the way in which Lacan conceptualizes perspective and its manifestation in *Las Meninas*. I will then discuss the representational problems that surface from the various interpretations of the painting and examine the way in which Lacan reads the paintings as a "representative of representation" (*Vorstellungsrepräsentanz*), a term which he borrows from Freud. The third issue I will address relates to the manner in which critics interpret the exchange of glances in the painting and its reflections. I will conclude my analysis of Lacan's discussion by comparing the Lacanian interpretation of the painting to Lacan's discussion of the prisoners' dilemma in his essay "Logical Time and the Assertion of Anticipated Certainty".[3]

Las Meninas and perspective

The relation between spatial organization and the principles of perspective is a major theme in the interpretations of *Las Meninas*. The following questions have been at the center of an ongoing debate: does the painting follow the laws of Albertian perspective, or does it violate them? Does it represent a perspectival paradox? Who is reflected in the mirror and from where? And from which point of view is this painting painted? As I stated in the previous chapter, perspective, as a way of representing space, is seen as a "key" to the understanding of the painting. Moreover, it functions under the supposition that if we attend to the principles according to which this perspective is implemented, we can arrive at the point of view from which the painting was created and make it possible to recreate its original historical moment. Since *Las Meninas* offers an impossible challenge to these kinds of tasks, the interpretative effort dedicated to it has been immense.

Different interpretations that deal with the perspectival representation of *Las Meninas* attempt to locate the painting's vanishing point. The wish to recreate the vanishing point is related to the impossible wish to extract the original point of view, the truth behind the painting. This difficulty points to an inherent incongruity in the painting, a perspectival lack in *Las Meninas,* which is immanent to the painting and also constitutes its complex meanings. The different interpretations offer several possible interpretations of the painting's perspective, and all of them, in their various ways, attempt to resolve that which cannot be settled.

John Searle argues that the painting is constructed as a paradox. He claims that *Las Meninas* breaks the laws of Albertian perspective and presents a visual paradox since the point of view from which the painting is painted is situated in a place that is taken by someone who is not the painter.[4] The paradox stems from the fact that if the vanishing point is in the mirror, then the reflection in the mirror should be that of the painter. Since the mirror reflects the royal couple, the painting depicts a paradoxical state in which the person standing before the mirror is not the one reflected in it. The solution to the paradox, according to Searle, is that much like in the literary medium, in *Las Meninas* the narrator is not the same as the artist.[5]

Ted Cohen and Joel Snyder argue against Searle, claiming that *Las Meninas* does not break the laws of Albertian perspective, but rather follows them.[6] They argue that the painting's vanishing point is not located in the mirror, but rather in the elbow of the image at the door. They conclude that the canvas itself must be the source of the mirror image; that is, the source of the painting is the hidden side of the canvas on which the King and Queen are painted.[7]

According to Amy M. Schmitter, both arguments regarding the position of the vanishing point are true, and the conclusion is hence that perspective representation in painting is not fixed to one vanishing point; rather, the viewer moves between several vanishing points.[8] She offers two readings of the painting which support each other. She believes that we should not dismiss the vanishing point in the mirror, since this is not an empirical location that can be exactly reconstructed. The painting refers to a point that is external to it, but this point is not concrete. Schmitter also claims that when the viewer turns his gaze to the right, the painting does not represent in a simple manner the position of the viewer or the place of the painter as a reflection in the mirror. The mirror represents something else: the painting on the canvas. Thus, the painting offers a multiplicity of representations.

Svetlana Alpers offers another interpretation of the perspectival representation of *Las Meninas*. She believes that the painting involves two antagonistic pictorial models: the window model, related to the Renaissance conception of painting and Albertian perspective, and the *camera obscura* model, which relates to paintings of the Northern Baroque.[9] According to this interpretation, the strength of the painting lies in the impossible cohabitation of these two opposites.

The debates over perspective in *Las Meninas*, which attempt to locate its pictorial vanishing point, also aim, in fact, to give formal validation to the painting. In this sense, I find a relation between these interpretations and the interpretations that attempt to explain what happened in the palace gallery and where Velázquez placed his easel on the day he chose the subject of the painting, that is, interpretations that offer a narrative to explain the picture as a documentation of a real situation.[10] Even though the debate over the figures and objects in the painting is different in almost every respect from the debate around the painting's implementation of the principles of perspective, these debates share a common denominator: the search for an Archimedean point outside the painting that can be unequivocally validated. In the case of identifying the figures, this point is located in historical truth, while in the case of perspective, it is located in geometric credibility. In the first case of identifying the elements in the painting, this wish has probably been satiated through testimonies from the period. In the second case of the vanishing point, no unequivocal ruling can be found. Interpretations that attempt to simply locate the vanishing point in the painting fail, since the painting is not organized around such a point in any clear way.

Most interpretations identify an unresolvable discrepancy in the painting: Alpers posits that this discrepancy stems from the use of two antagonistic models of viewing; Schmitter relates it to two flickering vanishing points, while Searle finds it in a visual paradox. In this sense, Snyder, who relates the complexity of the perspective representation to the allegorical nature of the image, is the exception. In fact, critics who participate in the debate on perspective in *Las Meninas* are unsuccessfully trying to untangle a knot. However, the perspectival failure in the painting testifies to its fundamental incongruency.

Perspective according to Lacan

Before discussing Lacan's analysis of perspective in *Las Meninas*, I wish to outline the way he treats perspective and its interpretation as a whole, which precedes his analysis of *Las Meninas*. This outline makes it possible to trace the logic of his argument: while the different critics discussed above treated perspective representation in *Las Meninas* as a riddle that should be solved or at least trace the principles that guided its creator, perspective representation, in Lacan's conceptualization, places the split subject within the scopic field. This can be extrapolated from Lacan's logical trajectory, which I began to unfold in the previous chapter. Perspective representation does not constitute a problem that can be solved; rather, it is a mode in which the painting represents what cannot be represented.

Lacan opens his discussion with the relation between the position of the subject and the visual structure of the subject. He asks what exactly is involved in the classical position of the subject and answers:

> It is here that the visual structure of this subject ought to be explored… and in the first place the screen, the screen that our analytic experience teaches us to be the principle of our doubt, what is seen does not reveal but hides something. This screen, nevertheless, supports, for us, everything that presents itself.[11]

The interest that Lacan finds in the discussion of perspective stems, then, from the relation between perspective and the position of the subject, while the key to understanding this relation can be found in the visual field, specifically in the concept of the screen. The screen that Lacan theorizes is not one that makes it possible to expose what supposedly lies behind it. Rather, it is the only thing possible for the looking subject. That is, the screen is the world; it does not hide a secret real world. At the same time, however, the screen is what makes sight possible. Lacan argues that in a similar fashion, we cannot understand representational relations as a problem that needs to be deciphered. Rather, we need to examine representational relations in another manner. Perspectival representation, then, is related to Lacan's conceptualization of the screen in that it does not represent something that can be deciphered but itself articulates the subject within the field of vision. This is not about a three-dimensional representation in two-dimensional means, and what is seen does not represent something else that is actually behind it, but "this is what there is".

Lacan postulates three planes in his discussion of perspective in accordance with conventions of perception in the history of art. First, There is a horizontal plane parallel to the picture's horizon line. This plane is the ground on which we stand, along with the painting itself. In addition to the horizontal plane, there are also vertical, parallel planes that are perpendicular to it: the plane of the picture and another plane that I will call the plane of sight. The plane of sight is the place from which the viewer looks at the painting. The two vertical planes, the plane of sight and the plane of the picture, meet with the ground plane. The line formed as a result of the encounter of the picture plane with the ground plane is the central line. This line has a special significance as it forms a meeting point between the represented world and the real world. It represents the earth's ground plane, while the horizontal plane of the pictorial space refers back to it. The viewer is marked as a point on the plane of sight and that is where the point of sight is located. From this point emerges another line, perpendicular to the plane of sight and the plane of the picture in 90 degrees, it crosses them and continues to infinity. This is the line of infinity. The point where this line crosses the picture plane is the vanishing point.

This is how Lacan outlines the elements of perspective representation that can be extrapolated from the different formulations of Albertian perspective. Perspective, as it has been conceived throughout history, demonstrates the imaginary sight attributed to the eye. This sight belongs to a unified subject that controls his field of vision. However, Lacan contends that perspective does not attribute sight to a unified subject; rather, it represents, in its structure, the split subject. As stated previously, in his eleventh seminar Lacan describes the split between the eye and the gaze, which manifests the split of the subject in the field of vision. Perspective constitutes a manifestation of the split subject within the field of vision.[12]

The vanishing point assumes a fixed and still line of vision as if we are like the prisoners in Plato's allegory of the cave and can only see the world when bound to our seats with iron chains. The vanishing point is supposed to represent the looking eye, but human sight is more complex: there are more things between the picture and the viewer.[13] In his attempt to articulate the other things that can be found between the viewer and the picture, Lacan articulates the point of the looking subject, which he calls point S. This point exists in the gap between two parallel lines: the line that connects the ground plane and the lower edge of the picture, and the line on which the subject stands. Lacan states that unlike the vanishing point, this point cannot be articulated and remains hidden from us.[14] This is because it is located between two parallel lines, whereas the vanishing point is a point of convergence. The vanishing point is the point of the looking subject, which represents the imaginary vision of the eye, whereas the point of the subject represents the gaze, a point that falls between the subject and the picture plane.[15]

The point of the subject is a failure built into perspectival representation, and despite its failure or precisely because of it, perspective is seen as a realistic representation. This can be explained as follows: the representation of the relation between the central line, which links the picture and the ground plane, and the line parallel to it, which is the picture's horizontal line, determines how the distance of sight between the subject and the painting is articulated through the painting. However, the subject is located at a point that cannot be represented. The manner of looking and the object we see are located on the same plane, while geometry creates the illusion that a line crosses these two parallel lines. The central line is both the subject's horizon line and a represented element. The subject is located at two points: on the picture's horizon line and the central line. The central line is impossible since it belongs to the ground plane and the picture plane, or the observer's plane and the picture plane.

Perspectival representations assume an imaginary system of projections. When we look at a perspectival painting, we assume the existence of this system of projections, even though it is only an imaginary system, according to which we suppose relations between subject and object. Point S, which represents the subject, is located on an imaginary plane that is parallel to the picture. This means that the subject stands before a picture that he grasps as existing on a vertical plane, and on which he is only partially registered. This partiality stems from the fact that the subject is fundamentally split, and ocular sight, which is the traditional way to conceive of looking at a picture, is related to sight on this "frontal" horizontal plane. This is the window that art theoreticians relate to when they speak of painting as a window to a fictional world. However, as Lacan states, the point S already encapsulates within itself a lack, a failure that is built into the perspective painting itself, and which stems from the fact the subject is split between the ego and the unconscious. In his eleventh seminar, Lacan conceptualizes this split through the split between the eye and the gaze:

> Indeed, there is something whose absence can always be observed in a picture.... This is the central field, where the separating power of the eye is exercised to the maximum in vision. In every picture, this central

> field cannot but be absent, replaced by a hole.... Consequently, and in as much as the picture enters into a relation to desire, the place of the central screen is always marked, which is precisely that by which, in front of the picture, I am elided as subject of the geometral plane. This is why the picture does not come into play in the field of representation. Its end and effect are elsewhere.[16]

While the eye's imaginary vision relates to a vision that, as perspective supposes, is holistic and complete, this coherent vision raises the possibility of a vision that is not in my control and eludes me. Lacan shows how the split itself is embodied within the subject's S point on the picture plane and can be extrapolated from perspectival representation. The subject present in the visual field is divided between being a looking subject himself and being an object to an external gaze that is looking at him.

Perspective, according to Lacan, provides a means of making the painter present in the picture as a subject, just as in other paintings other painters made themselves present through one of the depicts figures. Thus, Lacan explains how perspective aligned with the subject in the visual field: the significant aspect here is that while theories of art treat perspective as an "objective articulation of a subjective point of view", Lacan views perspective not as way of turning the subject into an abstract theoretical structure, but as a a way of making the artist present as a subject. Lacan underscores this argument by distinguishing a mirror image from a perspectival image through the way in which space is organized in each of them. While perspective in the mirror image corresponds to our experience of looking in reality, in perspective painting, the painter as a subject is inscribed in the scopic field.[17] This means that the very attempt to articulate vision through seemingly objective, geometric means raises other aspects of this vision that do not belong to an objective articulation but to a subjective articulation intertwined with desire. In its very structure, the articulation of perspective space contains the subjective split, the distance between the eye and the gaze.

The presence of the gaze emerges in the very same place where the attention is drawn to the imaginary vision of the eye. That is, the very places where imaginary vision describes a complexity or difficulty in vision are the places where we may think of the presence of the gaze. This assertion is critical for this discussion, as it engages with Jay's argument. Unlike Jay, who claims that perspective has a de-eroticizing effect,[18] Lacan argues the exact opposite: a perspectival image means the inclusion of the subject within the scopic field. Lacan later connects perspective and painting to the way in which painting and phantasy are analogous:

> The artist, like every one of us, moreover, renounces the window in order to have the picture, and this is the ambiguity that I gave the other day, that I indicated about the function of phantasy, phantasy is the status of the being of the subject and the word phantasy implies this desire

> to see the phantasy being projected, this space of withdrawal (*espace de recul*) between two parallel lines, thanks to which, always insufficient but always desired, at once do-able and impossible, the phantasy can be summoned to appear in some way in the picture.[19]

Painting and phantasy share, to a certain extent, the same status, that they both exist between two parallel planes that will never meet. The analogy lies in the distance between the picture plane and the plane of sight and the distance between the phantasy and its realization. Another analogy relates to the manner in which both cases are expressed through vision. Phantasy, like a picture, supposes the sight of the phantasy, its projection. The subject is similarly registered in phantasy and painting since, in both cases, it is an articulation of an impossible manifestation.

To understand this analogy, we need to return to Freud's conceptualization of the structure of phantasy. Freud extrapolates from a great number of patients who reported a similar phantasy of being present in a situation in which an adult beats the naked bottom of a child.[20] In his analysis of these cases, Freud outlines three stages to the constitution of the phantasy. The earlier stage relates to a state of competition between the child and his brother over their father's love. The patient then interprets the scene of his father beating another child as "my father loves only me, that is why he beats my brother". This stage is conscious and has a sadistic inflection. The child being beaten is anonymous and not the author of the phantasy. The second stage of the phantasy is a direct product of guilt, in which sadism is turned to masochism. This is the most complex and significant step and can only be reconstructed in the course of analysis. The image of the child changes. Now it is the author of the phantasy himself, and the relevant sentence is "I am being beaten by my father". As Freud explains, in the first stage the child experiences the sentence "My father loves only me, and not the other child, and so he beats him". However, the sense of guilt leads to the reversal of the victory – the patient is now the one being beaten. Now it involves an experience with a masochistic inflection that carries immense satisfaction. However, as Freud claims, this stage is not just about the sense of guilt but a regression to an earlier stage, in which the sentence "my father loves me" is substituted with the sentence "my father beats me".[21] The third step resembles the first. However, now the person carrying out the beating is not the father but a representative of the father, for instance, a teacher. The image of the child as the author of the phantasy no longer appears in it; rather, it is about watching the act of beating. The distinguishing feature in this stage is the clear sexual character this phantasy now has. The first and third stages are similar, while the second is the exception: it is the only unconscious stage in which the author of the phantasy is turned into its "protagonist", and the phantasy receives a masochistic aspect. As Freud claims, this stage never receives real existence, since it is unconscious and can only be reconstructed during analysis.

The structure of phantasy, then, is made of different and detached stages. The transition from one stage to another includes a few transformations and reversals with a complex relation between them, thus, we cannot directly infer one stage from the previous one. Freud sketches the logic of each stage and connects them only retroactively. The stages of the phantasy contain a certain relation to viewing the phantasy, as the author of the phantasy watches the scene. The relation between the subject as a viewer and the subject as the "protagonist" is complex since the viewer becomes not only an active actant in the scene but also the one being acted on. The analogy to perspectival structure, then, touches several aspects. In both cases, there are parallel planes that will never meet, just as the picture plane and the visual plane are parallel to the distance between the stages of the phantasy. In both cases, the representational relations cannot be reconstructed directly. In both cases, the representation does not simply mark the represented. Moreover, in both cases, there is an essential link to sight, which plays a role in the realization of the phantasy.

Lacan's discussion of perspective yields three central points: perspective presents the split subject, the perspective image is the place in which the subject is registered in the scopic field, and the structure of a perspectival painting is analogous to the structure of phantasy.

After showing how perspective includes an impossible point, Lacan defines the presence of Velázquez in the painting *Las Meninas* in relation to this point. As stated above, Lacan argues that perspective is a means of making the painter present in the painting, much like incorporating him as one of the painted figures. As he states:

> Velázquez...gives the impression of putting himself into it [the picture], but you only have to look at him to see ... the point to which he is in it in a state of absence. He is in it at a certain point that I precisely describe ... which is the other point of presence, the other subject point in the field of the picture, which is this point which is determined ... in taking into account precisely the fact that there is a point and a single parallel to the plane of the picture which can in no way be inscribed in the picture.[22]

Through Velázquez, Lacan shows how the painting can embody the subject as point S, but this articulation of the subject is merely partial. According to Lacan, we can understand the line that intersects the ground plane and passes through point S also in the inverse. Just as we assume a certain relation between the horizon line and the infinity line, through which the vanishing point is articulated, thus we can treat the second, impossible point of the split subject through the horizon line in relation to the infinity line that functions in the inverse. Velázquez's image, as it appears in the painting, returns from this point. According to Lacan, Velázquez returns to the picture from the opposite pole, after having split his group of people. The cleavage line shows us through its passage how the split arises from a place external to the picture.[23]

As mentioned in the previous chapter, Bryson also treats the vanishing point as bidirectional. However, while Bryson assumes a symmetrical bidirectionality, in which the vanishing point returns a gaze directed to the viewer in the same way that the viewer looks at the painting, Lacan argues that Velázquez returns to the pictorial scene, but in a different manner, which fashions part of the Mobius strip structure that he assigns to the painting. Velázquez is simultaneously the creator of the painting and is one of its elements. The one who appears on the painted canvas is the same one who determines vision through his gaze, and this yields the painting's Mobius structure.

The figures of the companions, the *Meninas*, Lacan states, turn to Velázquez in a demand: let us see. Different interpretations have assumed that the figures of the *Meninas* look at the king and queen, whom Velázquez paints. Lacan claims that the *Meninas*, with their unfocused looks, turned outside the painting, are pleading to Velázquez, who is painting behind them. We could have understood things more simply if we assumed that Velázquez paints the *Meninas*, who are in front of him with the back of the canvas turned to him, and that they turn to him with a request to see. However, in the painting itself, Velázquez appears on the same plane on which the *Meninas* are located, and the canvas seems to be in their line of sight. Yet, according to Lacan, Velázquez is located at a point external to the painting, a point that is not represented. Lacan explains this through the two axes that he draws – one begins with the figure at the door and creates a diagonal toward the inversed painting. The other axis stretches from the mirror in the background toward the figure of the *Infanta Margarita*. Velázquez is not located on either of these axes, he is rather located outside of them.

Lacan claims that Velázquez's answer to the figures of the *Meninas* is: "You do not see me from where I am looking at you (*tu ne me vois pas d'ou je te regarde*)". Yet, Velázquez says this without saying where this "where" is. This is the place of a gap, of an unmarked space, and it is from there that Velázquez seemingly speaks.[24] Velázquez answers from a place of absence, a place that cannot be represented. In other words, Velázquez is painted in the painting, but the function that he fills cannot be explicated from the way he is marked on the canvas, but in a different manner. His marked image is a cover for the impossible point from which he answers the *Meninas*. This point is also supported by the fact that we can see the image at the door as a reflection of Velázquez. And indeed, as Snyder and Cohen claimed, and as Lacan notes, the painting's vanishing point is located at the elbow of the figure in the door. This figure is the image of Nieto Velázquez, who, according to historical testimonies, held a senior role in the King's court. Lacan claims that he is a double for the painter. He does not ask to see because he is the one who sees, who has seen too much, and so he is about to leave.[25] This duality will be explained in what follows through Lacan's model of the two mirrors.

According to Lacan, the painting sustains two meaningful gaps: the gap at the front, in the space before the *Meninas* figures, and the gap between Velázquez and his painting. The gap at the front of the painting constitutes an important part of the allure the painting holds over the viewers since we grasp ourselves as an integral part of the pictorial space. This is why different interpretations have tried to understand the mirror in the picture as an Archimedean point located outside, one that can reveal the truth of the painting. The gap between Velázquez and the painting, Lacan claims, is analogous to the gap at the forefront of the picture. Velázquez is significantly farther away from the painting he is supposedly painting; he cannot even touch the canvas with his long brushes.[26] The conventional readings interpret this distance as Velázquez moving backward to see better. According to Lacan, the fact that Velázquez is not within touching range of the picture has crucial significance. This is the place in which one of the most significant cracks in the painting appears. It is here that we can catch a glimpse that Velázquez's image is not a representation of him, but rather manifests a contradiction: the canvas is not even within the reach of the painter, and its location tells us that we do not see it from where he is looking at us.

The image of the painter in the painting demonstrates how perspective, as an articulation of the subject's position in painting, does not make it possible to turn him into an abstract construct, a represented point, but only in a limited fashion. The painter here is not a result of the relations of representation but signifies the manner in which subjectivity emerges despite the attempt to abstract it into a theoretical articulation. This distinction is expressed in the painting in the discrepancy between the image of the painter as the creator and the actual painting, both in Velázquez's distance from the canvas and in the Mobius structure that arises from this: Velázquez paints himself painting himself.

Lacan, then, diverts the discussion of perspective in *Las Meninas* from attempts to extrapolate the truth of the circumstances behind the painting. He shows how perspective, as a mechanism designed to reduce the subject to an abstract theoretical point of view, eventually leads to the conclusion that the subject cannot be erased in such a fashion. The very attempt to articulate the subject as an abstract point introduces desire into the picture. In this sense, we may understand Lacan's statement, which he made already in his eleventh seminar, according to which the painting is a trap for the gaze.[27] The painting, as an imaginary system of projections, tempts the viewer to put down his gaze, much like putting down a weapon, but exactly in the place where it will resurface as disguised or as what cannot be articulated. Every painting, according to Lacan, consists of this imaginary system. Thus, by relying on this system, the viewer assumes that he himself is a product of a complex of gazes. What is unique in *Las Meninas* is that the complex of gazes that fashion both themselves and the viewer also functions as the subject of the painting.

***Las Meninas* and representation**

Las Meninas is a painting that challenges the paradigm which dominated the relation of representation in Western culture up to the seventeenth century.[28]

Indeed, in his interpretation of the painting, Foucault claims that it constitutes an example of a system of signs that no longer coincide with their signifiers. *Las Meninas* is the visual manifestation of a paradigm shift, while a literary example of this shift can be found in *Don Quixote*, where the madman is the protagonist, the fool is the wise man, and so forth.[29] Foucault's discussion of *Las Meninas* is different from the interpretations outlined above since he situates the discrepancy that rises from the painting at its center, which he also does not attempt to resolve. *Las Meninas*, in Foucault's way of looking at it, is a painting that presents a paradoxical situation, since it is a painting of a representation that attempts to expose the process of its own representation, while simultaneously maintaining the illusion that it contains within itself a real point located outside of it. Moreover, Foucault claims that *Las Meninas* is ultimately a representation of lack, a claim that stems from the paradoxical structure of the painting.

We could have guessed, Foucault claims, what the painter sees if it were only possible to glance at the hidden canvas. It seems as though we could stretch a line from the eyes of the painter to the real picture and then to us, thereby connecting the views to the painting. It appears to be a simple center stemming from a reciprocal relationship. However, an entire network of uncertainty is unfolded here, one of exchange and deception. The painter looks at those who look at the painting, so long as the viewer takes the appropriate place. At the same time, the painter also ignores the viewer, as he is turned toward the one who was there before him, his model. The painter's gaze, in fact, refers to a number of possible viewers. There is a constant exchange of gazes, and none of them is fixed. This exchange of gazes stems from the fact that the hidden canvas does not allow one gaze to be fixed in a permanent position but supposes multiple and different possibilities. The painting, with its back to the viewer, leaves the question of whether we are watching or being watched open.[30]

On the symbolic register, the sovereignty of the figures in the mirror stems from the fact that they are King Philip and his wife. But this sovereignty, first and foremost, stems from the triple role that it fulfills in the painting. Through these figures, there emerges a precise superimposition of the gaze of the model when it is painted, of the viewer looking at the painting, and of the painter creating it. These three gazes meet at a point that is external to the painting, a point that is also real. In this very reality, this point cannot be seen. The reflection in the mirror in the painting preserves what has disappeared from all the gazes, but perhaps the mirror does not provide the ample information that we assume it does. It is possible that it is hiding more than it reveals. The painting never makes it possible to simultaneously represent the represented and the representing.[31]

In *Las Meninas*, Foucault claims, representation is represented in every point: the painter, the color palette in his hand, the back of the painting, the painting hanging on the wall, the viewers watching, who are themselves framed by other viewers watching them, and last, the heart of all representations, the distant mirror showing the viewers in the painting what is represented. But the mirror is present as a distant reflection, buried deep in an unreal space, foreign to all the gazes directed elsewhere, until the image that is formed is nothing but a pale copy of representation. All of the painting's internal lines, especially those emanating from the central reflection, point toward the thing that is represented, yet is also missing. This represented thing is simultaneously an object and a subject. On the one hand, it is an object, since it is the thing the painter copies to the canvas. Yet, on the other hand, it is a subject, since what the painter sees when he is painting himself is himself. The painted figures in the painting are all directed toward a fictional place occupied by the royal figures. But this is also the painter's real place, since the one who occupies this ambiguous place, in which the painter and the sovereign authority constantly alternate, is a pure representation of absence. However, this is an essential lack, whose essence is drawn from the way in which it never ceases to exist through the different figures, the hidden canvas and the viewers in the painting, who all revolve around this lack.[32] In other words, the "never-ending flicker" emanates from the fact that looking at the painting contains an attempt to follow the relations of looking that took place when the painting was painted, and, at the same time, an attempt to understand the scene that is unfolded before the eyes of the viewer. This is where the never-ending exchange of places between the King and the painter emanates from. Here again, the question concerning the status of representation appears from the very supposition that the painter is both the representing and the represented object.

The representative of representation

In his discussion of *Las Meninas*, Lacan provides a central place for Foucault's interpretation of the painting (Foucault was also present in this seminar) and pauses on one central argument with which he disagrees. Unlike Foucault, who claims that *Las Meninas* is a "representation of the world of representations",[33] Lacan argues that *Las Meninas* is, in fact, a "representative of representation" (*Vorstellungsrepräsentanz*). The concept originates in Freud's discussion of repression. According to Freud, repression consists of two stages. In the first stage, primal repression, what is repressed is expressed through its representative. In the second stage of repression, the psychic derivatives of the representative are repressed. The origin of these derivatives could be different from the repressed representative, but they retain a certain associative relation to the repressed, and so they share in its destiny.[34] This means that what was repressed does not represent itself but is fixed through its representation. It can be extrapolated through a signifier that registers repression in language. The signifier, then, is a representative of representation. In other words, repression takes place at a certain early stage. Repression constitutes a representation of a missing object that cannot be represented. The signifier which registers this repression in language is the representative of representation: it represents something that is missing. Fink explains that according to Lacan, we posit these repressed representations through signifiers that make it possible for the drives to be represented.[35] The meaning of the representative of representation lies in the unconscious relation between the signifier and the signified. Žižek explains this concept through a joke: a painting was hanging in a museum, depicting Lenin's wife in the arms of a young party member.[36] The title of the painting reads "Lenin is in Warsaw." When the museum visitor asks the tour guide where Lenin is, the tour guide answers, "Lenin is in Warsaw." Thus, the title of the painting does not refer to what is depicted in the painting, but marks that which the painting represses.

In his thirteenth seminar, Lacan makes use of the concept of the representative of representation when discussing the visual field. He demonstrates this by comparing Plato's myth of the cave to prehistoric cave paintings, and this analogy also extends to the customary manner of interpreting these images in philosophy and the history of art.[37] The history of art poses some questions regarding cave paintings, like the ones found in Lascaux or Altamira, since these sites are in areas that are very difficult to reach and were discovered by accident. Moreover, the paintings in these caves are not located by their entrances but in their depths. Art historians have grappled with the questions of why the paintings are painted in such hidden places, and what is the meaning behind the seemingly random arrangements of the groups of animals on the walls, which in some instances are painted one on top of the other. The answer they suggest is that these paintings were used for ritualistic purposes to ensure a successful hunt. According to this explanation, the cavemen treated the image as part of the animal, hence as a guarantee to catch the animal during the hunt. Another fact that the history of art turns to is the realistic representation of these paintings, which proves that man's ability to create realistic painting is not a result of an evolutionary developmental process. Historians postulate that cavemen thought of painting as a creational process, which is related to the existence of the actual animals. The cavemen believed that, through realistic wall paintings, they had the power to create animals or at least increase the frequency with which they appear.[38]

Lacan refers to the two aspects of this interpretation of the cave paintings, albeit implicitly. He offers an alternative explanation for the mystery of cave paintings by comparing them to Plato's myth of the cave. Like the cave paintings, the shadows in Plato's cave are artificial, a result of an act of projection on a wall. Plato, Lacan claims, takes us to the belly of the cave so that we can wake up to the fact that what we see before our eyes are mere shadows, reflections of that which takes place behind the backs of the prisoners of the cave. These cave paintings, he says, relate to the exact same thing, since they are similarly disconnected from the external world. They do not signify a reality that is external to the cave; they are, rather, signifiers that represent other signifiers.[39]

The cave paintings depict figures of different animals in a realistic representation, which impresses researchers. Lacan explains that these cave dwellers did not have to travel to the depths of the cave to understand that the signifiers that appear there represent the signifiers at the opening of the cave. Even though we could not know what the voice of the person who painted on the cave walls was, we have no doubt that he was a speaking being.[40] That is, according to Lacan, the most significant thing we may understand from the case of cave paintings is that they are representative of representation: the signifiers in the openings of the cave do not refer to a referent whose meaning can be extrapolated; they are signifiers representing something that has been repressed. That is why there is no need to travel to the depth of the cave to understand, through the signifiers found there, something about the signifiers that appear in its entrance because the cave paintings function as a language.

According to Lacan, cave paintings, like the shadows in Plato's cave, demonstrate the function of the screen. This does not mean that the shapes are similar to one another, but that we can discover consistencies between them:

> The screen, here, functions as what is interposed between the subject and the world. It is not an object like any other. Something is painted on it. Before defining what is involved in representation, the screen already announces to us, at the horizon, the dimension of the representative of the representation. Before the world becomes representation, its representative – I mean the representative of the representation – emerges.[41]

Lacan understands the cave paintings as a screen, and the only certain interpretation that we can postulate about them is related to the fact that the creator of these cave paintings is a speaking being. The conclusions about the lives of the cave dwellers from these cave paintings, or the attempts to decipher the meaning behind the images on the wall, belong to the imaginary order. However, there is also the possibility of understanding the cave walls as a screen behind which we may never reach, which reflects Lacan's famous saying that "the unconscious is structured like a language".

As Lacan states, while art historians may be enthusiastic about the representation of the images through cave painting, we should remember that art is fundamentally metonymical and shows something different than what it presents.[42] That is, by reading with the concept of the representative of representation, we can see, in a different fashion, the signifying status and structure of the shadow or image. Whereas, both in the case of cave paintings and in the case of Plato's cave, interpretations usually focus on the meaning of the image through its relation to its origin, Lacan claims that this is not a relation between the reflection and its origin, but between one signifier and another. The very presence of a screen demonstrates the fact that there is nothing behind it, or that we, at least, have no access to the thing that is supposedly behind it, the thing that is supposedly the origin of the shadow.

Like the images on the walls of the cave, the figures of the companions in *Las Meninas* function, according to Lacan, as representatives of representation.

Like actors on stage, these figures do not represent anything but show their presence. They ask Velázquez to let them see. He is supposed to show them the hidden canvas, on which they appear as figures that show themselves and ask to see. That is why they are representatives of representation: they are representations by proxies and not representations; and this is also what binds them together.[43]

The Infanta turns to Velázquez and asks to see what is behind the canvas, as we see it from behind. That is, the Infanta asks to see what we, the viewers, cannot see. She is the mirror reflection of the viewer, who tries to decipher the painting before him. The Infanta, in her demand to see, strengthens, according to Lacan, the claim that the figures in *Las Meninas* are there for show as representatives of representation. As discussed in the fifth chapter, in his eleventh seminar, Lacan mentions the story of Zeuxis and Parrhasius.[44] The Infanta, then, in her appeal to Velázquez to let her see what is painted on the hidden canvas, is like Zeuxis, who asked Parrhasius to draw the curtain.

Exchange of gazes and reflections

Another central theme in the painting that has received ample critical attention is the exchange of gazes and reflections in the painting. The various interpretations on this subject attempt to explain the gazes of the figures, understand whom they are looking at, and the meaning of their gazes in different degrees of sophistication. Jonathan Brown, for instance, interprets the gazes of the figures, which are directed toward an external point, with a sense of a "frozen moment", as in Rembrandt's *Night Watch* and *The Syndics*.[45] Snyder also interprets the exchange of gazes that are reflected from within the mirror. He claims that these gazes should be understood as part of the painting's allegorical structure, whose subject is the mirror reflection of the Infanta, who exchanges gazes with her parents. And the reflection is an allegory of the ideal every princess aspires to reach. This is a mirror that does not reflect anything physical but a mental image that is the product of a work of art.[46] Schmitter focuses on the King's gaze.[47] She argues that the King does stand in front of the painting looking at those whose gazes are turned toward him. The king's gaze unifies all the centers of the painting: the mirror reflection, the Infanta as an emissary of the King, and the viewer who is the King himself. The king stands at first before the mirror. He then moves to the right and takes the place of the viewer before the vanishing point at the elbow of the figure at the door. When the King looks at the painting that analyzes his presence, the representation is completed: this is a representation that represents for the King what makes him a King, that is, his natural body, his representation and the combination between them. The encounter between the King and the painting that describes the representational relation embodies sovereignty. The King, who is looking at the painting, fashions himself through his representation.[48]

Alpers connects the representation of the gazes of the figures in the painting with conventions of photography and claims that the association with the snapshot stems from the fact that the gazes of the figures look back at the viewer.[49] She argues that the outwards-turned gaze is a constant characteristic in Velázquez's painting. This is a gaze that is not narrational and is not turned toward anybody. The gaze marks, from within the painting, that the viewer outside the painting is subjected to sight, and, at the same time, marks that the gaze itself is conscious of the fact that it is seen from the outside.[50] Leo Steinberg shows that some of the figures in the painting are painted as not meeting the gazes of other figures in it.[51] For instance, the companion offers the Infanta water, while the Infanta's gaze is turned to an undefined point at the front, or the woman in the background turns toward the man beside her, who, like the Infanta, turns his gaze toward an invisible point. The unanswered gazes raise the question of what exactly in the painting causes immense interest in it since its explicit subject is seemingly negligible. Steinberg's answer is that *Las Meninas* operates as a metaphor, a mirror of consciousness. Steinberg shows how all the objects that appear in the painting revolve around sight: pictures, windows, door, mirror; and in fact, the painting does not depict any other object but these. In a similar vein, the figures in the painting are mapped in accordance with what they see. The three men supposedly see the royal couple; the Infanta, the servant by her right, and the female dwarf look straight forward, while the servant in the back and the companion on the left are busy with their own affairs. All these relate, according to Steinberg, to the theme of the painting. And, if the picture could speak, he argues, it would say:

> I see you seeing me – I in you see myself seen – see you seeing yourself being seen – and so on beyond the reaches of grammar. Confronted mirrors we are, polarized selves, reflecting one another's consciousness without end.[52]

Foucault describes a more complex exchange of gazes. As I have shown, Foucault addresses an endless exchange of gazes that cannot be fixed, and it is impossible to fix this exchange of gazes because the canvas is hidden from our eyes. This concealment makes possible the ceaseless games of metamorphoses between painter and model. The painter looks from a place that never ceases to change its content, form, face and identity from moment to moment. But his eyes' constant vigilance is turned toward another place – toward the canvas on which is copied, or has been copied, a portrait that will never be erased. Thus, the painter's sovereign gaze creates a virtual triangle whose outlines define this picture of a picture: the eyes of the painter are at the top of the triangle, in one vertex – the invisible model, and the other vertex – the model that is probably painted on the canvas. Once the eyes of the painter position the viewer in their field of sight, they hold onto him, forcing him into the painting and position him at a place from which escape is impossible. They project him onto the surface of the canvas in the painting. The viewer sees his invisibility become visible to the painter, turning into an image that will forever remain invisible to him.[53] Those who create the exchange of gazes, according to Foucault, are the royal couple, whose pale reflection is the source of the Meninas' awe-struck gazes. Even though these figures receive the smallest pictorial attention, since no one in the painting turns their gaze toward them, they provide the main axis around which the painting is organized.[54] That is, Foucault ties the Meninas' awe-struck gazes to the system of mutual exchange of gazes.

Schmitter, Steinberg and Foucault all argue that the exchange of gazes in the painting mutually constitutes each other without a fixed point of reference. Schmitter focuses on the figure of the King and claims that the painting revolves around the relation between representation and power. Thus, in her interpretation, the gazes of the figures are seen through the perspective of the King, who is looking at his own representation, while the Meninas' gazes establish his royal standing. While Schmitter outlines a complex network of gazes established around the status of the King, Steinberg describes a network of uncertainties with no anchor. Foucault finds a similar situation of a constant flickering between the different positions in the painting and makes use of this supposition to claim that the painting is a representation of all representations.

Unlike Fried's description of the concept of absorption, which relates to a phenomenon in which the figures in the painting are deeply immersed in their own activity, the gazes of the figures in *Las Meninas* demonstrate the exact opposite of absorption: the figures turn outwards, and it is difficult to determine for certain whether their gazes are directed toward a single point. The object and meaning of their gaze remain enigmatic. These gazes are also different from the gazes of the figures painted in group portraits. Riegl, who analyzes Rembrandt's group portrait *The Anatomy Lesson of Dr. Tulp*, from 1632,[55] argues that the figure in the back looks toward the viewer of the painting, and thus includes him in an imaginary space stretching from the picture to the viewer and beyond him.[56] A similar thing happens in *Las Meninas*; however, it is also inherently different: the enigma that appears in the encounter with the gazes of the figures does not stem from the fact that they take the viewer into account, but from the fact that they completely erase him. The gazes of the figures, as a central element in the painting, do not make it easier to decipher it; rather, they "refuse" to cooperate with the viewer. The gaze of most of the figures *in Las Meninas*, as the different interpretations state, looks toward a space that is not included in the picture. But they also do not clearly gaze toward a specific point, and this effect is exacerbated by the plethora of gazes. On the other hand, these are not dreamy gazes of inward reflection. The figures gaze through the viewer, as if he were not present, as if he were something translucent you could see through. In a certain sense, they reduce the viewer, not to an object, but to his ultimate reduction, completely erasing him while looking at something else, unknown.

The gazes of the Meninas erase the viewer in an incomprehensible fashion. The fact that, according to Lacan, they are "representatives of representation," means, as stated, that they do not represent anything but constitute a signifier for another signifier, as part of a chain of signifiers. Interpretative practices can explain these gazes in different fashions; however, according to Lacan, these interpretations will always function as veils to what cannot be deciphered but can only ever be represented.

Exchange of gazes as a veil

To elucidate the exchange of gazes in the painting, I will turn to Ruth Ronen's discussion on realistic art.[57] Ronen claims that the realistic effect, the position of the viewer or the reader in the face of the realistic work of art, should be attributed to the encounter of lack in the real – an encounter that cannot be contained by the representational value of the image. Thus, in a paradoxical manner, realistic art is art that veils the real of representation while at the same time striving to illuminate it. In light of Ronen's explanation of realistic art and the manner in which the realistic image does not represent but rather veils, and it is this very veiling is the only way to "represent", I would like to claim that we can understand the figures of the Meninas as a represented representation. I wish to show that this painting presents a similar procedure of vision as a veil to what escapes representation while exposing this process.

Ronen demonstrates this claim through a literary analysis of the genre of stream of consciousness, mainly Virginia Woolf. As Ronen shows, the effect of realism ascribed to Woolf does not stem from the way she reconstructs consciousness, but from the fact that the random, associative, unorganized thought process gives rise to a consciousness that is conceived as realistic. Ronen claims that the real of consciousness is identified with the screen of representation more than with what is marked by it. Thus, consciousness, as an effect of writing, makes possible the effect of the real.[58] In other words, the effect of the real does not emanate from the fact that the stream of consciousness represents or reflects human consciousness. On the contrary, the effect of the real stems from the fact that this form of writing represents the screen of its representation.

In the context of Ronen's argument, it should be mentioned that nineteenth-century theoreticians categorized *Las Meninas* as realistic because it supposedly represents a random moment of palace life.[59] These critics believed in a symmetry between the image and reality; however, as I showed, *Las Meninas* reveals the opposite, the very impossibility of representing reality. A reading of *Las Meninas* in accordance with this impossibility reveals that the gazes of the figures are isomorphic with the seemingly senseless thoughts that veil the real in an attempt to represent human consciousness. I would like to claim that the enigmatic gazes of the figures constitute a veil covering something else.[60] I do not suggest that these figures are a visual manifestation of the gaze, since the gaze exists only as a place of lack, of absence. I would like to claim that the gap in the painting, the miscreancy it presents that evades articulation, is a guise for the gaze, and this is where we may locate the impossibility of representation embodied in *Las Meninas*.

In his interpretation of the gaze in Hitchcock's films, Žižek points toward the relation between a seemingly distracted gaze and an encounter with the real.[61] In everyday reality, we suppose an object to which the gaze is directed, something in the object draws our attention toward it. Hitchcock, according to Žižek, creates a cinematic ruse, which turns the tables. He first shows the fixed gaze, attached to something unknown, and only then does he turn to the cause of the gaze. That is, the fixed gaze pollutes the object. The gaze is not a result of the traumatic object; rather, the fixing of the gaze preludes its cause.[62]

Žižek draws on Lacan's formulations of sight and the gaze in *Seminar XI* and argues that the uncanny look into the camera is a testimony to the victory of the gaze over the eye. This victory is manifested via this inversion, in which he presents the traumatic object as dependent on the gaze. Žižek turns to other instances in Hitchcock's films in which the hero, who finds himself in a certain situation, suddenly fixes his gaze on something. He claims that this is the gaze that is distinguished from the eye, "a surplus of the Real over the Symbolic".[63] However, the gaze is not constituted by what it sees; rather, its very fixation is the object a.

One of the examples Žižek turns to is a scene from the film *Suspicion* from 1941. In this scene, two female friends of the female protagonist "are chatting at the church entrance, the atmosphere is idyllic and calm… when, all of a sudden, the gaze of one of the girls is 'petrified', transfixed by what she sees".[64] The camera moves to what the girl sees only after showing her gaze: the male protagonist forcing his embrace on the female protagonist, and then, suddenly, with no realistic context, the wind begins to blow again. A similar, though less dramatic, state of affairs takes place in the film *The Wrong Man*, from 1956. The lawyer explains to the protagonist and his wife his complex situation, and suddenly his gaze is transfixed, and the camera shows that he is looking at the woman who is losing touch with what is happening in the room.[65] These examples show that Hitchcock manifests the trauma not through its representation or a cinematic image that describes a traumatic event, but through a seemingly insignificant detail, which comes to mark what cannot be represented. As Žižek argues, the petrified gaze is isolated as a stain of the real, an underscored detail that is extracted from symbolic reality, or a surplus of the real over the symbolic. The significant trait in these scenes is that the detail has no meaning in itself but is fashioned as a result of the gaze that is transfixed on it. The object a in these scenes, then, is the gaze itself, the gaze that is forced on the viewer for a brief moment.[66] Žižek's argument points toward a similar procedure to the one Ronen describes: an effect of the real that emerges through the cover, as a stain that covers its object. This is an object that is present through its inability to be represented.

We can explain the veil as what cannot be represented through a description of another fixation of the gaze, which both covers and shows: the gaze of the wolves looking at the dreaming child, in the case of Freud's patient. As

I have stated, this is a repetition of a representation of a traumatic scene from the Wolf Man's childhood, which was hidden in the unconscious and came to the surface later, while the moment of fixation is an encounter between the gaze, the object and the phantasm. Sight is a fixation on a particular detail, which fashions a link between the object and something of the real, while sight constitutes the cover story of what was repressed and barred from access.

Lacan's two mirrors model

After showing how different critics analyze the exchange of glances in the painting and offering a view of it as a veil to what cannot be represented, I will now examine Lacan's treatment of this central aspect in *Las Meninas*. Lacan's discussion of the exchange of glances in the painting relates directly to his essay on the mirror stage and the optical model that followed the mirror stage, in his first seminar. This optical model serves Lacan to show how the subject is constituted through the gaze of the other.

Lacan finds the justification for using optical models for psychoanalytic inquiry in Freud's writings. As Lacan shows, visual images play a crucial part in Freud's work since, as he claimed in various contexts, we can grasp mental processes as images.[67] Lacan turns to the two-mirror model in his conceptualization of narcissism, following Freud. Through this model, he shows the relation between the imaginary and symbolic orders in their relation to the subject and the prominence of the symbolic order in the imaginary structure. Moreover, this model makes it possible to demonstrate the relation between the ego ideal and the ideal ego, which I elaborated on in the sixth chapter.

The eye in this model represents optical vision. The definition of an image in optics, according to Lacan, is that every point in the object should have a corresponding point in the image.[68] The eye, then, which is associated with the imaginary order, exemplifies how Western thought reduces the subject to an abstract eye, to a process of seeing that is limited to its strictly imaginary aspects, and this process is also manifested in the canonical conception of geometrical perspective. The model that Lacan proposes is a device used to create optical illusions. This device is constructed from a concave mirror in the shape of a bowl, which produces, from a certain point, a three-dimensional image. Within the concave mirror is an inverted vase, hidden under a box. A bouquet of flowers is located above the box. Through the play of rays of light, the vase turns over to its proper position and reappears as a real image, and the flowers seem as if they are placed within it. The image produced by the concave mirror is hence defined by its real appearance. Unlike the mirror image, which is flat, the object produced by the concave mirror seems, from a certain angle, to be three-dimensional. As Lacan explains, the imaginary vase that contains the flowers is like the ego, which is grasped as containing something.[69] In other words, the two-mirror model is a developed demonstration of the Lacanian mirror stage, in which the infant's reflection in the mirror, which is symmetrical and complete, does not correspond with the fragmentary way he experiences his body. This relation is represented in the model by the relation between the flowers and the inverted vase.

Lacan adds to the two-mirror model a third, flat mirror, which he places between the flowers, the inverted vase and the place where the real image is produced. This third mirror faces the concave mirror. That is, the image will be reflected another time, as a virtual mirror image. Thus, the object "exists" in three states: an object hidden in space, an image reflected on the concave mirror, and the reflection of the virtual image in the flat mirror. The concave mirror and the flat mirror operate in inverse manners. When you look at the image in the mirror, you see it where it is not. In the concave mirror, on the other hand, you see it where it is – under the condition that the eye is positioned at a certain point.[70] That is, the rays that are refracted by the mirror operate in a 360 degrees angle, thereby producing a three-dimensional image, and the flat mirror reflects this image. The two reflections have different statuses. While the concave mirror returns the rays of light that create the image, the flat mirror reflects a virtual reality, a reflection of a reflection, showing an image where, in fact, there is nothing. Thus, Lacan states, if we place a flat mirror in the middle of the room, and stand with our back to the inverted mirror, we may see the image of the vase of flowers reflected clearly, even though we will not see it directly but only through the mediation of the mirror. The mirror will reflect our face where it is not. The real image will appear where it is, as a virtual image.[71] The image produced by the concave mirror, then, can only be seen from a certain point, and the viewer has to be located at a certain angle to see the illusion. This image demonstrates how "in the relation of the imaginary and the real, and in the constitution of the world such as results from it, everything depends on the position of the subject".[72]

As stated, Lacan links the two-mirror model to his theorization of narcissism. He argues that narcissism is related to a corporal image. This image endows the subject with his form, unifying his perception and his sense of his body. This kind of narcissism is expressed in the model through the real image, produced by the concave mirror.[73] The reflection formed by the flat mirror presents a secondary narcissism, which determines the manner in which the subject relates to the other. Identification with the other makes it possible for the subject to locate himself in relation to the world in general, it promises him a unified image of himself and thus makes it possible for him to see his being.[74] Unlike animals for which the image and the real are the same, for man, the image receives its validation through a reflection in the other.

Lacan argues that the human creature can only see his form as material and complete as a mirage of himself, seemingly located outside himself.[75] Seeing oneself involves a complex process in which the mirror image is but one component. The subject requires the gaze of the other to see himself, and through this gaze, he will only see himself "outside himself". But in fact, the subject will never see "himself". As will be shown later, in *Las Meninas*, the painter and the viewer are positioned in an isomorphic manner to the two-mirror model, and the viewer takes an active part in it.

The two-mirror model is most relevant to Lacan's discussion of *Las Meninas*. As in the case of perspective, in which the painting demonstrates how the subject is only partially registered in the perspectival representation, this painting also demonstrates the way in which the subject sees himself through a system of reflections that are external to him. This model shows us how the viewer constitutes part of the painting. Two figures in the painting are especially relevant for Lacan's description of the model: the Infanta and the painter. The Infanta is similar to the inverse flower vase, a product of the return of the rays of light from the concave mirror. The glowing Infanta, covered in her garments, constitutes the picture's central object, which presents a lack. Her existence in the painting stems from the exchange of glances between the reflection of the king and queen in the mirror on the wall, who function as the Other, and the viewer, who is looking at the picture. If we return to Lacan's description in "The Mirror Stage", we can see in the Infanta a manifestation of the infant who discovers his reflection in the mirror and turns back to the mother, who supports him, and, through her, receives his being, while the couple reflected in the mirror is an empty Other.[76]

Lacan starts his discussion of the painting by claiming that looking at *Las Meninas* is akin to a game of cards, in which the painting is the face-down cards of the opponent, according to which the viewer must plan his next move. Lacan refers to the way the inverse canvas is positioned before the mirror. We cannot see what is painted on it; we cannot see the origin of the mirror reflection. We are called to a series of speculations that are based on the reflections of other speculations. This logic, through which we understand or attempt to understand the painting, and through which the pictorial figures receive their meaning, relates to Lacan's conceptualization of the subject, who receives his being through the Other that constitutes him.

The Infanta constitutes the focal point of the painting, in terms of the composition, the light she is submerged in, and the bright colorfulness that makes her stand out from the other figures in the painting. However, according to Lacan, the image that receives the most pictorial attention is an imaginary image produced through reflections. Like the vase of flowers in the model, the Infanta is perceived as an image that is produced as a result of rays of light reflected from the concave mirror. Her lighted image, her seemingly floating appearance and her central position in the painting support this claim. Lacan refers directly to Foucault, who, in his analysis of the painting, argues that we may extrapolate the shape of an X from it. The center of the X is the eye of the Infanta Margarita, and the top-left-hand point is in the mirror in the background, from which a straight line can be traced to the bottom right corner of the painting. The top-right-hand point is located in the figure at the door, from which emerges a line that connects to the reverse canvas at the bottom left corner of the painting.[77] However, in his analysis of the painting, Lacan leaves the Infanta outside of the X, between its lines. As he explains, these lines can never cross each other since they exist on different planes.

To demonstrate this claim, we can return to the schema of the two triangles in *Seminar XI* and examine it in light of the model of the two mirrors. As I will show, the painting employs the two models in an almost literal sense. As noted, the two triangles demonstrate the split between the eye and the gaze. When they are placed one on top of the other, they show the nature of the image as something not fixed, which flickers between two modes of looking, while the screen and the image are located between them. The Infanta is the image that is projected on the opaque screen, which does not make it possible for us to see what lies behind it, and at the same time, she is the image of the flickering rays of light that return to us from the concave mirror. She is a virtual image since her figure is a product of the exchange of glances between the viewer and the reflection of the royal couple in the mirror. That is, the Infanta, with her beautiful garments, is a veil for the object of the gaze, the very same thing that slips from representation and articulation:

> What resembles more this sort of secret object, in a brilliant garment (*vêture*) which is on the one hand, here, represented in the bouquet of flowers hidden, veiled, taken, encompassed, around this enormous dress of the vase, which is both a real image and a real image seized in the virtual due to the mirror, than the clothes of this little Infanta....[78]

As I have stated, the two-mirror model is also relevant to the way Lacan depicts the painting when stating: "You do not see me from where I am looking at you."[79] Lacan claims that if we place a regular mirror in front of the concave mirror and stand with our back to it, we will first see our face where it is not, while also seeing the real image where it is, as a virtual image. Velázquez, then, is a virtual subject, whom the figures in *Las Meninas* cannot see, since he looks at them not from a place of human existence, but as a mere reflection.

Velázquez's figure in the painting and its relation to the viewer unfold before us the model of the two mirrors in its entirety, since in this model the viewer takes an active part. The virtual subject is added to the system through the viewer, and the painting is constituted through every particular and concrete act of looking at it. Thus, the painting is constituted at each given moment when someone is looking at it. In other words, what is particular to *Las Meninas* is the way in which a certain procedure that takes place in every concrete act of looking turns into the painted subject in a Mobius structure. As Lacan states:

> If you do not recognize what the picture is the representative of, it is precisely by missing this function that it has, of reminding you that with respect to reality, you yourself are included in a function analogous to the one the picture represents, namely, caught up in phantasy.[80]

Las Meninas shows how the viewer discovers that he is already included within his object of observation.

Lacan argues that the distance between the painting and the canvas within it is crucial. Given that the painter cannot truly touch the canvas in the painting, the painting is not about representation. He claims that the distance between the painter and the canvas marks the passage of the fantastic presence of the painter as a viewer:

> If I tell you that it is somewhere at the level of the intersection of the fundamental line and the ground plane and at a point in infinity that the look of the subject is going towards, it is indeed also from this point that Velázquez made, in this ghost-like form which specifies this self-portrait among all the others, one of the traits which is distinguished undoubtedly by the style of the painter. He will tell you himself: "Do you believe that I would paint a self-portrait from this drop, from this oil, with this paintbrush."[81]

Lacan also discusses the gap he finds between the Infanta and her companion on the right. This gap, he states, is created by the "passage" of the painter "into the painting". That is, it is as if Velázquez stands before the painting, in the place of the viewer, and then "enters" the painting while crossing the group of figures to take his phantasmatic place within the painting. In this sense, Velázquez is the "mirage in which the subject sees himself outside himself". Velázquez's figure, then, articulates the eluding point of the subject, which is located between two parallel planes, the plane of the painting and the plane of sight, in a structure that is analogous to the structure of the phantasm. Velázquez does not represent the manner in which he paints the painting but presents the exact opposite: the manner in which his figure shows what cannot be represented.

Lacan draws a parallel between Velázquez and Descartes. Velázquez is the subject who validates himself through the act of painting, and the royal couple reflected in the mirror is analogous to God. Much like Descartes, who bases his existence on God, Velázquez bases his existence on the royal couple reflected in the mirror. However, the other is empty, it is a reflection in a mirror behind which there is nothing. As Lacan states:

> what is inscribed here in the structure, is this vision of an other who is this empty other, pure vision, pure reflection ...this other [is] complementary to the "I think" of Descartes.... namely, the truth which is there, in the picture, as I have described it for you. This other void, this God of an abstract theology, pure articulation of a mirage, /...is here the point of inscription, the surface upon which Velázquez represents for us what he has to represent for us. But as I told you, in order for this to hold together, it remains that it is necessary that there should also be the look. And that we are still playing ball between our look, God's look,

> and some other tiny object like the one that the Infanta presents us with, in this picture.[82]

That is, *Las Meninas* presents the Cartesian validation of the existence of the subject through the supposition of the existence of God as an Archimedean point, which makes it possible for the subject to find certainty in his own being. In a similar fashion, the mirror in the painting supposedly presents an Archimedean point to the painting. The status of God is analogous to the status of the royal couple reflected in the mirror: in both cases, they constitute an external Other that makes it possible to fashion a reflective vision. Human vision, then, is composed of three elements: subject, Other and gaze. And the three elements are necessary for the process of vision. In *Las Meninas* an even more complex situation takes places. While the place of the painter and the viewer overlap in every painting, in this instance, Velázquez also adds the painted painter, the reflection in the mirror and the exchange of glances between the Meninas. Thus, the painting itself revolves around the various exchanges between these components.

Las Meninas depicts Velázquez seeing himself through the gazes of the Meninas. This painting, then, demonstrates an anti-dualistic stance in which it is impossible to separate the painter from the image, and the viewer from the painting. The painter paints himself as he is reflected to himself through the object, or the object reflects the painter to himself. In each of these possibilities, *Las Meninas* manifests the asymmetry in the process of sight itself, which cannot be reproduced. Moreover, it clearly delineates the claim that the Lacanian subject, split between ego and unconscious, is invested in an external object. The subject, watched by an Other through the object, is both an object and a subject. That is, the subject is not only a subject toward himself, but part of him is invested in an object that is seemingly external to him.

Velázquez stands before the painted figures, which return his gaze. Lacan describes a similar situation in his analysis of the case of the Wolf Man:

> It is not only that the subject is fascinated by the sight of these wolves.... It is that their fascinated gaze is the subject himself.... Remember the adventure of the father, the sister, the mother, and the servant-woman Groucha. So many different stages that enrich the unconscious desire of the subject with something that is to be put, as signification constituted in the relation to the desire of the Other, in the numerator.[83]

Lacan explains that the different characters in the case of the Wolf Man represent different subject positions of the Wolf Man himself. They represent different forms or stages in the subject's unconscious desire. Lacan describes this in terms of a numerator and a denominator. The denominator is the primal repressed, and the changing numerators are the different representations of this repressed. In a similar vein, the Meninas, the Infanta, the figure of the painter and all the other figures in the paintings are the changing numerators, possible representations of the denominator – the particular phantasm of the viewer of the painter as a subject of the unconscious.

Speculations on time and space

In his discussion of *Las Meninas*, Lacan undermines the distinction between a "real" space and a pictorial "illusionary" space. He also refutes the supposition that representation depicts something whose meaning we can attain, thus, we are left with a chain of representation that represents other signifiers. We have access to a screen, and through its holes, we can see the veils of what escapes articulation. *Las Meninas* shows us that as viewers, we are completely devoid of our weapons. The painting is a game of cards in which we can also speculate on our opponent's next move, who, at the same time, also speculates on our next move, and the only thing that exists is this mutual relationship of speculations that constitute each other, with no possibility of settling in a fixed position.

In an earlier article on logical time, Lacan relates to a story revolving around three prisoners and their warden.[84] The warden tells the prisoners that he intends to free one of them. But to decide which prisoner, he posits a test. "I have five disks", says the warden,

> three white and two black. Without letting you know which I will have chosen, I will fasten one of them to each of you between the shoulders.... The first to be able to deduce his own color will be the one to benefit from the discharging measure at my disposal.[85]

The three prisoners see each other; however, they cannot communicate with one another. There are no mirrors in the room, so they cannot discover the color of their disks by looking at themselves. The warden fastens a white disk to the back of each of the prisoners, and the game begins.

After the prisoners look at each other for a while, all three of them walk toward the door together. Each of them thinks the following:

> I am a white... had I been black each of them would have been able to infer the following: 'If I too were a black, the other would have necessarily realized straight away that he was a white and would have left immediately; therefore, I am not a black.' And both would have left together, convinced they were whites.[86]

We may isolate three stages in the prisoners' thought process. In the first stage, every subject says to himself: "if I would see two black disks, I could deduce with certainty that I have a white disk, but since I see only two white disks, that possibility is off the table". In the second stage, each subject says to himself: "if I had a black disk on my back the two other prisoners would have seen this and reached the conclusion that they have white disks and walk out before me". In the third stage, each subject reaches a decision: "I will hasten to declare myself as carrying the white disk, so the others will not beat me by reaching the conclusion about their identity before me".

Lacan shows here a series of moves that lean on the way in which each of the prisoners draws what constitutes him and determines his status in relation to the other, as stemming from the instructions of the other from precisely what he does not see.[87] This essay, then, presents a state of affairs that is homologous to the act of looking at *Las Meninas*. Each one of the prisoners constructs his conclusion based on an array of speculations he posits concerning his friends. Since no one can reach a conclusion based on what he can see, each must suppose what he believes his friends see when they look at the disk fastened to his back. The only way to construct a supposition in this given situation is based on the action of the rival. But since none of the prisoners can reach an instant decision, there is a delay, and the prisoners attempt to base their conclusions on this very delay. Time, in this situation, has a double role, both as a signifier of hesitation and as the temporality of the action in general.

Like *Las Meninas*, the story of the prisoners constructs the structure of a Mobius strip. In *Las Meninas*, the pictorial space functions as a Mobius strip also in relation to itself, through the relation between the hidden canvas, on which the painting itself is painted, which the Infanta wishes to see, and the relation to the space occupied by the viewer, who becomes a part of his specular object, that is, the painting itself. As Lacan explains, the relation between the painting within the painting and the painting in general is that they both satiate each other.[88]

In both cases, the painting and the story of the prisoners, every subject is also a mirror image of another subject, thus creating an endless string of reflections with no fixed stopping point. The subject sees the others without being able to determine with certainty his own identity, but only in relation to others, only in relation to what he does not see, to what he supposes exists in the other as his mirror image. In the story of the prisoners, the concept of space is replaced with the concept of time, which is the main cause of the Mobius strip structure, while the representation of time is one of the components for the solution of the riddle: the hesitation of each prisoner points toward the solution his friends will reach, and vice versa.

In both cases, the prisoners and the Meninas, sight has a critical function, since it is precisely what sight does not show that makes it possible to extract knowledge. In a similar vein, time in and of itself does not yield knowledge; what yields knowledge is its very suspension. As Lacan states:

> What the suspended motions disclose is not what the subjects see, but rather what they have found out positively about what they do not see, the appearance of the black disks. What constitutes these suspended motions as signifying is not their direction, but rather their interruption [*temps d'arret*].[89]

Lacan refers, in both cases, to a game of cards, to the player who constructs his assumptions based on his opponent's hidden cards. In both cases, there is a higher authority that produces the situation. In the story of the prisoners, this authority is the warden. In *Las Meninas,* we can think of the royal couple in a similar fashion, as entities endowed with titles and representing power.

Las Meninas is a painting that shows the viewer the veil, what cannot be seen or represented. Moreover, it demonstrates the place of a particular instance of looking at a painting; it shows how the viewer functions as an inseparable part of the painting. New interpretations are usually seen as offering an improved interpretation. In this case, my reading of *Las Meninas* draws on the many previous interpretations of the painting, in two distinct ways. First, the interpretation I offer, following Lacan, does not distinguish between the painting and the interpretations that were previously given to it, but rather asks to read the painting in congruence with the various ways in which it was understood. Second, the previous interpretations given to the painting lead to my main argument – that the plethora of attempts at a solution only demonstrates the fact that the solution itself remains inaccessible and impossible. My reading of *Las Meninas* is not supposed to replace the interpretations presented in this chapter or even future interpretations; rather, it views them as an inevitable product of painting, layers that come to veil that which escapes articulation.

Notes

1 Lacan, Jacques. 1965–1966. *The Seminar of Jacques Lacan, Book XIII: The Object of Psychoanalysis*. Trans. Cormac Gallagher from unedited French manuscripts. [Unpublished].
2 Foucault, Michel. 1994 [1970]. *The Order of Things: An Archaeology of the Human Sciences*. New York: Vintage Books.
3 Lacan, Jacques. 1988 [1945]. "Logical Time and the Assertion of Anticipated Certainty: A New Sophism". *Newsletter of the Freudian Field* 2: 4–22.
4 Searle, John. 1980. "*Las Meninas* and the Paradoxes of Pictorial Representation". *Critical Inquiry* 6: 477–488.
5 Searle, 1980, p. 487.
6 Snyder, Joel, and Ted Cohen. 1980. "Reflections on *Las Meninas*: Paradox Lost". *Critical Inquiry* 7: 429–447.
7 Snyder, Joel. 1985. "*Las Meninas* and the Mirror of the Prince". *Critical Inquiry* 11: 539–572.
8 Schmitter, Amy M. 1996. "Picturing Power: Representation and *Las Maninas*". *The Journal of Aesthetics and Art Criticism* 54: 255–268.
9 Alpers, Svetlana. 1983. "Interpretation without Representation, or, The Viewing of *Las Meninas*". *Representation* I:1, February 1983, pp. 36–37.
10 See for example, Carl Justi, who claims that King Philip the IV chose the subject of the painting himself while sitting for Velázquez to take his portrait and then the princesses Infanta Margarita entered the room. The king decided that this moment should be immortalized, and the scene was transposed in its entirety to the gallery, where Velázquez painted it while standing before a large mirror that contained every detail of the painting. Justi, Carl. 1933 [1903]. *Diego Velázquez*. Zurich: Erschienen im Phaidon-Verlag.

11 Lacan XIII, lesson of 4.5.1966, p. 233.
12 Lacan XIII, lesson of 4.5.1966, p. 239.
13 Lacan XIII, lesson of 4.5.1966, p. 241.
14 Lacan XIII, lesson of 4.5.1966, p. 242.
15 Lacan XIII, lesson of 4.5.1966, p. 242.
16 Lacan, Jacques. 1981 [1964–1965]. *The Four Fundamental Concepts of Psychoanalysis: The Seminar of Jacques Lacan, Book XI*. Trans. Alan Sheridan. New York and London: W.W. Norton and Company, p. 108.
17 Lacan XIII, lesson of 22.5.1966, p. 283.
18 Jay, Martin. 1988. "Scopic Regimes of Modernity". In *Vision and Visuality*. Edited by Hal Foster. Seattle: Bay Press, p. 8.
19 Lacan XIII, p. 284.
20 Freud, 2001e [1919]. "A Child is Being Beaten". *S.E.* 17: 179–204.
21 Freud, 2001e, p. 189.
22 Lacan XIII, lesson of 18.5.1966, p. 276.
23 Lacan XIII, lesson of 18.5.1966, p. 277.
24 Lacan XIII, lesson of 18.5.1966, p. 285.
25 Lacan XIII, lesson of 18.5.1966, p. 256.
26 Lacan XIII, lesson of 18.5.1966, p. 279.
27 Lacan XI, p. 89.
28 Foucault, 1994. Schmitter also raises the issue of representation in painting while addressing Foucault's discussion of the subject. In her reading, she connects the concept of representation to the concept of power. She claims that the painting revolves around the representation of power, and its purpose is to provide the king with his representation, which would make it possible for him to take his place as King. Unlike Foucault, representation, for Schmitter, is a thematic concept and not a structural one (Schmitter, 1996).
29 Foucault, 1994.
30 Foucault, 1994, pp. 4–5.
31 Foucault, 1994, p. 15.
32 Foucault, 1994, pp. 307–308.
33 Lacan XIII, p. 271.
34 Freud, 2001c [1915]. "Repression". *SE* 14: 148.
35 Fink, Bruce. 1995. *The Lacanian Subject: Between Language and Jouissance*. Princeton: Princeton University Press, p. 74.
36 Žižek, Slavoj. 1987. "Why Lacan is not a 'Post-Structuralist'". *Newsletter of the Freudian Field* 1: 31–40.
37 For another reference to cave painting in Lacan's seminars, see Lacan, Jacques. 1986 [1959–1960]. *The Ethics of Psychoanalysis 1959–1960: The Seminar of Jacques Lacan, Book VII*. Trans. Dennis Porter. New York and London: W.W. Norton and Company, pp. 139–140.
38 Janson, Horst Woldemar. 1995. *History of Art*. London: Thames and Hudson, pp. 49–51.
39 Lacan XIII, lesson of 4.5.1966, pp. 235–236.
40 Lacan XIII, lesson of 4.5.1966, p. 236.
41 Lacan XIII, lesson of 4.5.1966, p. 235.
42 Lacan XIII, lesson of 4.5.1966, p. 236. According to Lacan's conceptualization, which is based on Jakobson, language is founded on two basic operations: metonymy and metaphor. While metonymy constitutes a lateral movement within the chain of signifiers in which the signifier does not cover the entire sense of what is said, and that is why there is a movement to the next signifier, metaphor is a vertical movement, in which the signifier substitutes another signifier. These two operations originate in displacement and condensation, the two major mechanisms of the dream work according to Freud. (Lacan, Jacques. 1977 [1966]. *Écrits:*

A Selection. Trans. Alan Sheridan. New York and London: W.W. Norton and Company, p. 160).
43 Lacan XIII, lesson of 11.5.1966, p. 255.
44 Lacan XI, p. 103.
45 Brown, Jonathan. 1978. "On the Meaning of *Las Meninas*". In *Images and Ideas in Seventeenth-Century Spanish Painting*. Princeton: Princeton University Press, pp. 90–91.
46 Snyder, 1985, p. 564.
47 Schmitter, 1996.
48 Schmitter, 1996, p. 264.
49 Alpers, 1983, p. 31.
50 Alpers, 1983, p. 32.
51 Steinberg, Leo. 1981. "Velázquez' *Las Meninas*". *October* 19: 45–54.
52 Steinberg, 1981, p. 54.
53 Foucault, 1994, p. 5.
54 Foucault, 1994, p. 14.
55 Mauritshuis Museum, The Hague.
56 Riegl, Alois. 1999 [1902]. *The Group Portraiture of Holland*. Trans. Evelyn M. Klein and David Britt. Los Angeles: The Getty Research Institute for the History of Art and the Humanities, p. 256.
57 Ronen, Ruth. 2002. *Representing the Real*. Amsterdam and New York: Rodopi, pp. 164–202.
58 Ronen, 2002, p. 179.
59 Justy expresses this position in his interpretation. Brown and Alpers also tacitly refer to this interpretive model.
60 The field of cultural research has a long history of comparative debates between verbal and visual systems of signs. My intent here is not to create this kind of comparison but to point towards a parallel trajectory.
61 Žižek, 1992a, pp. 211–272.
62 Žižek, 1992a, p. 235.
63 Žižek describes two operations of treating this "surplus of the Real": the first, which I described in the fourth chapter, relates to the way in which vision incorporates within itself a stain, an element that is external to vision and which disturbs vision itself. The second operation relates to the gaze as an object (Žižek, 1992a, p. 236).
64 Žižek, 1992a, p. 235.
65 Žižek, 1992a, p. 235.
66 Žižek, 1992a, pp. 235–236.
67 Lacan, Jacques. 1988 [1953–1954]. *The Seminar of Jacques Lacan, Book I: Freud's Papers on Technique 1953–1954*. Trans. John Forrester. New York and London: W.W. Norton and Company, p. 123.
68 Lacan, 1988, p. 123.
69 Lacan, 1988, p. 79.
70 Lacan, 1988, p. 78.
71 Lacan, 1988, pp. 124–125.
72 Lacan, 1988, p. 80.
73 Lacan, 1988, p. 125.
74 Lacan, 1988, p. 176.
75 Lacan I, p. 40.
76 Lacan XIII, lesson of 25.5.1966, p. 291.
77 Foucault, 1994, pp. 12–13.
78 Lacan XIII, lesson of 25.5.1966, p. 290.
79 Lacan XIII, lesson of 25.6.1966, p. 285.
80 Lacan XIII, lesson of 25.6.1966, p. 287.

81 Lacan XIII, lesson of 11.5.1966, p. 258.
82 Lacan XIII, lesson of 25.5.1966, pp. 291–292.
83 Lacan XI, p. 251.
84 Lacan L.T. *Écrits*, pp. 161–175.
85 Lacan L.T. *Écrits*, p. 161.
86 Lacan L.T. *Écrits*, p. 162.
87 Lacan, in his early teaching, does not yet distinguish between the other and the Other. In this instance I chose to leave this as other.
88 Lacan XIII, lesson of 11.5.1966, p. 255.
89 Lacan L.T, p. 166.

Bibliography

Aiken, Jane Andrews. 1998. "The Perspective Construction of Masachio's *Trinity* Fresco and Medieval Astronomical Graphics". *Masaccio's Trinity*. Edited by Rona Goffen. Cambridge: Cambridge University Press, pp. 90–107.

Alberti, Leon Battista. 1966 [1435–1436]. *On Painting*. Trans. John R. Spencer. New Haven: Yale University Press.

Alpers, Svetlana. 1983. "Interpretation without Representation, or, the Viewing of *Las Meninas*". *Representation* I: 1, February 1983, pp. 31–42.

Alpers, Svetlana. 1983a. *The Art of Describing: Dutch Art in the Seventeenth Century*. Chicago: University of Chicago Press.

Alpers, Svetlana. 1988. *Rembrandt's Enterprise: The Studio and the Market*. Chicago: University of Chicago Press.

Aristotle. 1932. *Poetics*. Aristotle in 23 Volumes, Vol. 23. Trans. William Hamilton Fyfe. Cambridge: Harvard University Press; London: William Heinemann Ltd. https://www.perseus.tufts.edu/hopper/text?doc=Perseus%3Atext%3A1999.01.0056%3Asection%3D1450a [section 1450a].

Aristotle. 1997. Trans. S. H. Butcher. New York: Dover Publications, Inc.

Arnheim, Rudolf. 1988. *The Power of the Center: A Study of Composition in the Visual Arts*. Berkeley and Los Angeles: University of California Press.

Bal, Mieke. 1985. *Narratology: Introduction to the Theory of Narrative*. Trans. Christine van Boheemen. Toronto, Buffalo, London: University of Toronto Press.

Bal, Mieke. 1990 "The Point of Narratology". *Narratology Revisited. Poetics Today* 9–10: 727–753.

Bal, Mieke. 1991. *Reading Rembrandt: Beyond the Word-Image Opposition*. Cambridge: Cambridge University Press.

Barthes, Roland. 1977. *Image, Music, Text*. Trans. Sthephen Heath. New York: Hill and Wang.

Baudrillard, Jean. 1988. "The Trompe-L'Oeil". *Calligram: Essays in New Art History from France*. Edited by Norman Bryson. Cambridge: Cambridge University Press, pp. 53–62.

Bell, Clive. 1961 [1914]. *Art*. London: Arrow Books LTD.

Bernheimer, Charles. 1989. "Manet's *Olympia*: The Figuration of Scandal". *Art and Literature. Poetics Today* 10: 253–277.

Berressem, Henjo. 1995. "The 'Evil Eye' of Painting: Jacques Lacan and Witold Gombrowicz on the Gaze". *Reading Seminar XI: Lacan's Four Fundamental Concepts of Psychoanalysis*. Edited by Richard Feldstein, Bruce Fink and Maire Jaanus. Albany: State University of New York Press, pp. 175–182.

Biberman, Efrat. 2005. "The Self as Other". *Consciousness, Literature and the Arts*, 6(1).
Biberman, Efrat. 2017. "Inside-Out Stories: On Geometrical Perspective and Narrative Representation". *Image and Narrative* 18(2).
de Bolla, Peter. 1996. "The Visibility of Visuality". *Vision in Context: Historical and Contemporary Perspectives on Sight*. Edited by Teresa Brennan and Martin Jay. New York and London: Routledge, pp. 63–79.
Božovič, Miran, 1992. "The Man Behind His Own Retina". *Everything You Always Wanted to Know about Lacan but Were Afraid to Ask Hitchcock*. Edited by Slavoj Žižek. Trans. Martin Thom. London and New York: Verso, pp. 161–177.
Brennan, Teresa and Martin Jay (eds.). 1996. *Vision in Context: Historical and Contemporary Perspectives on Sight*. London: Routledge
Brilliant, Richard. 1986. *Visual Narratives: Storytelling in Etruscan and Roman Art*. Ithaca and London: Cornell University Press.
Brown, Jonathan. 1978. "On the Meaning of *Las Meninas*". *Images and Ideas in Seventeenth-Century Spanish Painting*. Princeton: Princeton University Press, pp. 87–110.
Bryson, Norman. 1981. *Word and Image: French Painting of the Ancien Regime*. Cambridge: Cambridge University Press.
Bryson, Norman. 1983. *Vision and Painting: The Logic of the Gaze*. New Haven: Yale University Press.
Bryson, Norman. 1984. *Tradition and Desire: From David to Delacroix*. Cambridge: Cambridge University Press.
Bryson, Norman. 1988. *Calligram: Essays in New Art History from France*. edited by Norman Bryson. Cambridge: Cambridge University Press
Bryson, Norman. 1988a. "The Gaze in the Expanded Field". *Vision and Visuality*. Edited by Hal Foster. Dia Art Foundation. Seattle: Bay Press, 87–108.
Bryson, Norman. 1990. *Looking at the Overlooked: Four Essays on Still Life Painting*. Cambridge: Harvard University Press.
Caillois, Roger. 1984 [1935]. "Mimicry and Legendary Psychastenia". *October* 31: 17–32.
Damisch, Hubert. 1994. *The Origin of Perspective*. Trans. John Goodman. Cambridge: MIT Press.
Diderot, Denis. 1994. *Selected Writings on Art and Literature*. Trans. Geofrey Bremner. London: Penguin Books.
van Dijk, Teun. 1975. "Recalling and Summarizing Complex Discourse". University of Amsterdam. Mimeograph, pp. 50–91.
van Dijk, Teun. 1980. "Story Comprehension: An Introduction". *Poetics* 9: 1–21.
Dolar, Mladen. 1996. "At First Sight". *Gaze and Voice as Love Objects*. Edited by Slavoj Žižek and Renata Salecl. Durham and London: Duke University Press, pp. 129–153.
Elkins, James. 1994. *The Poetics of Perspective*. Ithaca and London: Cornell University Press.
Evans, Dylan. 1996. *An Introductory Dictionary of Lacanian Psychoanalysis*. London and New York: Routledge.
Faulkner, William. 1977 [1930]. "A Rose for Emily". *Collected Stories by William Faulkner*. New York: Vintage Books, pp. 119–130.
Feldstein, Richard, Bruce Fink and Maire Jaanus (eds.). 1995. *Reading Seminar XI: Lacan's Four Fundamental Concepts of Psychoanalysis*. Albany: State University of New York Press.

Fink, Bruce. 1995. *The Lacanian Subject: Between Language and Jouissance*. Princeton: Princeton University Press.

Foster, Hal. (ed.). 1988. *Vision and Visuality*. Dia Art Foundation. Seattle: Bay Press.

Foucault, Michel. 1994 [1970]. *The Order of Things: An Archaeology of the Human Sciences*. New York: Vintage Books.

Freud, Sigmund. 2001. *The Standard Edition of the Complete Psychological Works of Sigmund Freud*. Trans. James Strachey et al. London: Vintage, 24 Vols. Henceforth SE.

Freud, Sigmund. [1900]. "The Means of Representation in Dreams". *SE* 4: 310–338.

Freud, Sigmund. [1900a]. "The Psychology of the Dream-Processes". *SE* 5: 509–511.

Freud, Sigmund. [1906]. "Delusions and Dreams in Jensen's *Gradiva*". *SE* 9: 7–93.

Freud, Sigmund. [1908]. "Family Romances". *SE* 9: 237–241.

Freud, Sigmund. [1914]. "On Narcissism: An Introduction". *SE* 14: 73–102.

Freud, Sigmund. [1915]. "The Unconscious. Appendix C: Words and Things". *SE* 14: 209–215.

Freud, Sigmund. [1915a]. "Repression". *SE* 14: 146–158.

Freud, Sigmund. [1915b]. "Instincts and their Vicissitudes". *SE* 14: 117–140.

Freud, Sigmund. [1918]. "From the History of an Infantile Neurosis". *SE* 17: 7–122.

Freud, Sigmund. [1919]. "A Child is Being Beaten". *SE* 17: 179–204.

Freud, Sigmund. [1919a]. "The Uncanny". *SE* 17: 219–256.

Freud, Sigmund. [1937]. "Constructions in Analysis". *SE* 23: 257–269.

Fried, Michael. 1987. *Realism, Writing and Disfiguration: On Thomas Eakins and Stephen Crane*. Chicago: University of Chicago Press.

Fried, Michael. 1988. *Absorption and Theatricality: Painting and Beholder in the Age of Diderot*. Chicago: University of Chicago Press.

Genette, Gerard. 1980. *Narrative Discourse*. Trans. Jane E. Lewin. Ithaca, New York: Cornell University Press.

Goffen, Rona. (ed.). 1998. *Masaccio's Trinity*. Cambridge: Cambridge University Press.

Gombrich, Ernst. 1972 [1960]. *Art and Illusion: A Study in the Psychology of Pictorial Representation*. Princton: Princton University Press.

Gombrich, Ernst. 1994 [1982]. *The Image & the Eye: Further Studies in the Psychology of Pictorial Representation*. London: Phaidon Press Limited.

Greenberg, Clement. 1986 [1939]. "Avant-Garde and Kitch". *The Collected Essays and Criticism: Vol. 1 Perceptions and Judgments, 1939–1944*. Chicago and London: The University of Chicago Press, pp. 5–22.

Greenberg, Clement. 1965 [1944]. *Art and Culture: Critical Essays*. Boston: Beacon Press.

Greenberg, Clement. 1986 [1940]. "Towards a Newer Laocoon". *The Collected Essays and Criticism: Vol. 1 Perceptions and Judgments, 1939–1944*. Chicago and London: The University of Chicago Press, pp. 23–38.

Greenberg, Clement. 1995 [1967]. *The Collected Essays and Criticism: Volume 4 Modernism with Vengeance, 1957–1969*. Chicago and London: The University of Chicago Press.

Greenberg, Clement. 1973. "Seminar One". *Arts Magazine* 48: 44–46.

Iversen, Margaret. 1993. *Alois Riegl: Art History and Theory*. Cambridge: MIT Press.

Janson, Horst Woldemar. 1995. *History of Art*. London: Thames and Hudson.

Jay, Martin. 1988. "Scopic Regimes of Modernity". *Vision and Visuality*. Edited by Hal Foster. Dia Art Foundation. Seattle: Bay Press, pp. 3–23.

Jay, Martin. 1997. "Lacan and the Crisis of Ocularcentrism". *Image, Word and Self*. Edited by Maria Letizia Proietti. New York, Washington D.C., Baltimore: Peter Lang, pp. 169–198.

Justi, Carl. 1933 [1903]. *Diego Velázquez*. Zurich: Erschienen im Phaidon-Verlag.
Kant, Immanuel. 1952 [1790]. *The Critique of Judgment*. Trans. James creed Meredith. Oxford: Clarendon Press.
Kant, Immanuel. 1966 [1781]. *Critique of Pure Reason*. Trans. F. Max Müller. New York: Anchor Books, Doubleday & Company.
Kemp, Martin. 1990. *The Science of Art: Optical Themes in Western Art from Brunelleschi to Seurat*. New Haven and London: Yale University Press.
Koerner, Joseph Leo. 1993. *The Moment of Self-Portraiture in German Renaissance Art*. Chicago and London: University of Chicago Press.
Lacan, Jacques. 1965–1966. *The Seminar of Jacques Lacan, Book XIII: The Object of Psychoanalysis*. Trans. Cormac Gallagher from unedited French manuscripts. [Unpublished].
Lacan, Jacques. 1977 [1949]. "The Mirror Stage as Formative of the Function of the I as Revealed in Psychoanalytic Experience". *Écrits: A Selection*. Trans. A. Sheridan. New York and London: Norton and Company, pp. 1–7.
Lacan, Jacques. 1977 [1966]. *Écrits: A Selection*. Trans. Alan Sheridan. New York and London: W.W. Norton and Company.
Lacan, Jacques. 1981 [1964–1965]. *The Four Fundamental Concepts of Psychoanalysis: The Seminar of Jacques Lacan, Book XI*. Trans. Alan Sheridan. New York and London: W.W. Norton and Company.
Lacan, Jacques. 1986 [1959–1960]. *The Ethics of Psychoanalysis 1959-1960: The Seminar of Jacques Lacan, Book VII*. Trans. Dennis Porter. New York and London: W.W. Norton and Company.
Lacan, Jacques. 1988 [1945]. "Logical Time and the Assertion of Anticipated Certainty: A New Sophism". *Newsletter of the Freudian Field* 2: 4–22.
Lacan, Jacques. 1988 [1957]. "Seminar on *The Purloined Letter*". Trans. Jeffrey Mehlman. *The Purloined Poe: Lacan, Derrida, and Psychoanalytic Reading*. edited by John P. Muller and William J. Richardson. Baltimore and London: Johns Hopkins University Press, pp. 28–54.
Lacan, Jacques. 2006 [1957]. "The Instance of the Letter in the Unconscious or Reason since Freud". *Écrits*. Trans. Bruce Fink. New York and London: Norton and Company, pp. 412–441.
Lacan, Jacques. 1988 [1953–1954]. *The Seminar of Jacques Lacan, Book I: Freud's Papers on Technique 1953–1954*. Trans. John Forrester. New York and London: W.W. Norton and Company.
Lacan, Jacques. 1988 [1954–1955]. *The Ego in Freud's Theory and in the Technique of Psychoanalysis 1954–1955: The Seminar of Jacques Lacan, Book II*. Trans. Sylvana Tomaselli. New York and London: W.W. Norton and Company.
Lacan, Jacques. 2005 [1963]. *Des Nomes-du-Père*. Paris: Seuil.
Lacan, Jacques. 2014 [1962–1963]. *The Seminar of Jacques Lacan, Book X: Anxiety*. Trans. Adrian Price. Cambridge: Polity Press.
Lacan, Jacques. 2019 [1958–1959]. *The Seminar of Jacques Lacan, Book VI: Desire and its Interpretations*. Trans. Bruce Fink. Cambridge: Polity Press.
Laplanche, Jean, and Jean-Bertrand Pontalis. 1988 [1973]. *The Language of Psychoanalysis*. Trans. Donald Nicholson-Smith. London: Karnac Books.
Lee, Rensselaer W. 1967 [1940]. *Ut Pictura Poesis: The Humanistic Theory of Painting*. New York: Norton Library.
Lessing, Gotthold Ephraim. 1887 [1766]. *Laocoön: An Essay upon the Limits of Painting and Poetry*. Trans. Ellen Frothingham. Cambridge: Cambridge University Press, John Wilson and Son.

Levi-Strauss, Claude. 1963 [1958]. *Structural Anthropology*. Trans. Claire Jacobson and Brooke Grundfest Schoepf. New York: Basic Books.

Leupin, Alexandre. (ed.). 1991. *Lacan and the Human Sciences*. Lincoln: University of Nebraska Press.

Melville, Stephen. 1996. "Division of the Gaze, or, Remarks on the Color and Tenor of Contemporary 'Theory'". *Vision in Context: Historical and Contemporary Perspectives on Sight*. Edited by Teresa Brennan and Martin Jay. London: Routledge, pp. 101–116.

Merleau-Ponty, Maurice. 1993 [1961]. "Eye and Mind". *The Merleau-Ponty Aesthetic Reader: Philosophy and Painting*. Edited by Galen A. Johnson. Trans. Michael B. Smith. Evanston: Northwestern University Press, pp. 121–149.

Merleau-Ponty, Maurice. 1997 [1968]. *The Visible and the Invisible*. Trans. Alphonso Lingis. Evanston: Northwestern University Press.

Mitchell, William John Thomas. 1986. *Iconology: Image, Text, Ideology*. Chicago and London: University of Chicago Press.

Muller, John P. and William J. Richardson (eds.). 1988. *The Purloined Poe: Lacan, Derrida, and Psychoanalytic Reading*. Edited by and Baltimore and London: Johns Hopkins University Press.

Mulvey, Laura. 1989. *Visual and Other Pleasures*. Bloomington and Indianapolis: Indiana University Press.

Nietzsche, Friedrich. 1910 [1872]. *The Birth of Tragedy*. Trans. William A. Haussmann. Edinburgh and London: T.N. Foulis.

Nobus, Danny (ed.). 1996. *Key Concepts of Lacanian Psychoanalysis*. London: Rebus Press.

Panofsky, Erwin. 1991 [1927]. *Perspective as a Symbolic Form*. Trans. Christopher S. Wood. New York: Zone Books.

Panofsky, Erwin. 1955. "Iconography and Iconology: An Introduction to the Study of Renaissance Art". *Meaning in the Visual Arts*. New York: Doubleday Anchor Books, pp. 26–54.

Proietti, Maria Letizia, (ed.). 1997. *Image, Word and Self*. New York, Washington D.C., Baltimore: Peter Lang.

Quinet, Antonio. 1995. "The Gaze as an Object". *Reading Seminar XI: Lacan's Four Fundamental Concepts of Psychoanalysis*. Edited by Richard Feldstein, Bruce Fink and Maire Jaanus. Albany: State University of New York Press, pp. 144–145.

Ragland-Sullivan, Ellie, and Mark Bracher. (eds.). 1991. *Lacan and the Subject of Language*. New York and London: Routledge.

Regnault, François. 1991. "Lacan and Experience". *Lacan and the Human Sciences*. Edited by Alexandre Leupin. Lincoln: University of Nebraska Press, pp. 43–58.

Riegl, Alois. 1999 [1902]. *The Group Portraiture of Holland*. Trans. Evelyn M. Klein and David Britt. Los Angeles: The Getty Research Institute for the History of Art and the Humanities.

Rimmon Kenan, Shlomit. 1983. *Narrative Fiction: Contemporary Poetics*. London and New York: Methuen.

Ronen, Ruth. 1994. *Possible Worlds in Literary Theory*. Cambridge: Cambridge University Press.

Ronen, Ruth. 2002. *Representing the Real*. Amsterdam and New York: Rodopi.

Sartre, Jean-Paul. 1972. "Saint George et le dragon". *Situations,* IX. Paris: Gallimard, pp. 202–226.

Sartre, Jean-Paul. 1992 [1956]. *Being and Nothingness: A Phenomenological Essay on Ontology*. Trans. Hazel E. Barnes. New York: Washington Square Press.

Schniderman, Stuart. 1988. "Art According to Lacan". *Newsletter of the Freudian Field* 2: 17–26.

Soler, Colette. 1995. "The Subject and the Other (1,2)". *Reading Seminar XI: Lacan's Four Fundamental Concepts of Psychoanalysis*. Edited by Richard Feldstein, Bruce Fink and Maire Jaanus. Albany: State University of New York Press, pp. 39–53.

Schmitter, Amy, M. 1996. "Picturing Power: Representation and *Las Maninas*". *The Journal of Aesthetics and Art Criticism* 54: 255–268.

Searle, John. 1980. "*Las Meninas* and the Paradoxes of Pictorial Representation". *Critical Inquiry* 6: 477–488.

Snyder, Joel, and Ted Cohen. 1980. "Reflections on *Las Meninas*: Paradox Lost". *Critical Inquiry* 7: 429–447.

Snyder, Joel. 1985. "*Las Meninas* and the Mirror of the Prince". *Critical Inquiry* 11: 539–572.

Steinberg, Leo. 1981. "Velázquez' *Las Meninas*". *October* 19: 45–54.

Vasari, Giorgio. 1991. *The Lives of the Artists*, trans. Julia Conaway Bondanella and Peter Bondanella. Oxford: Oxford University Press.

Vasseleu, Cathryn. 1998. *Textures of Light: Vision and Touch in Irigaray, Levinas and Merleau-Ponty*. London: Routledge.

Volk, Gregory. 2010, "Neo Rauch", edited by Marcia Vetrocq. In: *Art in America,* Brant publications.

White, Hayden. 1987. *The Content of the Form: Narrative Discourse and Historical Representation*. Baltimore and London: Johns Hopkins University Press.

Wölflin, Heinrich. 1929 [1915]. *Principles of Art History: The Problem of the Development of Style in Later Art*. Trans. Marie Donald Hottinger. New York: Dover Publications.

Žižek, Slavoj. 1987. "Why Lacan is not a 'Post-Structuralist'". *Newsletter of the Freudian Field* 1: 31–40.

Žižek, Slavoj. 1991. "The Truth Arises from Misrecognition". *Lacan and the Subject of Language*. Edited by Ellie Ragland-Sullivan and Mark Bracher. London: Routledge, pp. 188–212.

Žižek, Slavoj (ed.). 1992. *Everything You Always Wanted to Know about Lacan but Were Afraid to Ask Hitchcock*. London and New York: Verso.

Žižek, Slavoj. 1992a. "In His Bold Gaze My Ruin Is Writ Large". *Everything You Always Wanted to Know about Lacan but Were Afraid to Ask Hitchcock*. edited by Slavoj Žižek. London and New York: Verso.

Žižek, Slavoj. 1994. *The Metastases of Enjoyment*. London and New York: Verso.

Žižek, Slavoj and Renata Salecl. (eds.). 1996. *Gaze and Voice as Love Objects*. Durham and London: Duke University Press.

Žižek, Slavoj. 1998. "The Seven Veils of Fantasy". *Key Concepts of Lacanian Psychoanalysis*. Edited by Danny Nobus. London: Rebus Press, pp. 190–218.

Žižek, Slavoj. 1998a. (ed.). *Cogito and the Unconscious*. Durham and London: Duke University Press.

Index

Note: *Italic* page numbers refer to figures.

For Product Safety Concerns and Information please contact our EU representative GPSR@taylorandfrancis.com Taylor & Francis Verlag GmbH, Kaufingerstraße 24, 80331 München, Germany